Dwelling in the Archive

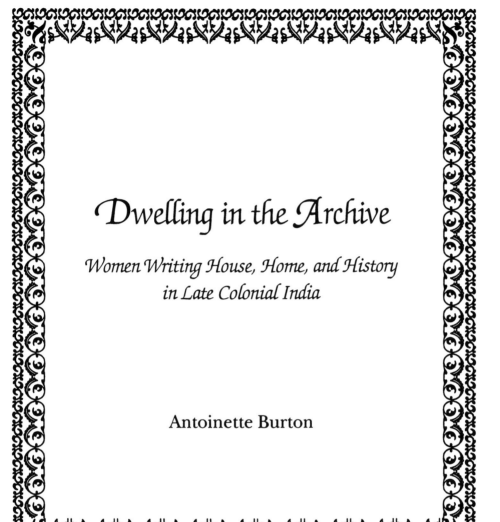

Dwelling in the Archive

Women Writing House, Home, and History in Late Colonial India

Antoinette Burton

OXFORD

UNIVERSITY PRESS

2003

OXFORD

UNIVERSITY PRESS

Oxford   New York

Auckland   Bangkok   Buenos Aires   Cape Town   Chennai
Dar es Salaam   Delhi   Hong Kong   Istanbul   Karachi   Kolkata
Kuala Lumpur   Madrid   Melbourne   Mexico City   Mumbai
Nairobi   São Paulo   Shanghai   Taipei   Tokyo   Toronto

Copyright © 2003 by Antoinette Burton

Published by Oxford University Press, Inc.
198 Madison Avenue, New York, New York 10016

www.oup.com

Oxford is a registered trademark of Oxford University Press

Parts of chapter 2 were published originally as "House/Daughter/Nation: Interiority, Architecture and Historical Imagination in Janaki Majumdar's 'Family History,'" *Journal of Asian Studies* 56, 4 (November 1997): 921–46, and are reprinted with permission.

Parts of chapter 3 were published originally as "'The *Purdahnashin* in Her Setting': Colonial Modernity and the Zenana in Cornelia Sorabji's Memoirs," *Feminist Review* 65 (Summer 2000): 145–58, and are reprinted with permission.

Library of Congress Cataloging-in-Publication Data
Burton, Antoinette M., 1961–
Dwelling in the archive : women writing house, home, and history
in late colonial India / Antoinette Burton.
p. cm.
Includes bibliographical references (p.) and index.
ISBN 0-19-514424-4; ISBN 0-19-514425-2 (pbk.)
1. Indic prose literature (English)—Women authors—History and criticism. 2. Women and literature—India—History—20th century. 3. Women—India—Biography—History and criticism. 4. Majumdar, Janaki Agnes Penelope, 1886–1963. Family history. 5. Hosain, Attia, 1913– Sunlight on a broken column. 6. Sorabji, Cornelia, d. 1954– India calling. 7. Family—India—Historiography. 8. Women—India—Historiography. 9. Autobiography—Women authors. 10. Family in literature. 11. Home in literature.
I. Title.
PR9492.6.W6 B87 2003
820.9'355—dc21   2002070077

1 3 5 7 9 8 6 4 2
Printed in the United States of America
on acid-free paper

for Paul:
finally, a book of his own

Acknowledgments

I have struggled with the ideas in this book more than with any project I've undertaken to date, yet even now I am sad to see it done. Many people have helped me find my way into the lives of the women whose work I have explored here, but their families undoubtedly deserve the most thanks—not only because they shared their memories and their archives, but because they graciously let me into their homes as well. Richard Sorabji hosted me in Oxford, Amar and Sally Singh in suburban Philadelphia, and Waris Hussein in London. Shama Habibullah was an extraordinarily generous e-mail correspondent, providing me with a virtual genealogical archive of her family and helping me gain access to the BBC Written Archives in Reading as well. I feel exceptionally privileged to have been permitted some glimpses into these family histories, and I hope that what follows in these pages does justice to the memory of Janaki, Cornelia, and Attia.

Without the assistance of Malavika Karlekar, Karin Deutsch Karlekar, and Anita Desai I would not have been able to contact Hosain's family, and I am grateful to them for the connections they made available. Sandra Ponzanesi, Paola Marchionni, Sylvia Albertazzi, and Alberta Grube all helped me to track down Laura Bondi's M.A. thesis, which was crucial to my understanding of Attia's life. The fact that Laura was willing to send it to me is evidence, among other things, of the generosity that Hosain inspired among those who knew her. The Singhs have been equally warm and cooperative with respect to Majumdar's "Family History." Indeed, it is thanks to them that this project got started in the first place. I am especially grateful to Sally for her correspondence with me about Janaki and her ongoing interest in my work. Anita Money treated me to tea in the Grosvenor Hotel and offered me a fascinating window onto "colonial Bloomsbury." Anuradha Needham shared interview notes and impressions of Attia, both personal and intellectual, for which I am grateful. Rozina Visram was uncommonly generous with both India Office references on Sorabji and her knowledge of generations of Indians in Britain. Her support for me and my research goes back many years, and I feel lucky to know her.

To Lucy Knauer and my mother, Gerri Burton—whose persistence first enabled me to meet the Singhs—I am profoundly indebted. Geraldine Forbes, Gail Minault, Frances Pritchett, Veena Oldenburg, Barbara Ramusack, and Mrinalini Sinha answered all manner of historiographical and bibliographic questions with tremendous forbearance, and I thank them for it. Gerry, Gail, Barbara, and Minnie deserve special thanks for having read the manuscript in its various incarnations; the book as a whole is much better for their comments and suggestions. Angela Woollacott, George Robb, Madhavi Kale, Laura Mayhall, Jed Esty, Meera Kosambi, Devoney Looser, Mary Poovey, Ania Loomba, David Prochaska, Sonita Sarker, Steve Johnstone, Mark Micale, Lara Kriegel, Ann Curthoys, Philippa Levine, Mahua Sarkar, Jim Barrett, and Tony Ballantyne also read either parts or all of the manuscript. Their critiques were spirited, challenging, and ultimately invaluable. Tony's passion for archives, for history, and for "home" is unmatched, and it is frankly hard to imagine how this book would have become what it has without his tireless interest and support.

My colleagues in the Department of History at the University of Illinois have indulged my endless "archive talk" in ways that I appreciate beyond measure. These include Jean Allman, Tony Ballantyne, Marilyn Booth, Clare Crowston, Augusto Espiritu, Peter Fritzsche, Kristin Hoganson, Craig Koslofsky, Kathy Oberdeck, Elizabeth Pleck, David Prochaska, Dana Rabin, Cynthia Radding, Leslie Reagan, and Adam Sutcliffe. Clare has been especially patient, supportive, and helpful: thank goodness our offices were next to one another. I have benefited from presenting parts of the book at the Cultural Studies Reading Group and the Gender and History Reading Group at Illinois; at Bryn Mawr College; the University of Washington; Indiana University; Southern Illinois University; the University of Minnesota; Old Dominion University; Johns Hopkins University; the Institute of

Historical Research, London; SUNY Binghamton; and panels at the American Historical Association, the Conference on South Asia at the University of Wisconsin in Madison, and "Locating the Victorians" in London. I have also incurred debts along the way to Sanjam Ahluwalia, Sally Alexander, Nicole Anderson, Tom Bedwell, Kate Bullard, Matti Bunzl, Catherine Candy, Dipesh Chakrabarty, Gary Daily, Chandra de Silva, Jen Edwards, Rosemary George, Rob Gregg, Catherine Hall, Sanjay Joshi, Suvir Kaul, Jan Langendorf, Marilyn Lake, Devoney Looser, Saloni Mathur, Rebecca McNulty, Sonya Michel, Rob McLain, Mickey Moran, Laura Neil, Andrew Nolan, Maura O'Connor, Aprel Orwick, Fiona Paisley, Judy Patterson, Doug Peers, Adele Perry, Uta Poiger, Srirupa Prasad, Nicole Ranganath, Anu Rao, Simona Sawhney, Cris Scarboro, Sudipta Sen, Nayan Shah, Nilufer Smith, Beth Starr, Hsu-Ming Teo, Lynn Thomas, Lisa Trivedi, Alison Twells, Judy Walkowitz, Jamie Warren, and Kerry Wynn. Generous funding from the Research Board at the University of Illinois made R.A. support and an archival trip to England possible, for which I am most appreciative.

Some of the labor in the earlier stages of this project was done by Heather Samples; I am grateful for her work and for her continued friendship. Raka Nandi and Françoise Labrique Walusis spent many hours at the microfilm reader and the Xerox machine: to them I owe a huge debt and an even greater thanks. Debbie Hughes did some last-minute, life-saving library work for me as well, and I am grateful. Susan Ferber is simply an extraordinary editor: her attention to detail and her consistent intellectual engagement have been nothing less than astonishing and have had a huge impact on the pages that follow. Without the help of Tasha Fast, much of the research for this project would have gone undone. She is a babysitter par excellence, whether in London or Urbana. Lori Hedberg's late-afternoon stints also made work possible, for which I thank her. When it comes to labor, no one deserves more recognition than Nagwa El Bassiouni, who has fed and watered me and mine for three years, and none more lovingly than her special charge, Nicholas. As a caregiver, a neighbor, and a friend she is without equal. She and Mahomed Samy have become our family and we theirs, as they are wont to remind us. Words cannot express my appreciation for them in our lives.

Dana and Clare and Kathy—and Jonah and Lily and Fiona and Cara—have quickly become essential, in so many ways. Dana has given sisterhood a whole new meaning to me. Herman Bennett and Jennifer Morgan are indispensable to my intellectual, emotional, and political life: this, I trust, they know. Philippa Levine continues to be inimitable. Laura Mayhall and George Robb remain true through thick and thin. To Hannah and Madhavi: you are always in my mind and my heart. My parents have been ever supportive. My mother in particular has set up several "homes away from home" that have been memorable as well as life-transforming—in Oaklands Close, on Fairbank Avenue, in Gwendwr Road, and last but not least, on Ambroseden Avenue. I hope she knows how much of this belongs to her. Mellow Oak has long felt like home, thanks to the hospitality and friendship of Eric and especially Audrey Matkins. Thanks to Vicki and Monica for their love and support. Nicholas, for his part, makes dwelling in the archive both possible and desirable—in more ways than I could have ever expected, and as only he can do.

This book is dedicated to Paul: at last.

Contents

When they had gone, the house on Cabral
Island became very quiet, but the walls, the
furniture, the rugs were still a-crackle with the
electricity generated by the recently departed;
there were parts of the house so highly
charged that just to enter them made your hair
stand on end. The old place released the
memory of the mob slowly, slowly, as if it half-
expected the bad times to return. But in the
end it relaxed, and peace and silence began to
think about moving back in.

—Salman Rushdie, *The Moor's Last Sigh*

Dwelling in the Archive

Chapter One

MEMORY BECOMES HER

Women, Feminist
History, and the Archive

Architecture is full of doubt, innuendo,
inexplicable visual suggestion, all ideas that
elude forthright documentation.

—Gautam Bhatia, *Silent Spaces*

Several years ago, my mother came to me with an intriguing tale. Someone she knew had told her that the great-grandson of the first president of the Indian National Congress (INC), W. C. Bonnerjee, was living in the suburb where I grew up. What's more, this great-grandson, Amar Singh, and his wife, Sally, had in their possession an unpublished diary written by Amar's grandmother, Janaki Agnes Penelope Majumdar, née Bonnerjee. Thanks to the good offices of my mother and her friend, I was eventually introduced to the Singhs, who after several cups of tea produced what was in fact a family history, written in Janaki's hand and running to about two hundred pages. As I sat in their living room scanning through this heirloom, I could not help marveling at both my good luck and the serendipity of history. Clearly what I had in front of me was rare and remarkable evidence—not just of Bonnerjee family history but of the domestic contexts of late Victorian Indian nationalism, at least in its Congress form. Yet it was hardly housed in a conventional archival site, and (like many artifacts of colonialism) it had traveled a long way from "home." All of that has led me to the questions that motivate this book. What counts as an archive? Can private memories of home serve as evidence of political history? What do we make of the histories that domestic interiors, once concrete and now perhaps crumbling or even disappeared, have the capacity to yield? And, given women's vexed relationship to the kinds of history that archives typically house, what does it mean to say that home can and should be seen not simply as a dwelling-place for women's memory but as one of the foundations of history—history conceived of, that is, as a narrative, a practice, and a site of desire?

In the face of such daunting questions, this project has a modest aim: to explore the ways that three twentieth-century Indian women—Janaki Majumdar (1886–1963), Cornelia Sorabji (1886–1954), and Attia Hosain (1913–1997)—made use of memories of home in order to claim a place in history at the intersection of the private and the public, the personal and the political, the national and the postcolonial. All three were preoccupied with domestic architecture, its symbolic meanings and its material realities, because they were keenly aware that house and home were central to their social identities and the cultural forms through which they experienced both family life and national belonging. Such an interpretation is common enough in the literature on home, even in its anthropologically richest scholarship.[1] This book resists the temptation to ghettoize women's memories as either privatized commemorations of family forms and domestic life or as expressions of a purely "psychic" state.[2] As the narratives examined here testify, the material culture of house and home that looms so large in the work of these women cannot be dismissed merely as memorabilia. To the contrary: all three used domestic space as an archival source from which to construct their own histories and through which to record the contradictions of living as Indian women in the context of colonial modernity. Indeed, each of the women under consideration here, writing either in or about the 1930s in India, responded to "the pressure of historical placement" by using their memories of house and home as the basis for writing histories about the impossibility of dwelling comfortably "at home."[3] Occupying a unique place at the intersection of home and history by virtue of their relationships to imperialism and nationalist projects (not to mention their complex identities as "Indian women"), all three women produced histories that preserved the domestic—not simply to commemorate it but also to critique the present in which they lived and, with it, facile notions of home itself.

To this end, the term "archive" as I use it in this book works in two ways. I intend it first in its conventional, disciplinary meaning: that is, as the source of evidence from which each woman produced historical accounts of life in colonial India. In this sense, for example, Majumdar's "Family History" relies on memories of the various homes her family inhabited, which in turn constitute an archival basis for her historical account. I use the word "archive" also to indicate that a text like the "Family History" is itself an enduring site of historical evidence and historiographical opportunity in and for the present. This book suggests that, in addition to serving as evidence of individual lives, the memories of home that each woman enshrined in narrative act—for us—as an archive from which a variety of counterhistories of colonial modernity can be discerned. I want to emphasize, in other words, the importance of home as both a material archive for history *and* a very real political figure in an extended moment of historical crisis.[4] I hope thereby to indicate a pathway out of one of the most vexing impasses of postcolonial history: the apparent dichotomy of "discourse" versus "reality." For if we take seriously the dynamic relationship between what are deemed discourses and what are designated material realities—between history and home, for example—we can begin to more fully appreciate them as mutually constitutive sites of cultural knowledge and political desire. We can begin, in short, to understand discourse and reality not as opposing domains but as a vast, interdependent archive:

a space where contests over colonial domination can be discerned and historicized.[5] That women and gender are the analytical categories at the heart of this critical approach—and feminist history its method—there can be little doubt. For if nothing else, the writings of Majumdar, Sorabji, and Hosain are useful reminders that the word "archive" derives from the Greek *arkheion*, that is, the house, residence, domicile of the archon (superior magistrate), and that this dwelling-place marks the liminal space between public and private— those typically, if unstably and contingently, gendered domains—as the characteristic feature of critical historical consciousness.[6]

The frequency with which women writers of different nations have made use of home to stage their dramas of remembrance is a sign of how influential the cult of domesticity and its material exigencies has been for inhabitants of structurally gendered locations like the patriarchal household. This strategy is neither unique to white elite North American women nor limited to the West—a phenomenon that suggests that home is one of those "ideological configurations that loop and spread across 'national' boundaries," even as it requires those boundaries for its ideological work and remakes them for expressly political purposes.[7] Obviously it is not enough to observe that "women do this," because the domain that home houses has its boundaries drawn for it by the larger culture, as well as by the political economies of race, nation, sexuality, and empire that shape it. Nor would I wish to suggest that women writers resort to home in their family memoirs more commonly or consistently than men—witness, for example, Kwame Anthony Appiah's evocative title *In My Father's House* or V. S. Naipaul's equally suggestive *A House for Mr. Biswas.*[8] But as a number of scholars have demonstrated, women writers have typically figured women's lived experience—however various and complex, however idyllic or tortured—through architectural images, top-to-bottom reconstructions, and "chants" that remodel as they move from room to room.[9] Critical analyses of home that do not wish either to essentialize or romanticize its allegorical power must therefore be attentive to the specific languages, metaphors, and tropes through which it is articulated by historical subjects. And they must visualize the stories/storeys through which women writers have attempted to make home permanent in memory and, beyond that, to establish it in history. No. 124 Bluestone in Toni Morrison's *Beloved* is among the most powerful examples of how memory can be stored in the physical places of home, as well as how one imaginary dwelling-place can be reconstituted in another across time and across texts. "Sweet Home"—the house in

Beloved—stands, quite literally, at the intersection of past and present, serving as the concrete yet ghostly site for the reenactment and the reproduction of African American history.[10]

What was it that compelled these three women to use their memories of house and home as archival sources for the writing of histories that tried to capture the rifts and fissures of modernity in late colonial India? Surely their own diasporic experiences go some way toward explaining their attachment to home as both an architectural trope and a material witness to history. Janaki Majumdar was born in India but spent her childhood and early womanhood traveling back and forth between India and Britain, in part because of the transnational character of her father's role as president of the INC. Cornelia Sorabji was a Parsee "by nationality" who was born in India to Christian missionary parents. Educated at Oxford, she spent her life shuttling between India and Britain and was proud to say that she warmed her hands "at both fires."[11] Attia Hosain, the youngest of the three, was a Muslim from a *taluqdari* (landed) family who lived through the partition of India, in response to which she left Lucknow for Britain. Though she traveled back and forth between the subcontinent and London after 1947, she retained a Chelsea apartment and raised her two children in Britain. For Majumdar and Hosain, as I will show, the disappearance of the family residence in the wake of both conjugal choices and the upheavals of history undoubtedly helped to shape the way they housed their childhoods in powerful tales of home. Sorabji's story is a bit different. Her law practice, which kept her on the move from client to client and case to case, produced a kind of perpetual homelessness—a self-confessed "hotel" existence that contributed to the fetish of the stable orthodox home that structured her reform agenda, her political writings, and her personal memoirs. While the specifics of their lives are distinctive, they all lived a highly mobile existence, which makes them significant, if not necessarily representative, figures in the history of late colonial India. The mobility that characterized each of their lives thus accounts, at least in part, for why house and home became touchstones for their apprehensions of historical time and space— revealing, in the process, the gendered politics of the diasporic historical imagination.

It would be a mistake, however, to fall back on such a particularized and individual notion of identity in order to understand why home provided the foundational archive for the histories they left behind. For one thing, house and home had long been highly charged ideological categories in the context of the Raj. The "orien-

tal" *zenana*, or women's quarters, was pathologized as dark, unhy-
gienic, and indicative of Indians' incapacity for self-rule throughout
the nineteenth century, with Victorian feminists taking the lead in
extrapolating from this domestic space a host of judgments about
the character of Indian men, women, and children from the 1860s
onward. Whether feminist or not, Western women focused on, and
most often demonized, the spatialized domestic practices of their
colonized "sisters," either to enlarge the domain of their own social
responsibilities or to justify the imperial mission of their govern-
ments, or both.[12] Elite Indian male nationalists, for their part, refracted metropolitan anxieties about the status of home into concerns about the integrity of "Indian" domestic space, in part because
they shared many of the patriarchal convictions at the heart of the
British colonial project.[13] What is significant for my purposes is that
the gender ideology of British colonialism in its nineteenth- and
twentieth-century manifestations compelled male Indian reformers
to specify the parameters of conjugality in spatial terms that, in turn,
mapped the colonial domestic as feminine, private, spiritual, in contrast to the imperial public, which was masculine, secular, and mate-
rialistic.[14] The home carried the contradictory political burden of
standing in for the nascent Indian nation as well as of marking domestic space as evidence of an authentic India rooted in (an implicitly) Hindu past. The civic secularism of much nineteenth-century
Indian nationalism, particularly the Indian National Congress variety, is potentially misleading precisely because it leaves the (Bengali)
Hindu character of the "Indian" home either unmarked, as in Victorian nationalist discourse, or underplayed, as in some scholarly as-
sessments today.[15] In any case, the struggle over house and home
that shaped debates about Indian modernity undoubtedly staged domestic space as historical time, thus guaranteeing that it would be
seized on as an opportunity for modernizing interventions. Whether
it was the "old fashioned zenana" or the reformed nationalist space,
home offered testimony about the ability of the reforming male elite
to manage their personal lives and hence evidence of their capacity
for self-government. By the time Majumdar, Sorabji, and Hosain put
it to use in their own histories, then, "the Indian home" had become
a well-established archive—one that mostly male nationalists insisted
Britons and fellow Indians read as justification for the historical departures that even conservative Indian nationalism represented
under British colonial rule.[16]

If house and home were scrutinized by Victorian Britons and
Indians alike, domesticity and its practical forms came under even

more intense surveillance in late colonial India, where the evidence that home housed was critical to debates about how modernity could and should be played out. As Geraldine Forbes has documented, although women's organizations had been active in India since the nineteenth century, it was Sarojini Naidu's deputation to Sir Edwin Montagu and Lord Chelmsford in 1917 to demand the franchise for Indian women that arguably galvanized Indian women's suffrage and linked it inextricably to nationalist claims on the imperial state.[17] The 1920s and 1930s witnessed a series of legislative inroads in this regard, with Bombay, Madras, the United Provinces, the Punjab, Bengal, Assam, the Central Provinces, and Bihar and Orissa extending the vote to women between 1921 and 1930.[18] Muthulakshmi Reddy was elected deputy president of the Madras Legislative Council in 1927, the same year that the Simon Commission was convened to assess the state of representative institutions in British India. It is not too much to say that the imperial public sphere was saturated with the "woman question" in these heady and tumultuous decades. The centrality of domestic space to the rhetoric, ideologies, and practices of Indian feminism in all its diversity during this period is striking. The All-Muslim Ladies' Conference regularly met "under strict purdah arrangements," thus quite deliberately mobilizing "seclusion in public" for political purposes, despite internal division about what degree of purdah was prescribed by Muslim law.[19] Meanwhile Sarojini Naidu, in her capacity as resident of the INC, declared in 1925 that:

> Mine, as becomes a woman, is a modest domestic programme: merely to restore India to her true position as supreme mistress in her own home; sole guardian of her vast resources, and sole dispenser of her own rich hospitalities as a loyal daughter of *Bharat Mata*.
>
> Therefore it will be my lovely, though difficult, task through the coming year to try to set my mother's house in order; to reconcile the tragic quarrels that threaten the integrity of her old history, joint family, the life of diverse communities and creeds; and to find an adequate place, purpose and recognition, alike for the lowliest and mightiest of her children and foster-children, the guests and the strangers within her gates.[20]

Here, Naidu figured India itself as a home whose true mistress had been usurped by "guests and strangers": a house that had to be restored to its rightful proprietors, one whose orderliness depended on the ministrations of the Indian woman-as-mother. In this sense, twentieth-century feminists reappropriated the discourses of house and home that had been seized by male Indian nationalists since the nineteenth century, linking domesticity expressly to their own reform agendas in ways that both consolidated that "traditional" idiom and refigured it as a new subject of public political discourse. It is practically a commonplace in the scholarship of this period that the relationship between "Indian" feminisms and "Indian" nationalisms was evolving and complex, as was the relationship between Muslim organizations and Hindu-dominated "all-India" feminist groups. Less frequently commented on is how, like Indian nationalism, Indian feminism in all its variety involved "a reworking of territorial and social space" based on a demarcation of boundaries that was both new and familiar—with the imaginative and material spaces of house and home at the heart of such reterritorializations.[21]

How do the rhetorical maneuvers of the interwar period help us to situate Majumdar, Sorabji, and Hosain and historicize their determination to make home the archive for their accounts of the period? Quite simply, public debates about home raised the stakes of the house-as-archive, transforming domesticity from a woman's question into the very centerpiece of public debate about the promises and limits of all manner of reform agendas. As Tanika Sarkar's work has shown, this was a long historical process that depended as much on rhetorics of conjugality as on those of domesticity per se. But events of the 1930s intensified the relationship between the "woman question" and the nationalist question, blurring the lines between the two in historically new and politically quite specific ways.[22] Preoccupation with the zenana in particular as an increasingly outdated interior space not only dominated but actively framed the "domestic" discourses of nationalism, imperialism, and feminism in these decades and thereby helped to guarantee the heightened archival value of house and home by making them evidence of both a disappearing past *and* a promising "progressive" future. Imperial Britons, for whom companionate marriage (with its valorization of free "social intercourse" for women) was a marker of civilizational progress, had been anticipating and prophesying the end of zenana life since at least the late nineteenth century; not surprisingly, perhaps, its demise was the fondest hope of British feminists, even as some also fetishized seclusion as the distinctive mark of Indian "tradition" and "national" culture. The first several generations of elite and especially English-educated Indian nationalists shared such ambivalences, but by the 1920s many recognized in nationalist leaders' confident embrace of the "passing away of purdah" a pathway toward political recognition. Although the zenana (a spatial location) and purdah (a social practice) are not one and the same, the so-called erosion of purdah was seen as conclusive evidence of the capacity to govern the house in ways that might presage national self-rule.[23] Meanwhile, over the course of the 1920s the zenana became a site of programmatic medical, scientific, and educational intervention, mostly in service of a male bourgeois modernizing and nationalist project—though it continued to be appropriated by female reformers in and outside India as well.[24] Even more critical for my purposes is the impact of Katherine Mayo's *Mother India* (1927) on the imperial public sphere of the 1920s and 1930s. Thanks to the scholarship of Mrinalini Sinha, we are to able to appreciate the ways that Mayo's attack on Hindu child-marriage brought the interiors of domestic space into national (and international) view. Sinha's work has also pointed to the uses Indian feminists made of the controversy to seek a set of newly articulated political demands from both the nationalist movement and the imperial state.[25] To the extent that the zenana came under scrutiny in this debate, it emerged both as an archive of what was and, by extension, as a repository of a past that nationalists, imperialists, and feminists agreed should be confined, at least in its earlier forms and manifestations, to history.

Despite newspaper headlines like "Purdah Must Go!" and "Purdah Disappears from Villages," purdah as a socioeconomic and cultural practice was far from obsolete by the 1930s.[26] Rumors of its disappearance were nonetheless fueled in that decade by the very public spectacle of women leaving hearth and home to participate in political activities that flew in the face of ideologies of a respectability long held dear by elite Hindus and Muslims alike. Again, it is worth underscoring that purdah and the zenana are not equivalent terms, though (as will become clear) a conceptual slippage between the two was a fairly consistent feature of interwar imperial and, to a lesser extent, colonial reform discourse. Gandhian nationalism, with its invocation of the Hindu woman as a political subject and its invitation to her, as the events of 1930s unfolded, to leave the sanctity of the home for the hazards of the street (all in the name of India), was clearly crucial for rearticulating the relationships between seclusion, domesticity, history, politics, and the emergent postcolonial nation.[27] Writing about the United Provinces in the 1930s, Uma Rao argues that the dominant image was of "hordes of women pouring out of their houses."[28] Ishanee Mukherjee makes a similar case for Bengal, where the phenomenon of "zenana participants in agitational politics" dated from 1907 and the aftermath of partition in Bengal.[29] As I will show, Cornelia Sorabji revived this specter in the

1930s precisely to make her point about the dangers of linking women, feminism, and the political to the ongoing stability of the zenana as a characteristically "Indian" domestic form. With Subhas Chandra Bose calling for women to carry daggers for the cause, to be trained in target-shooting and armory caretaking, and eventually to be enlisted as assassins, the "extra-domestic activism" of nationalist women made them nothing less than "full-fledged comrades-in-arms" well before World War I.[30] As Mukherjee also argues, the political sedition of the 1910s was a model for student activism of the 1920s and in turn for Gandhian activities of the 1930s—a trajectory that suggests the long history of anxieties about the zenana's erosion, as well as the culturally freighted meanings it had accumulated by the 1930s.

It is quite possible that the *swadeshi* campaigns of the 1920s and 1930s (that boycotted British goods) were themselves enough to refigure domestic practices by turning consumption—heretofore a largely private, feminine domain—into an area of highly public political contribution to the nationalist cause. Like protocols of violence, these practices drew on a longer cultural memory in which the boycott of goods and the highly politicized manufacture of alternative domestic commodities would have lived large, at least for Bengalis, who first embraced it in response to the partition of Bengal in 1905.[31] As Lisa Trivedi's research on the advertisement of *swadeshi* (homemade) goods demonstrates, much of the Indian subcontinent would have had occasion to see patriotic consumables come to life in visual and even spectacular forms over the course of the 1930s.[32] In any case there can be little doubt that the idiom of political action was not just domestic but involved the transformation and reimagination of the very notion of dwelling at home as well. Helena Dutt, a Bengali revolutionary, recalled in an interview with Geraldine Forbes in 1975 that "[we] were like caged tigers." According to Forbes, "Women more conservative than Helena and her friends were told 'the house is on fire' and that they should leave it in order to help douse the conflagration."[33] The traditional Indian (read upper-caste Hindu) home, had it ever existed, was fast beginning to look like a historical form, a sign of the past. Its most recognizable incarnation, the zenana, was therefore becoming more and more a charged ideological space. The value of house and home, their political and ideological valences, were, in short, matters of highly visible national and imperial concern—a fact that made their archival value all the greater, and all the more competed for and argued over, among nationalist promoters and their critics alike.

It is in this context—that is, during an extended historical moment when the traditional "Indian" home and its seclusionary practices enjoyed a kind of cult status as emblems of a culture of disappearance—that two of the women writers examined here wrote histories putting the architecture of home to use as an archival source and documenting the relationship between domesticity and nationalist politics. Janaki Agnes Penelope Majumdar's "Family History" was written in 1935, the fiftieth anniversary of the founding of the INC. Majumdar's father, W. C. Bonnerjee, had married Hemangini Motilal when she was a young girl, in the late 1850s. Influenced by her mother's conversion to Christianity, Janaki was herself a Christian, educated first at the Croydon High School for Girls and later at Newnham College, Cambridge. She not only reconstructed the "family history" by reassembling the various houses the Majumdar clan had inhabited, she staged the story of her parents' life together as a drama about the variety of homes they established in fin de siècle Bengal and suburban London. Majumdar's "Family History" is a vital, evocative archive of the interior spaces of family life organized around detailed recollections of the material culture of this peripatetic Victorian household. It is also a repository for Janaki's own conflicted views of her father's political career and its effect on her mother and in turn on the family at large—all read through memories of specific rooms and the architectural arrangements of the family houses in Britain and India. In Janaki's version of this history, W. C. Bonnerjee's public profile is effectively eclipsed by the drama of the orthodox Hindu, then Christian, woman (Hemangini) struggling to maintain her identity, to guarantee her family's coherence, and above all to establish a viable, stable home for herself and her children amid the upheavals of temporary exile. In this respect, Janaki's account provides what we could call a thick descriptive counternarrative to the discourses about companionate marriage that underpinned many of the arguments for Indian self-government produced by elite, progressive Hindu men like Bonnerjee himself in the fin de siècle period.[34] As chapter 2 illustrates, Majumdar's "Family History" works the concept of archive in the double sense outlined earlier. It does so first by mobilizing the family home as an archive of Indian nationalist history and second by serving as the basis for a heretofore unavailable historical narrative—thereby testifying to the painful and sometimes contradictory effects of nationalism's modernizing project on one famous nationalist's daughter, as well as to her ambivalent embrace of modernity under late colonialism.

Cornelia Sorabji's writing offers a history of the same period from a different political position but also archives the interiors of house and home at a moment when contemporaries were preoccupied with the passing of the "traditional Indian home" into history. On the move as a professional woman rather than as the daughter of a nationalist politician, Sorabji repeatedly takes up the question of the zenana in both her memoirs, *India Calling* (1934) and *India Recalled* (1936). Trained as a barrister at Oxford in the late 1880s, she practiced law in India, most notably as a pleader for the Court of Wards, where her clients were *purdahnashin* (secluded women). In her writing, the zenana emerges as the quintessential emblem of home: the "vanishing monument" of an India that seemed to be disappearing before contemporaries' very eyes. The rhetoric of ruins she produced in these texts has a consistently romantic cast to it, signaling the nature of her historical perspective as well as her commitment to authenticating a dimly glimpsed yet eminently retrievable past. That rhetoric of ruins enabled Sorabji to claim authority about the past and, in turn, to critique the gender politics of Indian nationalism in the 1930s. In many ways Sorabji treats the zenana as an architectural wonder whose interiors and material culture make it worthy of being counted as a uniquely orientalist tourist site precisely because of its archival qualities—an archive for which she fashions herself the perfect historian-guide. She arguably turns the women's quarters into a museum in which tradition and its displacements—in the form of the Singer sewing machine, for example—could be consumed by an avid British reading public. The museological character of her memoirs is instructive here, insofar as it reflects her determination to understand the zenana and its inhabitants as relics of a bygone era and herself, by extension, as the representative of a modest, and also of course a deeply contradictory, modernity. Her mobility, together with her anglophilia and her status as a professional woman allow her to claim authority as a savvy traveler and to subject the Indian landscape to a Baedeker-type narrative of some of the subcontinent's most intimate spaces—raising questions about the relationship between tourist and historian, both then and now. Sorabji's repeated return to and disavowal of the zenana tells us much about the ways the public and the private, the home and the world, were being challenged and refigured in twentieth-century India. As I argue in chapter 3, Sorabji's work provides us with evidence of how politicized the zenana had become by the period, not merely as a site of social and cultural reform but as archival evidence of "authentic" India at the level of colonial and nationalist politics as well. Like Majumdar's "Family History," Sorabji's writings do double duty, first by archiving the disappearing zenana as a site of political contest in late colonial India, second by offering us the basis for a complex, multistranded historical account of how complex a figure in and of colonial modernity "the Indian woman"—both the zenana inhabitant and Sorabji herself—could be.

This book takes Attia Hosain, author of the partition novel *Sunlight on a Broken Column* (1961), as a final example of how house and home were enlisted as archives in the service of history, and more particularly in the project of memorializing the penultimate decade of British rule. Though it was not written in the 1930s, I read it as a memoir of the 1930s that represents itself as history of the period—thereby engaging the work of recent feminist historians of India about the relationship of autobiography to history as a personal and political enterprise.[35] Hosain's status as an "Indian" woman (someone born in Lucknow who left the subcontinent for England in the wake of partition) raises important questions about the fantasy of national categories and their domestic ramifications in a postcolonial, diasporic world. Here I use Hosain's novel to suggest that in the context of many partition narratives, home emerges as a very specific kind of space, a "telling place" through whose doors, windows, and passageways people's pasts are glimpsed, in whose rooms life-stories are relived and consequently re-membered.[36] The memory of attachment and the agony of rupture are associated with the materiality of the house, its grounds, its structures—literally, its emplotment in space and time.[37] Especially when it is the *ancestral* home, the family house is made to bear witness to the past; and often, its ghostly interiors are made to stand in for the unspeakable violence of what has come before. We can see this very clearly in *Sunlight*. At the center of the narrative is Laila's family's home, called Ashiana: "the arched, carved, latticed, pillared, sprawling house" to which she is fundamentally, yet uncomfortably, attached. It would be easy to see the interior of Ashiana as a refraction of Laila's emotional life, its corridors, passageways, and winding halls her route to freedom, its demise the end of her childhood innocence. And, as I shall illustrate, the house—crowded with furniture yet open to light and sound from outside—does compel her to cast beyond its walls, to break the patterns literally set in stone, and to conjure a future only dimly imaginable from the zenana. And yet *Sunlight* is not a bildungsroman, that classic novel of development that privileges the quest story through the biography of the individual/protagonist.[38] Hosain seems determined to resist the evolutionary model inherent

in that genre, in part because she does not represent Laila's pathway
as that from communal subject to modern secular citizen. Laila re-
grets the passage of history not because such is the bittersweet price
of modernity but rather because she is skeptical of the possibilities of
a postpartition, postcolonial modernity for herself and perhaps
more generally for women like her. As I suggest in chapter 4,[39] writing *Sunlight* allowed Hosain the means by which to commemorate a
kind of disappearing "home" that is different from those of Majumdar and Sorabji: a home at the intersection of political violence and
the trauma of history. As the archive of a house altered, if not destroyed, by the events of 1947, Hosain's novel furnishes us with evidence of how a catastrophic event like partition might grip—and, in
the end, shape—the postcolonial historical imagination.

Does the specter of their disappearance and destruction capture
the imagination as much, if not more so, than house and home itself? If so, it is perhaps not surprising that for the three women
whose work I deal with here, the preservation of the past that home
housed was a labor of love—love at last sight, if you will.[40] The political significance of this labor was, as I have suggested, considerable in
the last two decades of the Raj. This book juxtaposes several genres
(the family history, the memoir, the letter, the official report, the
oral history, the novel) in order to understand the various forms mobilized by these well-educated women from the Indian subcontinent
as they tried to register the costs of modernity—in both its imperialist and nationalist guises—for domesticity and the very possibility of
"home" as well. Arguably, the transformation of house and home
into durable archives was not just a way of rescuing domesticity from
the oblivion of history but also a means of rescuing History itself
from the triumphalist representations that dominant imperialist and
nationalist discourses had been producing about house and home
since the Victorian period. The writings of Majumdar, Sorabji, and
Hosain together represent a challenge to claims that British "civilization" and Indian nationalism could deliver Indian women from
the backwardness of zenana existence and the prison-house of
domesticity—documenting, as I will show, a quest for belonging that
required a concerted struggle against contemporary presumptions
about the self-evident comforts of home. In addition to their determination to archive the domestic, clearly what joins all three women
writers under consideration here is their elite status, which enabled
their mobility and hence the "bird's-eye" view they were able to take
of house, home, and history. Theirs was indubitably what Janet
Frame calls "the luxury of reminiscence."[41] In the case of Majumdar

and Hosain, their class status provided them with the very properties that became the stuff of memory and the touchstones of their historical imagination. Lest there be any doubt, I treat them in the chapters that follow not as subaltern figures but as the educated, diasporic subjects they were—not, in other words, as self-evidently resistant actors but as particular examples of the cosmopolitan woman writer who can tell us much about "the complex interaction of local and colonial structures" in the context of the bourgeois Indian modern.[42] Flagging their elite status is obviously not sufficient; assessing its historical significance, especially in terms of the gender politics it entailed, is what is called for. Here, the links between class status and mobility are critical to the kinds of histories they were able to write. Their privilege enabled them to move freely, inhabit transnational spaces, represent their worlds to an English-speaking public, and claim their perspective as exiles. Their structural location as women—the limits it imposed and the particular vantage points it offered—gave them the opportunity to discern the coercive power of nationalism, to critique the promises of modernity, and to historicize the paradoxes of being "modern Indian women" that had shaped their own experiences of the last decades of the Raj. If the histories they produced were tragic or dystopic ones, they serve as an instructive reminder of how imperfectly the linear development model of "civilizational" progress under imperial rule fit their historical experiences.[43]

At the heart of their particular visions of late colonial India and its prison-houses is, of course, a hierarchy of social relations—caste and class—that signal the "unstoried" experiences, especially of servants both in and outside the house, which shaped elite colonial women's gendered relationships to home and history.[44] The work that servants perform in Janaki's "Family History," Sorabji's official reports, and Hosain's novel dramatize the absolute dependence of elite women's mobility, worldview, and political desires on the labor of people doubly subordinated by caste and class in the Indian colonial context. Notwithstanding the complex relationships all three women had with religion, the sacred, and communalism, their writing offers evidence of the place of caste in cultural narratives of the aspiring secular self in twentieth-century India.[45] Drawing attention to the archival value of women's writing means confronting the full range of subjectivities that such an archive can yield, including those that it erases, suppresses, buries, denies. It involves, in short, coming to terms with the proposition that no archive, however antagonistic, fails to inscribe power—even and especially the power of some women over their social subordinates, both male and female. Reading home as an archive can be a political project subversive of "business as usual" only when domesticity is historicized both as a space where "the rescue and the retreat into an apolitical private sphere can be endlessly embroidered upon" *and* as a place through which the "social inequalities undergirding elite households can be critiqued."[46] The fact that all three women wrote in English, for an English-speaking audience, in which—at least in the case of Sorabji and Hosain—the implied reader was both Indian and British, also follows from their elite locations, and from the privileges of both dwelling and mobility that those locations allowed. While their privilege clearly shaped the dialectical relationship between what Inderpal Grewal has called "home and harem"—and, indeed, permitted the reproduction of their elite status in elite idioms—this does not necessarily diminish the archival value of their work for us. Indeed, that work now serves as evidence of a specific domain of "Indian" history in its bourgeois modern form—especially since, as any number of postcolonial writers have suggested, English is (for better or worse) a right and proper Indian language.[47]

As exceptional as their lives may have been, preoccupation with the physical spaces of house and home was by no means unique to them if we consider the history of writing by and about Indian women in India from the 1860s onward. The world of autobiography with which they might have been familiar and, at the very least, in which their own writing finds company—memoirs, devotional literature, personal narratives, and a variety of prescriptive texts—has been well detailed by scholars.[48] The image of place, and specifically of the physical layout and material culture of home, is a recurrent feature of the memory-work contained in this vast archive—a phenomenon that reminds us of how intimately connected spatial relations are to social relations, as well as of how constitutive architectural idioms can be of the practice of remembering. For some South Asian women writers, the house is the foundation for memory; for others, its courtyards, verandahs, and stairways plot not just space but also familial relations, personalities, and the cycle of birth and death.[49] Certainly, not every single personal narrative inscribes home at its heart or even consistently evokes domestic interiors as constituents of identity or family history. Neither Ramabai Ranade's *Himself* (1910) nor Muthulakshmi Reddy's *Autobiography* (1964), for example, privileges the space of home either rhetorically or affectively; though interiors are mentioned in passing, they do not dominate these works or give structure to their narrative form. And when they do, they do not always conjure happy memories, as in Lakshmibai Tilak's work *I Follow After* (1934–37).[50] At the same time, titles like *Inner Recesses, Outer Spaces* (1988) and *Courtyards of My Childhood* (1996) point to the enduring discursive influence of house and home on Indian women's autobiographical productions.[51] Clearly, the impact of history on home is different at different moments in time, with the 1920s and 1930s exercising a distinct, if not unique, kind of pressure, in ways that perhaps the 1980s and 1990s did as well.

What accounts for the consistent use of house and home as tropes in memory and history? As has been documented by Mary Carruthers and Jonathan Spence, architectural mnemonics have a long history in Western tradition, beginning with Aristotle and finding one of their most remarkable expressions in the "memory palaces" that the Italian Jesuit Matteo Ricci used as a strategy for evangelizing China in the late sixteenth century.[52] In a variety of regional and vernacular traditions in India, the role of *ghar* (household), *wada* (residence, typically Maharashtrian), *haveli* ("big house"), and *vitu* (house/household) in the history of memory, nation, and self has been equally, if differently constitutive, and certainly no less politically significant. Recent work in "Indian" epistemology suggests that memory is one of the feminine forms that display divine excellence in the *Bhagavad Gita*—behind only fame, prosperity, and speech as one of the ninefold stages of *bhakti* (devotion).[53] Not surprisingly, perhaps, given the hegemony of Bengali history in modern South Asian history in the last century, the domestic geography of the upper-caste Bengali home is the most well known. Sonia Amin has analyzed the role of the private sphere of Muslim households, while Himani Bannerji has parsed the *andarmahal* (the "inner quarters" and, in her view, the "social domain") against the grid of the *griha* (the sentimental moral space). Dipesh Chakrabarty has focused on the office versus the home, the clerk versus the wife, in his analysis of the family romance of Victorian *bhadralok* (middling class).[54] In part because these interior designs were part of "the normalization of a new patriarchal morality," they impressed themselves on women's subjectivities, and in turn on their representations of the past, well into the twentieth century.[55] Given the role of companionate marriage in nationalist discourses, the domestic was scarcely contained in or by "the private"; it was nothing less than a fillip to action in the public sphere on the local, regional, "national," or imperial stage. As Meera Kosambi has noted (in relation to Maharashtra), memories of home have enabled women across class and caste not simply to recall the domestic spaces that helped to shape them, but also to imagine and work for alternative social universes via political and cultural reform—against British imperial interests and, in some cases, against Indian nationalist prescriptions as well.[56]

Seen in this context, Majumdar, Sorabji, and Hosain were quite canny about what archiving the domestic meant in the context of British colonialism and its legacies—and equally prescient about the difficulties of claiming "History" (capital *H*) as women's work. Their reliance on memories of home as an archive for histories of late colonial modernity raises crucial questions about the relationship between memory and history, and about the role of colonialism itself in shaping what constitutes legitimate, "reliable" evidence of the past. Beyond the particular stories that this book examines, therefore, I want to engage the problem of who counts as a historian, what archives look like, and why memories of house and home should be recognized as crucial to what we think of as the historical imagination. For although the pressure of women's, gender, and feminist history on the discipline at large has been significant in the last quarter-century, in fact domesticity has traditionally been viewed as outside history both in Europe and beyond it during most of what is designated "modern time." This is not only because official discourses of the nation actively managed the domestic sphere so that it appeared as the timeless, universal "other" of modernity but equally because home, coded as inherently feminine and private, apparently eludes what the Indian architect and critic Gautam Bhatia calls "forthright documentation."[57] And although the status of women as rightful historical subjects is no longer in doubt, the capacity of women to write History has been considered dubious until quite recently, historically speaking. Hence what women wrote was conventionally designated "Literature" (the domain of memory, sentiment, and fiction) while men claimed the more "objective" task of writing truth-telling "History." As Bonnie Smith and Devoney Looser have effectively demonstrated, the emergence of Literature and History as distinct domains was a historical process that can be traced to a specific historical moment, namely the end of the eighteenth century. Their research has also demonstrated what a convenient ruse this distinction has been for marginalizing women from one of the chief centers of modern public discourse, namely historiography itself.[58] The segregation of History from Literature coincides, not incidentally, with the emergence of "archival rationalization"— a process whereby archives became part of the quest for a "truth-apparatus" that undergirded a variety of social science practices.[59] Just as the notion of separate spheres has come under criticism by feminist historians as the representation of white Western middle-class women's lived social experiences, so too has the application of that quintessentially Victorian ideology to the question of who may be said to count as a historian.[60] In this sense, then, recent scholarship has detailed the genealogies of Christina Crosby's claim that women have been "the unhistorical other of History," even while offering us an opportunity to consider how—under what historical conditions and with that discursive forms—women have made use of home to wrestle with the exclusions and possibilities of history as a public, political practice.[61]

Scholarly attention to memory in the past two decades has given women's historical experience a foothold in history, insofar as their testimonies—archived through oral narratives, autobiographies, and ethnographies—have been recognized as a supplement to the official record, whether in the context of cataclysmic historical events like the Holocaust or in the case of the so-called smaller, more localized experiences of daily life. At the same time, recent work on memory has relied, often in unspoken ways, on the longstanding template of fiction/feminine-history/masculine by gendering memory as female: by casting it as compelling but also "interested, provisional, and characterized by lapses of forgetting, silences, and exclusions." Memory has been represented, in other words, as dependent and mendacious (fictional, fickle) and therefore of dubious authority and reliability, all of which are hallmarks of conventional female identity in the context of a heterosexual symbolic economy.[62] In many respects this tendency to cast memory as unreliable/fictional represents the fate of most if not all testimonial evidence, even when such aspersions are not cast in explicitly gendered terms. An otherwise laudatory review of Suvir Kaul's 2001 collection on partition, for example, lamented that "although . . . oral history and unstructured interviews constitute the most fashionable discourse today, how far can the diagnoses of individual psyches be extended to form general conclusions? What about questions of reliability, validity and authentication?"[63] Starker still is C. W. Watson's question, aimed at the "autobiographical self" in the letters of Raden Ajeng Kartini (1879–1904), an Indonesian nationalist and feminist: "how do we know the narrator is telling the truth?"[64] The question of reliability continues to dog even the most respected work in oral history, in large measure because "properly" archival sources are still considered the standard against that all other evidence must be verified, or at least against which it must be measured.[65] Indeed, very few historians make, let alone accept, the case for "stories" (whether "fiction" or rumor or even gossip) as legitimate historical sources the way Luise White has done in her book *Speaking with Vampires (2000)*—despite (or perhaps because of) the capacity of such stories to "change the way . . . historical reconstruction is done."[66] Since official colonial archives are limited where the historical experiences and subjectivities of indigenous peoples are concerned, scholars of colonialism have been especially preoccupied with this question, though they are not necessarily less invested in the archival hierarchies that undergird the profession at large. As one historian of colonial Mexico argues, when one works one's way "down the documentary and institutional food chain to the most fragmentary, biographical, and folkloric data," one is in "murky" waters, seeking historical explanations from evidence that "looms like rusted hulks on the teeming ocean floor."[67]

Whether such evidentiary skepticism is reserved chiefly for the memories of non-Western, ex-colonial, or nontraditional historical subjects like people of color and women is a provocative question.[68] In any event, the presumption that memory is closer to fiction than history is to "truth" can disqualify it—or at the very least, call it into question—as *evidence* and, therefore, as an archival source, technically speaking.[69] Such reasoning is in danger of obscuring the historical processes through which "facts" and evidence became the grounds of professional history. It prevents us from appreciating, in short, the extent to which what emerged as "the archive" itself was the preoccupation of a modernizing, Western, bourgeois, Victorian professional class.[70] Equally obscured is how the hierarchical relationship between memory and history is embedded in the epistemological genealogy of the modern Western social science disciplines—a genealogy rooted, of course, in the history of colonialism. Although Pierre Nora admitted that "modern memory is . . . archival," he also prophesied the gradual decline of and disappearance of memory—a process that, however regrettable, was entailed by history's professional destiny.[71] What is telos for Nora is evolution for Jacques Le Goff; in his view, memory must be considered "the raw material of history"—a calculus that evokes not just the raw and the cooked but a kind of evolutionary progression, in that the primitive (memory) is supplanted by the civilized (history). If history is one of the central myths of Western modernity—that symptomatic sign of the colonial modern—memory remains its regressive, subordinated Other.[72] When rememberers and their memories challenge history (aboriginal peoples in Australia, Holocaust survivors around the world), they may produce a shift in historical consciousness among their listeners and even a critique of History itself, but their status *as Others* (vis-à-vis a presumptively male Western civilization) rarely, I would argue, changes, except insofar as they are incorporated as such into dominant historical narratives. Whether, and under what conditions, such folks wish to be part of academic history as "subjects" has been crucial to debates in Australia especially, where incorporation can be viewed as a form of neocolonialism.[73] Although most scholars who engage these questions fail to comment on it, it should come as no surprise that women and other "others" (working people, tribals, children, "subalterns") are memory's chief representatives, as well as its primary preservers. Questioning the verifiability of the evidence produced in sites of memory like oral histories, letters, autobiographies, and testimonies throws doubt on the narratives drawn from them *as history*, leaving women's (and others') accounts of their own experience—most often found in "unreliable" sources—in the realm of memory and clearing the way for an apparently superior, because disinterested, "History." Given the role of History in legitimating white, male, and middle-class hegemony, reading women's memories as supplements to History is not only unfortunate, it is arguably a continuation of the logic of Western colonial modernity.

Obviously, the big battles over the legitimacy of personal testimony and oral histories were fought and mostly won by the end of the 1980s: one of several legacies of social history to cultural history and cultural studies.[74] Feminist historians, for their part, have long used unconventional sources—letters, diaries, ephemera of various kinds—to write women's experiences (back) into history, and in doing so have tried to establish an alternative archive from which to challenge exclusionary local, national, and colonial histories. As Laurel Thatcher Ulrich has commented with respect to her 1991 book *A Midwife's Tale* (which uses Martha Ballard's eighteenth-century diary to reconstruct her working life), "I'm interested in what isn't there [in the archive], what can't be found, what's been lost."[75] Yet despite the extent to which women's history has entered into the mainstream of academic practice, it is also true that when such work is subjected to the "archive test" in job talks, hiring evaluations, and prize and promotion decisions, it is frequently found wanting. If this evidence of professional standardization is largely unarchived, its effects are nonetheless very real. Indeed, despite the fact that recognition of the false dichotomies of history and fiction has been addressed by social historians as prestigious and influential as Natalie Zemon Davis (her 1987 book *Fiction in the Archives* makes just this kind of case), such work is often categorized these days as "cultural studies" (rather than history) or accepted as a supplement to an extant "master narrative."[76] When primary sources are not housed in recognized repositories, there is, still, rarely a consensus about them, I would contend, as legitimately "historical" material in their own right.

In the South Asian context, Shahid Amin's work has done much to disrupt the alleged self-sufficiency of the official archive. In his account of events at Chauri Chaura (1922) he insists on the materiality of memory, emphasizing its peculiar "facticities." Rather than dismissing them as tainted evidence or holding them up as purified examples of "truth," he makes use of peasant memories to demonstrate where and how historical consciousness dwells in narrative and its various forms.[77] And yet the most common critique directed against memory, especially via oral history, is that recollection is suspect as historical evidence because "narrators . . . get it wrong." As Peter Heehs opined in his review of Wendy Singer's *Creating Histories: Oral Narratives and the Politics of History-Making*, narrative accounts are fine and good, but "when their basis of factuality departs, they transmigrate into something that is useless to the practicing historian." Moreover:

> The métier of the historian is to take the available materials, study them, find where they have been distorted by factors of various sorts — mendacity, forgetfulness, economic interests, discourse—and beat them back into shape by means of critical reading, collation, analysis and so on. The result will never be as shapely as the original . . . but it will at least have some utility.[78]

Although it is harsh, even extreme, Heehs's evaluation speaks to the empirical bias, even fantasy, that continues to influence history as a "social science" discipline. Book reviews can be quite ephemeral sites of judgment, to be sure; but they have disciplinary power that we ignore at our peril. Thus Tanika Sarkar's 1999 book *Words to Win* (a brilliant reading of the first Indian woman's autobiography in Bengal, Rassundari Devi's *Amar Jiban* [1876]) begins with the following confession: "it is not easy to convince oneself that the writing of an obscure village housewife has any significance as a subject of historical research, since it cannot uncover new or significant 'historical facts.'"[79]

Sarkar attributes her uncertainty to the fact that "the world of the institutionalised discipline of Indian history still refuses to accept" histories from below and histories of representation as legitimate history.[80] As I have suggested, I am not at all sure that this is a limitation unique to the profession in South Asia, though its manifestations elsewhere may be more subtle than Heehs's aforementioned review. Significantly, the Delhi-based feminist publishing house Kali for Women, which issued *Words to Win*, has committed itself to producing what it calls an "archive series": historical documents and texts written by women, often originally in Indian languages, that have been translated with extensive scholarly analyses to accompany them. In the words of one of Kali's founding editors, "the idea is to build up an archive of an archive, so to speak"—indicating her view that such work already constitutes an archival source but requires a public affirmation of that status.[81] Recent scholarship on women's experience of partition (1947) has forced us to reconsider not just the relationship between memory and history but how those categories have been gendered, and how that gendering has contributed to the continued marginality of "Indian" women in and by History. As the work of Urvashi Butalia, Ritu Menon, and Kamla Bhasin has shown, memory may have "become" her, in the sense that it was a nontransgressive, private realm in which to preserve the past. But it has also perhaps been in danger of "becoming" her—in the sense of being coterminous with her relationship to "real" history—as well.[82] Their insistence on reading memory as history signals an important epistemological break not simply with the divide between literature and history, or even with the pathologization of memory by history, but rather with the presumption that the problem resides in the *subject* or *contents* of an archive rather than with practices of recognizing a variety of materials as archival and *reading* them accordingly. By acknowledging that not all readers either can or want to read like professional historians, Butalia especially implies that women's historical memory has evidential status when and if it is read as an *interpretive* act: as neither truth nor fiction, in other words, but as a continual reminder of the historicity—and, of course, the political valences—of all traces from the past.[83] Her contribution lies in her determination to democratize what counts as an archive: to enlarge the scope of what we *recognize* as such and to include memory in it: not as a second-class citizen, as it were, but as a usable source of history. In doing so, she aims to challenge the colonial logic, with its constitutively gendered assumptions, of even postcolonial history-writing.

In keeping with these efforts, I hope to contribute to the prodigious literature on gender, memory, and history by arguing that women's memories of house and home, such as those that Majumdar, Sorabji, and Hosain have archived for us, can and should count as the grounds of history: as a constitutive, rather than just a supplemental, archive of the past. Extending their use of home as an archive, I insist that published and unpublished texts like the family history, the memoirs, and the novel examined in the following chapters are not mere "afterimages" of history.[84] Nor do they only articulate "the literary dimension of nationalist ideology."[85] Instead, they should be read *both* as archival sites *and* as history-in-the-making: as legitimate, and as subject to interrogation, as official policy documents or other artifacts of the state or, for that matter, other accounts of the past. The consequences of this maneuver are worth underscoring. First, by recognizing house and home as archives that produce histories, we interrupt the binary logic of the discipline that segregates primary from secondary sources and privileges the archive as some originary—and therefore somehow pure—site of historical knowledge or evidence. We acknowledge, in other words, that "the archive contains primary sources, at the same time that it is always already a secondary trace of historical discourse."[86] In doing so, we must concede the fundamental liminality of the archive: its porousness, its permeability, and the messiness of all history that is made by and from it. We might even think of it as a kind of "third space": neither primary or secondary because it participates in, and helps to create, several levels of interpretive possibility at once.[87] Embracing such indeterminance compels us to rethink the contingency of all archives, not just those that women create for the purposes of making history. For if we are to challenge the standards of judgment and evaluation to which Sarkar refers and to which Kali has so vigorously responded, we must commit ourselves to acknowledging that all archives are provisional, interested, and calcified in both deliberate and unintentional ways; that *all* archives are, in the end, fundamentally unreliable—the archive of women's memory no more or less so than any other. In contrast to what some critics of postmodernism have suggested, this need not mean the end of history. To the contrary: it is the very condition from which history, especially in the wake of colonialism and its archival silences, ruptures, and depredations, must proceed. If we are to preserve women in, for, and as history, we must allow that the discursive forms that their memories take are not incidental to the kinds of stories they tell. These are in fact the very *matériel* of history: "precious records," to borrow from Susan Mann's account of women's writings in Qing China; not simply representations but material evidence of the gendered experiences of domestic life and family culture that help to constitute the political past, the national story, the colonial narrative.[88] And if women's structural locations have meant that the domestic looms large in these accounts—if house and home, in all their symbolic and material complexity, are prime among the resources that women have used to imagine the past—then we must take them seriously precisely as archival forms in order to bring women's "private" experiences more fully into the purview of history. Otherwise the historicity of women's words will continue to be imperiled, and memory, like fiction, will continue to be viewed merely as the "counter-archive for the ephemeral and wayward" rather than as a full-fledged (if not self-standing) archive—one that displays a variety of historically contingent narrative strategies and provides an opportunity for a variety of intellectually responsible interpretive possibilities.[89]

In the face of the tangible connections between memory and politics, memory and reform, memory and history that this book unearths, it becomes impossible to dismiss autobiographies, family histories, and other memory-bilia as merely fictional and therefore as secondary or even supplemental to archival sources for getting at historical agency and conditions. This is especially true if such archives are read ethnographically—that is, interpreted as "real" cultural artifacts with systems of logic and representation. Conceptualizing memory as history involves recognizing that artifacts (like house and home) are carriers of memory and that the narratives people tell about them are the stuff of history, *if* we treat them as skeptically as we read official repositories of evidence, and *if* we read them with an eye for what they can tell us about the political desires and ambivalences to be found in the recesses of ostensibly "domestic" space.[90] Feminist historians have not succeeded in fully interrogating the supremacy of a male-patterned archive, in large part because they need certain kinds of archival grounding for their own legitimacy. Resituating the kind of memory-work undertaken by Majumdar, Sorabji, and Hosain as archival history is therefore critical to the project of feminist historiography, which has historically been devoted to interrogating false dichotomies like public and private and, presumably, their analogs—history and memory—as well. In a 1994 essay that anticipated much of what I am concerned with here, Paula Hamilton called this question "the knife edge" of the discipline: not just because contemporary societies are obsessed with remembering and forgetting but because history as a professional practice, even in its subspecialties, has been preoccupied with patrolling the borders between itself and memory.[91] Given the role of the traditional archive in excluding and distorting women's subjectivity—and of course, all historical subjectivities—making memory history is, arguably, one of the grounds from which discussions of women's agency in history must proceed.

Naming women's memoirs, autobiographies, family histories, and novels as historical forms addresses the limits and possibilities not just of feminist history but also of the demands of history as a discipline itself. As Mary Margaret Steedly has argued,

> the transcription of historical experience—in names, monuments, genealogies; in collective fantasy and in the repeated social intercourse of every day life; in law, property and desire; in stories inhaled with the common air of a shared place or time—is the movement through which subjectivity is produced.[92]

Far from being simply "personal," subjectivity is produced and lived as history, through historical processes embedded at least in part in everyday architectural apprehensions and imaginaries. And just as "storytelling is the making and remaking of the gendered self in social relations," so too is history implicated in the production and reproduction of women's cultural imagination.[93] Coming to terms with histories that materialize untold archives of the domestic with all their possibilities, suppressions, and limitations allows us to appreciate the role of material objects in creating and sustaining gendered historical imaginaries. It is also one way of pushing the claim that feminist history is more than business as usual, because the interiors that women's narratives house always look out onto, and are constituted by, history itself.[94] The fiction that History continues to tell itself is that there ever was such a thing as the "private"—that quintessentially gendered domestic space-in-time—when in fact the discipline has been instrumental in reproducing the private as women's domain. The extent to which critiques of the fictionality of the private (as opposed to discussions of its opposition to or relationship with "the public") have made their way to the center of historical practice or the historiographical imagination is one question that guides this book. To archive the domestic is to begin to prize open that fiction and face the radical historicity to which a critical engagement of all archives (whether grounded in memory or "history") commits us.[95] It also, inevitably, means interrogating the dreams of mastery and total knowledge—"truth-telling"—that have been at the heart of History's history as a discipline, as a profession, and as a site of political desire since its earliest origins.[96]

The stakes of memory are undoubtedly high, and the truth-status of its narrative forms, therefore, equally contestable. Rajeswari Sunder Rajan reminds us that English-language fiction-writing in India today operates in the shadow of Salman Rushdie's novel *Midnight's Children* (1980), and in some sense, so too does the work of scholars of twentieth-century South Asian history. Am I reading memory-as-history back through partition and the novel that concludes this book, *Sunlight on a Broken Column?* Very possibly. At the same time, I would argue, it would be a mistake to imagine that the intensity of memories of home—and with them, histories of the fantasy of dwelling in colonial modernity—were original or somehow particular to the upheavals of 1947 in the modern Indian colonial context. By juxtaposing Hosain's novel with other women's writing in and about the preindependence period, we can more fully appreciate, I think, the ways that partition was the culmination, even the manifestation, of a certain kind of colonial modernity rather than a break from it. We can also understand, by historicizing these archives themselves, what was at stake for elite Indian women writing in English as they laid claim to a certain kind of historical voice, forged out of their individual encounter with history but also produced from the crucible of domestic politics "at home"—politics, in other words, *as home*—as well. The insecurity and fragility of home as British imperialists and Indian nationalists viewed it thus reemerges as the ground for a different kind of domestication project: one that takes as its point of departure the very impossibility of home and thereby tracks its history as a story of the fantasy of safety that has always motivated its most powerful ideological manifestations. As I suggest of Hosain at the end of chapter 4, each of the authors under consideration here might well have agreed with Theodor Adorno's sense that home had grown intolerable by the third and fourth decades of the twentieth century. As Adorno himself put it, it had become "part of morality not to be at home in one's home"— and, by extension, in history as well.[97] In this respect, home had to, perhaps, become an archive—the dwelling-place of a critical history rather than the falsely safe space of the past—in order to be tolerable in the context of colonial modernity and its aftermath, for women and for men equally, if differently. And so whether it was a hybrid, transcontinental affair, the inner chambers of the zenana, or the ancestral abode, Majumdar, Sorabji, and Hosain made "home" a repository of historical knowledge—one that they could not simply or easily reside in, because of the challenge to comfort it invariably produced.

And yet each of the women in this study chose to cast her encounter with history as an account of domestic spaces—spaces that offer us, in turn, an unexplored archive of what it could mean to be a daughter both of and in history, as well as a glimpse of how seductive, in spite of their critiques, home ineluctably is. Like other colonized women grappling with their colonial pasts in the twentieth century, Majumdar, Sorabji, and Hosain (re)built homes on their own textual terms, "refusing to cede the authority of the interior" to nationalism, to imperialism, or even, in the end, to History *tout court*.[98] The fact that each of them had an ambivalent relationship to nationalism is itself a crucial feature of their political interventions. If, as Rosemary Marangoly George has argued, imagining home is as political an act as imagining the nation, the archival sources I am interested in calling "history" demonstrate how a certain class of Indian women tried to manage the political implications of the past by putting their own narratives of home within the realm of public memory.[99] It is my intention in this book to contribute to the literature on women, memory, and history-writing in the twentieth century by analyzing the generic forms and rhetorical strategies Indian women used to preserve themselves as remembering subjects, and by examining the larger problem of what kinds of memory colonial modernity required from Indian women—and how the historical imagination was made and remade through their engagements with it.[100]

Chapter Two

HOUSE, DAUGHTER, NATION

Interiority, Architecture, and Historical Imagination in Janaki Majumdar's "Family History"

My mother grew up in a small Punjabi village not far from Chandigarh. As she chopped onions for the evening meal or scrubbed the shine back onto a steel pan or watched the clouds of curds form in a bowl of slowly setting homemade yoghurt, any action with a rhythm, she would begin a mantra about her ancestral home. She would chant of a three-storeyed flat-roofed house, blinkered with carved wooden shutters around a dust yard where an old-fashioned pump stood under a mango tree. . . . In England, when all my mother's friends made the transition from relatives' spare rooms and furnished lodgings to homes of their own, they all looked for something "modern."

"It's really up to date, Daljit," one of the Aunties would preen as she gave us the grand tour of her first proper home in England. "Look at the extra flush system . . . Can opener on the wall . . . Two minutes' walk to the local amenities. . . ."

But my mother knew what she wanted. When she stepped off the bus in Tollington, she did not see the outside lavvy or the apology for a garden or the medieval kitchen, she saw fields and trees, light and space, and a horizon that welcomed the sky that, on a warm night and through squinted eyes, could almost look something like home.

—Meera Syal, *Anita and Me*

 In an age of virtual reality, cyberspace, and migration of global proportions, the very possibility of home is being vigorously contested. Whether it is identified as Africa, England, India, or, more subversively, the "black Atlantic," home is neither a stationary place nor a self-evident trope. Like all historical utterances, it is both fictional and contingent, inflected by the particular social contexts out of which it is fashioned and, of equal significance, defying the very materiality and permanence it appears to embody. Because it is one of the organizing fictions of national literatures and ideologies, the project of remembering home has produced elaborate interiors and imaginative architectures that are vivid and, as Meera Syal illustrates, ultimately approximate as well. These dwelling-places of the mind seduce but do not finally satisfy, precisely because they can only ever "*almost* look *something* like home."[1]

Like all memoirs, Janaki Agnes Penelope Majumdar's "Family History" is just such an exercise in approximation: an essay in remembrance whose objects of imagination and desire are the houses of her family's past. Majumdar was the daughter of W. C. Bonnerjee, the first president of the INC, and Hemangini Motilal, a Hindu woman who was betrothed to him as a young girl in the 1850s.[2] An English-educated Christian, Janaki grew up largely in Croydon, outside London, and earned a degree from Newnham College, Cambridge. Although she settled in Calcutta after her marriage to P. M. Majumdar, she spent her formative years either outside India or traveling between Calcutta and southeast England.[3] Memories of the Bonnerjees' family homes in India and Britain are at the structural heart of Janaki's "Family History," which was written in 1935 as the fiftieth anniversary of the INC was being commemorated in India. Her manuscript—which was unpublished for almost seventy years—raises questions about how and under what conditions home is recalled when a woman takes up the task of mapping domestic genealogies *as a daughter*. It prompts us to ask how the architecture she produces ends up figuring the nation in history as well. Unlike the memoir or the novel, the family history is a commemorative practice that creates a very specific kind of archive. Here, the (re)built environment has a specific ideological function: to house the interiorities of childhood and, by doing so, to bear witness to the fact of historical—and national and political—consciousness.[4] I would not like to deny that such histories are also fictional, or to suggest that they always assume a generic form that is, say, distinct from Western conventions of autobiography.[5] Nor would I wish to claim that women writers resort to home in their family memoirs more commonly or consistently than men—though in the case of British India, the village arguably eclipsed the house as the most memorable site for those male elites who committed their recollections to paper in the public sphere.[6] In the context of colonial Bengal, Janaki Majumdar's "Family History" acts as a counternarrative to the family romance that underpinned elite discourses of nationalism in the nineteenth and twentieth centuries.[7] As I will demonstrate, it is also a many-layered, many-voiced counterarchive of colonial modernity, assembled for private consumption to commemorate Indian nation-building by a daughter determined to rescue her mother from the recesses of a diasporic nationalist history. This chapter examines what this work of reconstruction meant in the context of 1930s Indian nation-building, in the hands of a prominent nationalist's daughter who was bold enough to chronicle her family's history and, in the process, to reveal her own persistent desire for the elusive fiction of home. My hope is to answer recent calls for attention to the role of remembering and forgetting in the "circuits of nationalist thinking" by regrounding the history of Indian Congress nationalism in the social life of "things" like house and home.[8]

Much has been written about the discourses of domesticity produced by reforming male elites in the context of colonial Bengal—most famously by Partha Chatterjee, who argued that the nationalist "resolution of the 'woman question'" was to affirm the domain of the Brahman home as the redemptive spiritual space that could resist the materialist values and incursions of a Western, colonizing culture.[9] This maneuver involved a crucial shift for the precincts of house and home at both the symbolic and the material levels: for it required the transformation of the household from kinship unit to spatial entity under the guidance of modernist reformers, chiefly men.[10] Dipesh Chakrabarty has elaborated on just what kind of patriarchal bargain such a project set in motion. For in addition to making the upper-caste Hindu home an archive for British imperialists (official and unofficial), it helped to focus the "natural" fraternity of Indian men on a shared investment in protocols of domesticity, including female beauty and "pleasantness" of demeanor.[11] Followers of this vein of analysis over the past fifteen years would be hard pressed to deny that the colonial/nationalist project outlined by Chatterjee and Chakrabarty failed to create an emancipatory space for the upper-caste Indian women who found themselves in the confines of the Bengali home. Indeed, feminist historians have been at pains to excavate both the world of women's print culture, in which such patriarchal bargains were discussed and negotiated, *and* the lives of a number of women who were outspoken opponents of the limitation of possibilities that such house discipline entailed. Significantly, perhaps, the most celebrated of those resistant and very public voices were not Bengali: Tarabai Shinde, whose pamphlet, *A Comparison between Men and Women* (1882), launched a blistering attack on patriarchal gender relations, was Maharashtrian. The same is true of Pandita Ramabai, whose peripatetic young life made her a kind of all-India, as well as a cosmopolitan, figure.[12] And yet there is a lingering presumption that the spiritual redemption to be gained by association and identification with the Brahman household, and especially with the household goddess Lakshmi, offered a pathway toward self-fulfillment that some privileged Hindu women might take advantage of. Tanika Sarkar's work on Rassundari Devi, the first Indian woman to write an autobiography (*Amar Jiban*, in Bengali, completed in 1868), would seem to bear this out. Although Sarkar's translation of and extended commentary on the autobiography together throw light on the "dark landscape of upper-caste domesticity," they also demonstrate how Rassundari's submission to devotional regimes produced a certain kind of freedom. As Sarkar argues, her subordination "ensured a space of relative autonomy . . . [She] goes through extremes of helplessness as well as great authority in the same lifetime. . . . she gets to know both subjection and the taste of ruling."[13]

I do not mean to suggest that Sarkar interprets Devi as an example of feminist consciousness. Such a reading would imply an equivalence between Victorian Britain and Victorian India that Sarkar adamantly rejects. And in any case, Sarkar is understandably more interested in explaining "why and how . . . women are, most of the time, compliant subjects of patriarchy" rather than its critics.[14] At the same time, Sarkar does see in Rassundari's text more than mere inklings of modernity; and by extension, she sees in her a certain kind of modern heroine, if only because of the "deeply transgressive departure" that her learning to read and the writing of her life symbolize for a respectable Hindu wife.[15] The same might be said of the diversity of personal narratives produced by the Bengali *bhadramahila* since just after midcentury, when middle-class women wrote short stories, periodical articles, and other texts that detailed their experiences and their observations of social and cultural life in British India and created "modern," semiheroic subjectivities for women in the context of colonial modernity.[16] Although it details a transnational lifestyle to which very few Indian women had access (and that many Hindus would have considered disrespectable because it involved crossing "the black waters"—bodies of water that high-caste Hindus were forbidden to cross—and thus guaranteed a fall from caste), Majumdar's "Family History" participates in this tradition of elite Indian women's writing from the nineteenth century, insofar as it focuses on the interior spaces of family life and their role in the political economy of the household.[17] But what distinguishes Majumdar's memoir is the fact that it unabashedly displays the differences and, at times, the outright tensions, between W. C. and Hemangini as characteristic of Bonnerjee family life. This is not to say that Bengali women's narratives did not critique either the ideal of Hindu conjugality or the house discipline concomitant with it. As Srabashi Ghosh has shown, Kailashbini's complaint to her husband—"from my childhood I follow your instructions as far as possible. If you can't find fault, how can you rebuke me"—echoes the plaintive cry of Bengali women writing from the Victorian through the postindependence period.[18] Janaki's chronicle departs from the work of the Victorian *bhadramahila* not because it places Hemangini's emotional well-being at the center of the narrative but because it constructs the Indian mother as a pathetic, helpless, and ultimately stranded subject of domestic discipline. It thus attempts to deflect attention from the daughter, who had traditionally been the resistant voice, in order to protest the conjugal face of the reformed household, companionate marriage: that "critical trope" of colonial modernity.[19]

As a counternarrative, then, the "Family History" is quite instructive, in part because it is not about just any family. Despite the fact that her adolescence was shaped by the exigencies of Bonnerjee's political career—and, of course, because of this fact—Janaki chose to represent the 1880s and 1890s not as the moment when organized Indian nationalism emerged but rather as a period of extended struggle for the preservation of the family household by her mother. Indeed, in the "Family History," W. C. Bonnerjee's public profile, though certainly never neglected, is arguably eclipsed by the drama of the orthodox Hindu (and, later, Christian) woman struggling to maintain her identity, to guarantee her family's coherence, and, above all, to establish a viable, stable home for herself and her children, despite the upheavals of temporary exile. If the physical spaces of home haunt Majumdar's archive, it is not, therefore, simply a historical accident. The recurrent architectural imagery of home is produced by a witness to the collision between "traditional" Hindu

family life and a particular strand of secular nationalist politics—
even as the cultural terms of that collision were reshaped by Hemangini's conversion to Christianity in the 1870s.

From the very beginning of the "Family History," Janaki recon-
structs her domestic genealogies by imagining the dwelling-places of
relatives past. The text opens with details of her husband's ancestors
and fixes immediately on the physical spaces of home that defined
P. K. Majumdar's *zamindar* (landowning) family existence in the
early nineteenth century. The Majumdar family house at Islampur
appears on the first page of the narrative, standing as both a symbol
of their prosperity and a sign of their social status. The family residence mirrored the family fortunes: P. M.'s father rebuilt the house
as he improved his estate, establishing a local school and dispensary
on the premises along the way.[20] P. M.'s youth, which takes up the
first twenty pages of the "Family History," is figured as a series of es-
capes from home—to the town of Behrampur, to pig-sticking meets,
and eventually to St. Xavier's College (Calcutta) where, we are told,
he developed his taste for things English and his ambition "to live
[someday] in Creek Row among the flower of Anglo-India."[21] Following a brief sketch of P. M.'s education at Birmingham University
and his call to the Bar comes the early history of W. C. Bonnerjee. In
Janaki's hands it is a tale that radiates from the family house at Kidderpore to his early education and then his betrothal to Hemangini
in 1859, when he was fifteen and she ten. In addition to their
middle-class origins, what her husband and her father had in common was a skepticism about religious orthodoxy of any kind—doubts
that would cause them both to fall away from Hinduism in later life,
despite the attachment of both of their wives to practical (Christian)
faith. The accounts of the two men are otherwise disjunctive. In contrast to the story of her husband's early life, which takes up almost
thirty pages of the "Family History," Janaki's account of her father's
young adulthood is brief (four pages) and clearly dependent on the
structure of P. M.'s, even though W. C. was the older and more famous man.

From the start, the "family" with which Janaki identified in her
"Family History" was first the Majumdars and then the Bonnerjees.
This maneuver is not entirely surprising, since the text was written
primarily for her children and grandchildren. Its audience was far-
flung, even diasporic, and its chief purpose was to testify to their collective past. The primary effect of this structural choice is the subordination of W. C.'s very public life to the "domestic" narratives of both
her mother's life and, eventually, her own. To this end Janaki privi-

leges the story of her courtship and 1908 marriage to P. M., the event that brings part 1 of "Family History" to a close. One could read this gesture as characteristic of Indian women's memoirs, which tend to sideline the conventionally political in their narratives and to privilege the woman's movement from family of origin to family of marriage.[22] But, given W. C.'s highly public profile in the nationalist movement in both Britain and India, his relative marginalization in the text is quite remarkable. Janaki's determination to structure the narrative around what are indubitably *conjugal* households and, in so doing, to try to keep the activities of the INC off-center, is a structural feature of enormous historical significance—not least because it signals the ways in which her "Family History" ends up recuperating Indian nationalism as a bourgeois project that is dependent on the privatization, as well as the domestication, of "the Indian woman."

If P. M.'s and W. C.'s ancestral homes represent the fixity of patriarchal property, Hemangini's tale makes visible the shifting and impermanent relationships a high-caste Hindu woman might have had to the "family home." At the heart of Janaki's narrative arc in part 2 is Hemangini's struggle to master a family household that was highly unorthodox according to the standards by which she was raised and, as if that were not enough, continuously dispersed and on the move as well. We are first introduced to Hemangini as the sweet, shy daughter who was raised in an orthodox Hindu family by a generous father and a strict mother. Although formal education was denied her, Hemangini "managed to pick up her letters from her elder brothers" and once even tried to stow away in the carriage that took them to school, a trick for which she was "ignominiously" punished. Her mother was such a disciplinarian that when Hemangini lost a silver chain she had been given, she and her father conspired to find an identical one to replace it so that the loss would never be known, and she would not have to face her mother's wrath.[23] Unlike either P. K. Majumdar or W. C. Bonnerjee, Hemangini had little choice about what her daughter later called "the fate that lay in store for her—early marriage, innumerable children, and hard work under a possibly cantankerous mother-in-law"—though Janaki emphasizes how lucky Hemangini was to secure such a handsome and well-educated bridegroom. In a touching instance of mother-daughter candor, Hemangini told Janaki that they were so shy and nervous in anticipation of their wedding night that "when the bridegroom and the bride were left alone together for the first time, she told me the only remarks exchanged by them was her question as to how far it was from Bowbazar to Simla and his reply!"[24]

But it is neither these early hardships nor her mother's girlish naïveté that makes her the sainted center of Janaki's "Family History." Rather, it is Hemangini's continual struggle against her limited education and unworldliness that earns her pride of place. While her timidity, her lack of schooling, and her apparently basic English might not have been particularly grievous handicaps had she been married to a less ambitious man, these "limitations" were thrown into bold relief because Hemangini was the wife of an aspiring barrister who was also a politically ambitious, unabashedly modern, and anglophilic Indian man. The theme of Hemangini's vulnerability is foreshadowed by her very early life, where Janaki describes her as a "plain child" whose unremarkable looks were apparently compounded by the onset of leukoderma, a skin disease that left disfiguring traces on the face and body. This was hardly the model of physical beauty or "pleasantness" valorized by elite male nationalist discourses of domesticity in Bengal. But in Janaki's narrative, it is Bonnerjee's first trip to England in 1864—when he was twenty and Hemangini was fifteen—that begins Hemangini's lifelong pattern of suffering and struggle. Bonnerjee was the Bengali candidate chosen to study law in England under the auspices of a scholarship established by a Bombay businessman. His family declared it out of the question, knowing that, for an orthodox Hindu, crossing the black waters meant becoming an outcaste. With the help of an Anglo-Indian attorney, Bonnerjee fled the country alone, unbeknownst to his parents and presumably to Hemangini as well. The Bonnerjees senior were horrified and unforgiving when they first discovered he had gone. According to one of W. C.'s biographers, "loud were the lamentations that echoed through the old house" when Bonnerjee's flight to England was discovered.[25] His father eventually forgave him and sent him money to help him with his studies, though still, according to Janaki, "strongly disapproving of his behavior."[26] The consequences fell disproportionately on Hemangini's head. "My mother told me she also came in for a lot of abuse at that time," Janaki wrote, "and was called an unlucky girl and taunted with the fact that her husband ran away rather than have to live with her." Hemangini, still a teenager, was taunted, her daughter recalled, especially "for having no children."[27]

What follows is a chapter-long description of Bonnerjee's first experience in London in the later 1860s, where he worked hard at law and at perfecting his English (by reading aloud to himself every evening, as he later told her). "My father was very happy in England," Janaki writes, "and in after life used to look back with pleas-

ure on his student days."[28] The contrast with Hemangini's life in the
Bonnerjee family household in that same period is striking. "In the
meantime," Janaki writes, "my poor mother was not having a happy
life during my father's absence. She was repeatedly blamed for being
'unlucky,' and she used to practice all sorts of austerities and perform all sorts of penances to make up for his having lost caste by
going to England . . . she suffered vicariously during all the years of
his absence."[29] The fact that Hemangini was, according to custom,
living in her in-laws' home meant that she might have been the object of family and perhaps even local community disapproval on a
daily basis, though Janaki does not specify who the taunters were.[30]
Nor does Janaki give any indication that Hemangini was embittered
by either Bonnerjee's absence or the criticisms it engendered from
her orthodox contemporaries. But she does allow that her mother's
suffering manifested itself in quite specific ways, visiting itself literally on her body:

> She told me that . . . she was hysterical, and sometimes used to suffer
> from regular fits during which she completely lost consciousness. At
> one time her elders decided that these fits must be due to devil posses-
> sion, and accordingly an Exorciser was summoned to drive away the
> devil; and this drastic treatment used to make her worse than ever.
> Once she was told, during treatment, to look into a certain mirror and
> report what she saw there, and to her horror she really saw the face of a
> terrifying old cook they used to employ, who had died years ago, with
> his head held at a characteristically crooked angle, as he used to carry
> it in life. This vision so frightened her that it took her hours to get over
> it then, and it remained an alarming memory throughout all her life.
> In later life she completely got over these hysterical affections.[31]

These difficulties were not to abate. When Bonnerjee returned to
India in 1868, he made it clear to his family that he would not seek
readmission to caste through the formal ceremony. He was therefore
not permitted to return to his parents' home and initially stayed in a
hotel.[32] The rift this caused between him and his relatives was by no
means untypical for "England-returned" students, who often went to
tremendous lengths to subvert Shastric provisions by seeking alternative scriptural interpretations from local pundits.[33] As a consequence of W. C.'s resistance in this matter, he and Hemangini moved
to a small house in Entally soon thereafter.[34] Of all the hardships
Hemangini had thus far endured, Janaki believed that this move—
from the family house to their own—was the hardest yet, in part because it represented such a departure from tradition, in part because
it foreshadowed the unconventionality of things to come. "Having

been brought up as a good Hindu, and taught that a husband's word was law, she was able to make a complete break with the past, though what a terrible effort it must have been for her is hard to realize."[35]

In Janaki's account, that break continued to require sacrifice and submission from Hemangini in a variety of enduring ways, most of them centered on the daily practices and rituals of the new and, by nineteenth-century orthodox Hindu standards, extremely unconventional household. The following excerpt enumerates some of the pressures facing an upper-caste Hindu woman married to an outcaste Brahmin in Victorian Bengal:

> In after life my mother often used to tell us how very difficult she found it to come out of purdah and live in English fashion. In the first place, she had to give up wearing a sari, and to wear English dress. . . . Then there was the difficulty about food. For an orthodox Brahmin girl to have to eat food cooked and handled by Mahomedan servants, and to have to eat meat—even beef—was a most terrible ordeal, as she had been brought up to think such behavior a most deadly sin. She used to say that she could never have surmounted these difficulties if it had not been for my father's great kindness and consideration. At first, he himself would bring her meals from the kitchen, so that the Mahomedan or low caste Hindu servants should not touch it, and in the desire to save him trouble, she got over her feelings of distaste.[36]

As Dipesh Chakrabarty has argued, debates about modernity in colonial Bengal centered around the internal discipline (and in this case, the internal geography) of the Western home. Bonnerjee's willingness to go into the kitchen—and thus to cross a boundary that separated women and servants from "the man of the house"— illustrates the depth of his commitment to refiguring traditional structures in order to have a "modern" household.[37] If such a gesture may be read as a demonstration of his love for Hemangini, it is also an indication of the lengths to which he was prepared to go to modernize her along with the conjugal household. Like the objects of sartorial improvements in other "enlightened" Bengali homes, Hemangini was in effect a "captive household female," subject to the determination of reforming elites to create an "appropriate social subjectivity" for Indian women.[38]

Negotiating the spaces, both public and private, outside the physical parameters of "home" also presented challenges for Hemangini, according to her daughter:

> Although she and her husband were now "outcastes" in the sense that their relations could no longer eat with them or take water from their

hands, they were all devoted to her and she loved them all just as much as ever, and used to go visit them frequently. Here again a difficulty arose. She could not be seen by her servants and neighbours leaving her house in a sari; but on the other hand she could not arrive at her Mother-in-law's or Mother's house in an English dress. She solved this problem by taking a sari with her in the carriage, drawing down the blinds and changing on the way, so as to arrive clad in a sari and barefoot. On the way home she had to change back to dress and stockings and shoes, and she went on doing this until her relations got used to her new ways.[39]

By 1872 the Bonnerjees had moved not once but twice from Entally and were living at No. 1 Store Road in Ballygunge, an area of Calcutta that, after the suburban railway opened up, became "a citadel of the educated Bengali middle-class."[40] Although both Entally and Ballygunge were technically suburbs of Calcutta until the late 1880s, it may be that this new environment did not exact the same kinds of punishing requirements—though expectations about dress would probably have remained the same on the part of her mother and mother-in-law. If Hemangini resented having to perform these acrobatics, her daughter did not record it. Janaki did, however, make it clear that some of her father's expectations could be a trial for her mother when it came to other innovations. Upon his return to India in 1868, Bonnerjee was keen for his wife to learn English as well— a subject she never really mastered. According to her daughter, Hemangini found English "extremely difficult, and never really managed to conquer it completely."[41] The failure took its toll: Hemangini "always deplored her lack of education, the fact that she had never really learned to speak English as an Englishwoman, though she began so young and had so much practice."[42] Janaki attributed her mother's persistence in the face of Bonnerjee's expectations to "her great love and admiration for her husband, and her feeling that whatever he ordered must be right, that enabled her to adapt to his wishes."[43]

These adjustments were the consequence of being married to a Hindu man who had crossed the black waters, fallen from caste, and refused to be reinitiated into the faith and hence the family community. They were also the result of Bonnerjee's attraction to and romance with English family life. He named their first son Kamal Krishna Shelley in honor of the romantic poet. By the time his second and third children were born (daughters Nalini and Susila, known as Nellie and Susie, respectively), he had decided that they should all be educated in England—despite the fact that he himself had to remain in Calcutta to oversee his thriving law practice. With the help of an English solicitor, he arranged for his wife and children to go to England and take up residence in Anerley with a family called the Woods. Colonel Wood was a retired army man who agreed to board the Bonnerjees, including Hemangini, in order to supplement his "meagre pension."

If the move to Entally and the break with her orthodox past was the first trauma in the narrative of Hemangini's heroism, the breakup of the household at Ballygunge and its relocation chez Wood represents the second. Again, a brief excerpt provides a sense of the courage such an undertaking required, as well as an indication of the anxieties and fears it engendered:

> My father could not possibly afford to take his family to England himself, as he was working far too busily to earn enough money to keep them in England, so my poor mother had to take the voyage alone, with three small children, in the summer of 1874, when Shelley was just 4, Nellie nearly 3 and Susila about 18 months old. She often told me what a nightmare that voyage was! My father knew one man who was traveling on the boat, Dr. Godeve Chakravati, and asked him to help my mother. He promised to do so, but my mother said he was a terrible snot, and was ashamed of knowing another Indian who could scarcely speak any English, and took absolutely no notice of her! She was terribly seasick and miserable and thoroughly scared. The only bright spot was that my father had written to the P. & O. agents at every port of call to look after my mother, and they came aboard at each port and helped her in various ways. She said the last straw was when playing with the children one day she asked the baby "Where's Papa?" and the baby solemnly replied, "He's dead"! However, at last the voyage came to an end, and she arrived at the Woods, who were then living at 8 Harcourt Road, Anerley.[44]

The story of the Bonnerjees' residence at Anerley in the 1870s is indeed a grim one in Janaki's chronicle. In the first instance, they were living in a home that was not their own—a situation that no doubt exacerbated the pain of displacement and exile, for Hemangini especially. In addition, the fact that W. C. was paying the Woods appeared to be the sole reason that they had agreed to take the Bonnerjees in. As Janaki put it, "They had a strong colour prejudice and disliked all orientals, classing them as 'natives' . . . both my mother and her children were subjected to numerous indignities, and never treated equally by the family."[45] Such indignities—which took place in the confines of the home on Harcourt Road—ranged from mockery, because they could never get their dark skin "clean," to outright physical abuse. In part because Janaki was not yet born when the family was first with the Woods, she includes testimony from her elder sister Nellie about her experience there. Nellie describes being "frightfully severely punished" by the Woods because they believed she was "willfully stubborn and obstinate." "I think I told you," she is quoted as saying, "I used to be locked up in cupboards." As late as the 1930s Nellie could claim, "I bear the marks of being pushed under an iron bed that cut my head open."[46] These incidents took place when the Bonnerjee children were left alone with the Woods, after Hemangini had returned to India, either in 1875 after the birth of her second son, or in 1878, in anticipation of the birth of her third son. Whether she knew about them is not clear. What Janaki found most significant was her mother's willingness to forgive the Woods. "The amazing part," she wrote, in chapter 6 (part 2), "Hemangini's First Visit to England, 1874–75," "is that my mother never bore a grudge against them, forgave all the indignities, and was extremely good to all the family later on, when she was wealthy and in an established position in her own house in England, and they were poor and unhappy."[47]

The extent to which having "her own house in England" (and the security that that entailed) enabled such generosity from Hemangini is impossible to know with any certainty. Janaki, for her part, interpreted the Bonnerjees' experience at the Woods' as a kind of morality tale. Not only did her mother rise above their treatment of her and her children but the Woods' sons and daughters ended up giving their parents unspecified "trouble." The sons in particular were "thoroughly unsatisfactory and later broke their parents' hearts by their evil conduct."[48] Crucial to this tale was the fact that Hemangini turned to Christianity while at the Woods, and went on to become a member of the Plymouth Brethren, whose services (conveniently located in the Drill Hall in upper Norwood) she preferred to those of the Woods' own Church of England.[49] As Nellie observed, W. C. had not reckoned with his wife's "religious strength of character" for "he did not realize what an ardent Christian she would become." According to her, Bonnerjee never tried to prevent his wife from being baptized—but, "though he did not object to our being brought up as a Christian, he would not allow us to be baptised or confirmed til we were 21."[50] Hemangini's newly found faith may well have sustained her as she struggled to find a place for herself and her family in England. Indeed, looking back on the Victorian era from the vantage point of 1935, Janaki emphasized that Hemangini's "great support and refreshment was her religion, first as a devout Hindu, and later as a devout Christian."[51]

As she recorded her mother's travels back and forth between England and India in the 1870s and after, it was not Hemangini's faith that Janaki foregrounded but the family dwellings—in India and in England—between which her mother migrated and through which she tried to establish stability and permanence for a family that was unusually mobile and scattered. Although their first nuclear family house was built in 1876 at Kidderpore, where W. C. Bonnerjee was born, Hemangini did not live there for long. Once W. C. returned from studying law in London, she was continually on the move. After the stillbirth of a son in 1878, she and W. C. returned to the Woods, bringing Susie to stay with them; they returned to India in 1882; and after the birth of their fourth son in 1883 they went to England again.[52] Perhaps because of all these displacements, Kidderpore remains in the shadows of the "Family History." In 1884 the Indian government developed a scheme for extending the Kidderpore Docks, upon which the family house stood, and the Bonnerjees had to sell their land and find a new home. They purchased a large house at No. 6 Park Street in what, as Janaki proudly recalled, "was the very best part of Calcutta."[53] More important, this house was to be the center of family life well into the next century. No. 6 was where Janaki was born in 1886, where all of Shelley's children were born, and where Hemangini died in 1910. Not only did it "shelter the family for many years," it "was considered a family dwelling."[54]

Janaki's description of the house at No. 6 Park Street is quite detailed, reflecting her personal attachment to the home in which she was born, her desire to revisit its interior spaces, and her commitment to reproducing them for future generations. Not just the house but its architectural design and geographic layout are all brought to life again as evidence of the family's prosperity and standing. She may have been particularly keen to re-create Park Street with such vividness because although she was born there, she did not return for the first time until 1899, and then only briefly. As a child she remembered "besieging [her sister] Milly with questions as to what 6 Park Street looked like," since Milly was the only one who could recall it at the time.[55] "It was really a beautiful mansion (no other word is grand enough) and had been Sir Elijah Impey's dwelling house, and the imposing gate had sphinxes on each side, put up by him," Janaki wrote in her chapter entitled "6 Park Street, Calcutta, 1885."

A long drive, flanked on one side by a row of servants' godowns discretely hidden behind a hedge, and on the other by an enormous coach-house, led up to the house, with its huge portico and imposing marble entrance hall and beautiful wooden staircase (with 80 steps?) built with galleries on each floor. On the ground floor was a large state dining room in the centre, to the east of that was a suite of three rooms, ante room, study, and bedroom, and a bathroom; to the west was a lesser dining room with a still smaller children's dining room beyond it; and to the west of this, a second suite of three rooms similar to the first. These rooms all led to a deep south verandah, with steps down to the garden. The middle storey consisted of an enormous billiard room, part of that was screened off and used as an extra sitting room, over the portico; a huge central drawing room, with a suite of bedroom, ante room and bathroom on each side of it, leading to another deep south verandah, with an extension westwards, over the ground floor western suite of rooms. The top storey was similarly arranged, with an open verandah over the billiard room. Above all was a flat roof that used to be a favourite playground for the smaller children. . . .

There was a pleasant garden with a tennis court on the east of the house, and a range of stables beyond it with stalls for eleven horses; and to the north of the house a flower garden, with narrow paths and two fern houses. On the west and south were narrow paths only.[56]

As vivid as the material objects of the house were her recollections of the servants, "who stayed on till they died or were pensioned off. Among these were Lakshmi Ayah . . . the Sudder Bearer, Ramjan Coachman, the old Kansamah, and Kumur-ud-din Kitmitgar, some of whom used to come and see us after we were married to get buksis on the strength of having carried us about when we were small."[57]

Here as elsewhere in the "Family History," the presence of servants is highly naturalized: like the furniture in the house, they are represented as belongings of the family. Nonetheless, they offer a revealing glimpse of the support staff that worked behind the scenes and suggest just how constitutive domestic labor was to the success of the Bonnerjee's transnational household.[58] Janaki's recurrent references to servants remind us that the Victorian home, whether in India or Britain, was by no means an exclusively middle-class space, even if its owners strove to make it look that way.[59] Her account of interiors, exteriors, and domestic servants re-members the house of the past, archiving the children's activities and the family's daily habits in the Victorian period. It also repeatedly underscores the privilege characteristic of the Indian nationalist diaspora and the bodies of working people who helped to make possible the happy childhood she largely credits to her parents. As with African Americans in Toni Morrison's account of modern American literature, the servants in the "Family History" are relatively invisible but absolutely foundational to the memories of house and home that Janaki's narrative preserves.[60] Like the ghost of the cook that haunted Hemangini as a child, they represent the suppressed archive of labor at the heart of the history of Brahmanical domesticity, even in its reformed and transplanted forms. For all her self-consciousness about Hemangini's imprisonment in and by the household, Janaki is not particularly attentive to the ways in which her mother's domestic lot was eased by those who work for her in both India and Britain. The ornamental role that the servants play is matched by Janaki's lavish descriptions of the storeys and verandahs and tennis courts of the house in Calcutta especially, quite literally displaying her pride in her parents' achievement, both financial and cultural. Their bourgeois, anglophile status is plainly evident in the variety of rooms differentiated by function and the various signs of upward mobility in the heart of British India: billiard rooms, tennis courts, and stables—each of which provided the equipment for quintessentially English Victorian pastimes. W. C.'s romance with Englishness was thus partially fulfilled, and the house on Park Street remained its most vivid embodiment in the Bonnerjee family history and memory. It was, however, very much a joint venture; for, as Janaki put it nearly fifty years later, "my parents became very fond of this lovely house."[61]

Beyond the house itself, the grounds that surrounded it are also marked out as evidence of No. 6's importance—not just because it belonged to "the Bonnerjees" but arguably because it was part of the patrimony of the aspiring Indian nation as well. In this sense, Park Street represents a "system of settings" that links the ostensibly domestic with the public domain.[62] The intimate connection between private and public, between home and the nation, is made inescapably clear when we realize where the passage just quoted is situated in the larger text: for the chapter immediately following is entitled "The Founding of the Congress, 1885." It is quite brief and matter-of-fact, giving the most basic outline of the origins of the INC movement and enumerating the major positions Bonnerjee staked out for it at the first meeting at Bombay, where he was elected president. It ends with a reminiscence by S. Sinha about Bonnerjee's speech on that occasion, praising his "splendid oration" and recalling that it had "brought the House down as I have seldom seen."[63] That the purchase of the new house at Park Street and the founding of the INC should have occurred almost exactly at the same moment testifies to the kind of historical coincidence that came to bear on the Bonnerjee family, and to the inseparability of their family narrative from the story of Indian nationalism. In keeping with the pressure of this historical coincidence, nowhere is Janaki's investment in ordering the relationship between her father's public life and her family's domestic history more evident than at this moment. The chapter immediately following the one devoted to Congress is called "Family Life at 6 Park Street," and it opens with the following disclaimer: "As this is only a Family Chronicle, and not a political history of the times, enough has been said to indicate my father's interests and activities at this time."[64] Not just the structural imagery but the very architecture of the memoir itself is designed to decenter the political narrative of Indian nationalism and to locate the family's history separately, inside the rooms and in the private domain of the Bonnerjee household.

Although Janaki takes great pains to segregate W. C.'s political activities from the story of family life, her narrative ends up being an archive of how and why nationalist politics entered into and shaped the domestic scene, in ways that were keenly felt by Hemangini. Janaki recalled that her father "was brought by his political works into contact with many new and interesting personalities" and that in consequence her mother, "while remaining essentially domestic in all her tastes, was obliged to come forward and act as hostess on several occasions. She was always very shy and nervous at such times, but enjoyed small parties and entertaining my father's intimate friends."[65] Even the small parties were evidently quite frequent. W. C. Bonnerjee liked to keep "open house" hospitality, and "every Sunday he had a dinner party of friends and rising junior barristers, that was to include the future Lord Sinha . . . and others."[66] On these occasions the house was by no means a private space: it was routinely intruded upon by nationalist reformers and their supporters. Although they were often friends of the family, this did not necessarily diminish Hemangini's anxiety, for she was "very shy and unready in society and very much afraid of people she considered superior in intellect to herself, and formal entertaining was a terror to her."[67] Janaki represented her father's house parties as exciting and obviously recognized how important they were for his political ambitions, but she routinely returned to her mother's discomfort in such settings—not just to emphasize Hemangini's unease, but to put it in the context of her larger life, and tellingly, to establish that it was not the sum total of Hemangini's personality or experience. "She was a good gossip with her own relations, and was shrewd in her judgment of people's characters," Janaki recalled in the chapter entitled "Family Life at Park Street." "When at her ease," she added, "she had a keen sense of humor."[68]

Meanwhile, the tenor and structure of Hemangini's life was enormously influenced by W. C. Bonnerjee's anglophilic tastes, which reached deep into the home on Park Street and, therefore, shaped the household Hemangini ran. According to Janaki, "the 6 Park Street house was beautifully furnished in solid mid-Victorian style, and all the appointments were in keeping and of the choicest character. My father had his crockery and cutlery and linen specially made for him in England, and we still have some pieces of his once famous Coalport china dinner service with a large monogram of W. C. and H. B. in the centre of each plate and dish; and the remains of a beautiful hand-painted dessert service."[69] If Hemangini did not pick the crockery she, like English mistresses of similar households, did choose the servants who helped her manage the household. Significantly, she staffed it with English nurses for the children whom she recruited during her sojourns to Britain—first Rose, who left India because she was ill, and then Fanny, who returned to England to marry a coal heaver.[70] Although their departures signal the class inequalities at the heart of transnational household management, and even (on the part of Fanny) resistance to the kind of service that made it possible, Janaki does not remark on it. She is however, however, quick to point out that Hemangini was "very competent in all household affairs and the management of servants [and] money."[71] Like many Indians of equivalent caste and class status, and like many aspiring middle-class English women of the time, Hemangini no doubt understood servants to be the background rather than the foreground of the household story. This was the very same historical moment when middle-class English women were being asked by a variety of reformers, architects, and medical professionals to come to terms with household management as an extension of their identities as women—and for the wife of W. C. Bonnerjee, that meant being mistress over servants who were to be seen and not heard.[72] Many years later, her daughter certainly understood that the task of the modern Western housewife was "to represent her husband, class and nation through the acquisition and use of appropriate goods."[73] At one interpretive level, this reminds us that the middle-class Victorian house was "one of the most consciously contrived creations of domestic space in history."[74] At yet another level, Janaki's attention to housing, interior decoration, and consumption practices, like her parents', marks out the bourgeois preoccupations of the Victorian nation-building project, as well as the connections the Bon-nerjees perceived between family patrimony and Indian self-representation.[75]

By the late 1880s Hemangini had borne eight children, seven of whom survived into adolescence. Three of those were being raised in England and educated in English schools. Despite the difficulty of raising a large family in two places, often with a husband in absentia, there were comforts to be had from family life nonetheless. "My Mother often told us," Janaki wrote at the end of her chapter on Park Street, "how proud she was of her well-balanced family—four boys and four girls, and an elder brother to look after each sister. I think these years about which I am now writing must have been the 'Golden Age' of my parents." She continued:

> My father was at the very top of the tree in his profession, with all his political interests and new friends. The eldest son was doing well at Rugby, the girls were very clever and rapidly acquiring English culture, the youngest children were at hand to play with, and the Nursery was presided over by a nice English nurse; the relations were all admiring, and grateful for monetary help, and all the prospects for the future were bright.[76]

Whether Janaki's admiration for her family's anglophilic achievements was shared by Hemangini, we do not know. In any event, this idyllic moment was fleeting, as the family was soon on the move again. In the spring of 1888, W. C. Bonnerjee decided that it was time for his wife "to move completely" to Britain, so that all the children could have proper English educations. Once again, Janaki's narrative focuses on the physical spaces of home. Hemangini initially took over the home the Woods had been renting, at 44 Lansdowne Road, Croydon. The Woods were moving and wanted to give up the house anyway, so the Bonnerjees decided, in Janaki's words, "to take it over from them 'lock, stock and barrel,'" while looking for a suitable property to purchase for themselves."[77] When W. C. came over during the Pujah holidays, as he usually did, the Bonnerjees bought a house at 8 Bedford Park, Croydon—a neighborhood that "was then a very good one, though it has deteriorated sadly now," lamented Janaki in 1935.[78] She spent several pages detailing the gardens, the stables, and the circular drive in front of the house; the property was so extensive that there was a kind of minibarn at the end of the lawn where Hemangini kept poultry. Significantly, Janaki felt that the house was so impressive—and important for the "Family History"—that it "must have a chapter to itself."[79]

The house at 8 Bedford Park was enormous: three storeys and ten bedrooms, with drawing room, dining room, "capacious basement" kitchen, scullery, wine and coal cellar, pantry, and china closet. What is interesting about Janaki's description of Bedford Park, compared to the one of the house at 6 Park Street, is the emphasis on the way the Bonnerjees remodeled the interior of this Victorian house to suit their particular needs. According to Janaki, "there was no bathroom at all, and only one lavatory . . . this was shocking to Indian ideas, so a bathroom was added on the first floor landing, and two more lavatories; and an extra wing was built on the house containing a billiard and smoking room."[80] The Bonnerjees acted very much in keeping with the times: the 1880s was a period of domestic architectural reform in Britain—when the attention of the middle classes "had been guided back to the interior [not just] as a work of art" but as an expression of cultural achievement as well.[81] The interior of Bedford Park was also remade to create a place for the children to play, and the servants' hall was renamed the Schoolroom and was later refitted so that the elder children could do chemistry experiments there. These rearrangements were made to accommodate a large family, but they also helped to make the house in Croydon resemble the one at 6 Park Street, architecturally at least—though in Janaki's memory it could never measure up. "The whole house was beautifully furnished by a London firm called Fox and Co., with good solid furniture, thick nailed-down carpets in every room and on the stairs, as was the fashion in those days. It made an exceedingly comfortable family home, though it was not of course half so grand or luxurious as the Calcutta house." This comparison with the family abode in India served as a continual reminder that the house in suburban London would never be more than a copy, never more than a temporary "home." Given what we know about how Victorian-English the house at Park Street was, it seems clear that there was no "model" or even originary house, either in India or England. Like Homi Bhabha's mimic men, the Bonnerjee homes were almost identical, "but not quite"—a likeness that was itself made possible largely through memory.[82] In Janaki's remembering, each interior acts as a mirror for the other, reflecting the growing family's particular needs and, above all, refracting the kind of hybrid cosmopolitanism required by W. C.'s political tastes and aspirations. Thus the trope of interiority that runs throughout the "Family History" signals a desire not just to rebuild the Bonnerjees' past but to remember their capacity for capital accumulation as well.

If national identity as experienced in everyday life is itself a form of "accumulated cultural capital," the Bonnerjee household in suburban London is an exemplary case.[83] Hemangini set herself up as the quintessential Victorian housewife at Croydon, and "everything in her province went on oiled wheels." In so doing she fulfilled expectations of what the "modern" woman would look like as that cultural icon was being remodeled at the century's end both in Britain and among upper-caste Bengalis.[84] Janaki emphasized her mother's housekeeping competency, recalling that

> there was never any servant trouble, as the same servants stayed on for years. Of course they used to quarrel among themselves sometimes, and there were various difficulties to cope with, but they always adored my mother. The food too was always of the choicest quality, and she invariably gave us the earliest strawberries, green peas, oysters etc. that were in the market. From her Hindu upbringing she used to enjoy giving us special food for special days, and we always had pancakes on Shrove Tuesday, and roast goose at Michaelmas. And Christmas Day used to be a time of gor[g]ing for the whole family, my mother making a special expedition to London to get as many dainties as possible from the Army and Navy Stores.[85]

Once again the servants break the surface of the narrative, this time as demonstrable evidence of the family's capacities for domestic engineering and especially of Hemangini's managerial skills and accomplishments, however tentative. Janaki's determination to represent the servants in Britain as happy and pleased with her mother's governance is also striking, especially in contrast to the difficulty the Bonnerjees had in retaining English servants in India. Though the story of an Indian family with English servants in Victorian Britain is one worthy of an extensive archive, Janaki's accounts of life "below stairs" in Croydon are allusive at best. This is evidence of the silences and violences of all archives, even those that act as counternarratives to dominant histories, as Janaki's does. Far from rendering all gendered subjectivities more legible, this archival source rescues some—like Hemangini's and Janaki's—from the recesses of nationalist history, only to obscure those others that make the Bonnerjee women's identities possible. Significantly, here as elsewhere in the "Family History," the servants come into view at the same time that the family's consumption patterns enter the narrative. Needless to say, servants' own memories—whether inside or outside "the comfort zone"—were not preserved in Bonnerjee family history.[86] Taken together, Hemangini's management of the servants and her patronage of the Army and Navy Stores are proof of the Bonnerjees' adaptation to English middle-class ways, and to their buying power as well.[87]

Sundays were special days at the house in Croydon, a time when the family was often all assembled and fellow Indians who were in temporary or permanent exile in London would flock to the house for food and hospitality. Janaki's account is worth reproducing in full:

> [The day began] with breakfast in bed, as when the elder sisters began their medical work in London they had a very early start and a late return all the week and liked to get up late on Sundays to make up, and we younger ones thought it a marvelous idea, so my mother would send up as many as 6 trays sometimes! Attendance at the Iron Room was compulsory for the younger ones, and on our return we usually found two or three young Indian students and other friends awaiting us who had arrived for lunch—Mr. K. N. and Mr. P. Chaudhuri were frequent visitors, also Basanta Mullick and his brothers, Sir B. C. Mitter, Sir B. L. Mitter, Mr. C. C. Ghose, and a great many others. After lunch . . . there was a "spread tea" in the dining room and after that "Hymn" in the drawing room. Each of us in turn chose our favorite hymn, and Nellie played the piano while the rest of the family sang. Sometimes we used the "Ancient and Modern" Hymn book and sometimes "Sankey and Moodie's." Immediately after this ceremony my mother used to go down to the kitchen to cook a real Indian dinner, and as soon as I was old enough I always used to help her. The servants were all given the evening off, and we used to dish up and carry up the things ourselves—My Aunts always sent the spices to us ready ground in tins and we and our visitors all greatly enjoyed this meal. Sometimes my father would come and help, and I remember him and Mr. R. C. Dutt once spending the whole evening cooking a wonderful duck curry that no one could eat because it was too highly spiced ("jhal")! At first the servants were rather "superior" about Indian food, and my mother always left plenty of cold meat and pudding out for their supper. But she gradually noticed that however many curries might be left over on Sunday nights, there was never anything on Monday morning, and at last a deputation came to her from the servants asking her to cook just a little more of everything if she didn't mind, as they all so much enjoyed it![88]

Given the otherwise obscured role of the servants in the "Family History," this glimpse of their "conversion" to Indian food is telling, as is the triumphalist tone in which it is told. Here the servants perform a very specific kind of ornamentalism, serving as evidence of the orientalization of the Croydon house below stairs. This anecdote also makes visible the centrality of the kitchen to the symbolic and material work of the household as a whole—in this case, as evidence of a kind of domestic charivari. The image of W. C. and R. C. Dutt, two English-educated barristers, in the kitchen cooking the duck for "family" dinner is just one indication of how the traditional world of the upper-caste Hindu home was recast, if not turned upside down, chez Bonnerjee in Britain. A contemporary of Janaki and a friend in later life, Mrs. Arthur Alexander, had vivid memories of these Sunday feasts, in which she was included as a young girl. "What an oasis . . . [the Croydon house] must have been to the dozens of young Indian students who came there on Sundays and were transported in spirit to their own country!"[89] No. 8 Bedford Park functioned as more than a gathering place for expatriate Indians, a communal space as well as a little bit of India in England: it was a showcase of the reformed spatial practices of the modern Indian home in diaspora. As Alexander's observation and, indeed, as much of the "Family History" itself illustrates, not only did nationalist politics leave its imprint on the Bonnerjee family, but the Bonnerjee family also helped to influence the cultural forms early Indian nationalism took in Britain, especially in terms of how new forms of domesticity were imagined and acted out.

Given her role in these proceedings, Hemangini may be said to have actively shaped the conditions under which those first generations of English-educated Indian men experienced the "Indian nation" in exile.[90] In this sense, she made a significant contribution to nationalist politics. This fact is illuminated by Janaki's account of the family's past and makes clear in quite concrete terms how domestic space is always inevitably public space as well. Significantly, Hemangini's contribution to the cultural politics of Indian nationalism is consistently framed by Janaki's insistence that her mother did not feel up to the task of participating in the "political" affairs of the household. For despite her obvious pride in being part of these historic gatherings, Janaki's refrain remained the same as it had through the beginning of the "Family History." "At best," she wrote of the days at Croydon, "it must have been a lonely life for [Hemangini]." She was "very much out of touch with her eldest children, who rather despised her lack of education—education having been made something of a fetish by them—and really had nothing in common with her, as they scarcely remembered their life in India and their relatives there."[91] The youngest children, for their part, "were only too ready to take their tone from the elders, and book learning and culture was the order of the day." The older ones brought their friends home at holidays, and Hemangini "liked some of them very much," but according to Janaki "it was not usual in those days for parents to be friends with their children . . . and my mother must sadly have missed my father and her own contemporaries."[92] Janaki does record that Hemangini made the house in Croydon her own kind of social space, sponsoring "Mother's Meetings" where neighborhood ladies met to read the Bible and discuss related matters in her living room on Thursday afternoons.[93] These local social connections notwithstanding, Janaki believed that "though my mother's life seemed so prosperous and happy on the surface, except for the inevitable separation of her husband, she really had many worries and anxieties to cope with"—specifically having to do with her children's lives and futures. In this way, Janaki directs our attention again and again to the most circumscribed, although by no means apolitical, definition of the domestic sphere, managing the children, and to the considerable emotional costs it entailed for Hemangini. Shelley was a rather mischievous young man, and although he ended up at Rugby and Oxford, he came close to expulsion from the former. An even greater sorrow was the death of her son Kitty from pneumonia in 1890 at the age of eleven—a death for which she always blamed herself and for which she wore mourning for the rest of her life.[94] So responsible and guilty did she feel that the first time W. C. returned to Britain after Kitty's death she could not bring herself to meet him, "because he had left his son under her care and she had let him die."[95]

The splintering and re-creation of the household continued apace in the Bonnerjee family. Janaki narrates this process again through an emphasis on the lives of the children, specifically as the elder ones married and set up their own homes, both in England and in India. W. C. and Hemangini traveled back and forth between India and Britain half a dozen times or more in the late 1890s. Using Croydon as the home base, they took several of the younger children on holidays in the British Isles and to Europe. They often rented houses while on holiday, as in the summer of 1903 at Harlyn Bay near Padstow, Cornwall, though these do not figure in any detail in Janaki's historical narrative. In the last years of his life, W. C. was more frequently in England. He worked at the Privy Council and made two attempts to stand for Parliament—evidence of his desire to inhabit the most important and influential House in the British empire. But his health began to fail, and despite a number of trips to spas in and around the southeast, he died in the house at Croydon in July 1906. In his death, as in his life, W. C.'s home at 8 Bedford Park became a pilgrimage site for Indians in exile; among those whom Janaki remembered coming to pay their respects were R. C. Dutt and G. K. Gokhale, who had been regular visitors during

W. C.'s last days. Bonnerjee was cremated at Golders Green, and his ashes were buried in Croydon cemetery without ceremony, according to his wish. His epitaph, which he dictated to his daughter Susie the day before he died, read as follows: "here beside the ashes of his son rest the ashes of Womesh Chunder Bonnerjee Hindu Brahmin who died on a visit to England."[96] His final words are tantalizingly ambiguous, for though they leave little doubt that he viewed himself as a visitor to Britain, they give no explicit indication of where he thought "home" might be. Like the Croydon house itself, England evidently only resembled "something like home."

The impact of W. C.'s death on Hemangini was enormous, not least because as the heir to his money she was left "in a sea of business and other worries."[97] In Janaki's account it was, significantly, No. 6 Park Street itself that served as the focus of anxiety. Shelley, who had been living there with his wife while working as a barrister, had let the upstairs apartment to "a couple of young English men" without informing his parents. Hemangini was "terribly upset and grieved about it" because "it seemed to her a sort of sacrilege that any part of my father's house should be let to strangers."[98] This contretemps was complicated by the fact that the upstairs flat had initially been intended as a nursery; but Shelley's wife, Gertie, had had a miscarriage, and they decided to rent it because they couldn't bear to leave the space empty.[99] By the time Hemangini returned to Calcutta after W. C.'s death, Shelley and Gertie "were still much estranged from the rest of the family, though still living in the same house, and my mother felt very sad about this."[100] Hemangini, Janaki, and Susie returned to Croydon, leaving Shelley and another brother and wife to share Park Street. The Bedford Park house proved to be too large for "our reduced numbers" and was eventually sold. Its owners turned it into an orphanage for army officers' daughters, which was still in operation when Janaki was writing her family memoir in the 1930s.[101] After that, Janaki and her mother returned to Park Street, where Janaki was married to P. M. in 1908 and where Hemangini died in January 1910. According to Janaki, "she was conscious up to the end, and so very thankful to be going to join her husband, as she said."

> I shall never forget her look of intense joy when the doctors thought it right to warn her that she only had a few hours to live. She was, as ever, far more thoughtful about the comforts of her children and nurses than about her own pain, and kept urging us to rest, to go down for meals. She died bravely and gladly, as one really "Going Home."[102]

If "home" was unspecified for W. C. Bonnerjee, Janaki, at any rate, believed it was self-evident upon her mother's death. Like a good Hindu and indeed like a good Christian wife, Hemangini followed her husband out of the world to join him in a final resting place—crossing boundaries that were "not delineated in space" in order to realize home.[103]

Hemangini's death does not bring an end to "Family History"; the narrative is not coterminous with either the Bonnerjees' marriage or their lives. Indeed, Janaki devotes several sections of the memoir to her own education, both in Croydon High School for Girls (est. 1872) and at Newnham College, Cambridge. While they provide a further glimpse of Janaki's subjectivity, these scenes also shed further light on other possible tensions between W. C. and Hemangini, especially where the figure of Dorinda Neligan, the first headmistress of the Croydon High School, is concerned. As one of Neligan's contemporaries recalled, Neligan had "a strong personality, a beautiful Irish voice, 'a dominating presence and great independence of character. She could work easily with men as few women of her generation could.'"[104] Janaki elaborated on the portrait as follows.

> She and my father were great friends, as they thought alike about politics, both being liberals and great admirers of Gladstone. Irish and Indian political problems had much in common in those days and there used to be great discussions of all sorts of interesting topics whenever Miss Neligan came to see us. . . . My father admired her greatly . . . [because] he was always a great advocate of "Women's Rights."[105]

Dorinda and her sister Annie were frequent visitors to the house at Croydon, and the Bonnerjees also stayed with them after Bedford Park was sold. "Miss Neligan" was the only person to be accorded her own chapter, suggesting how influential she was in Janaki's adolescence and, not incidentally, what kind of a foil she may have provided to Hemangini's faithful domesticity—for W. C., perhaps, as much as for his young and impressionable daughter.

Digressions about her education notwithstanding, Janaki's own story emerges as the central focus of the text only after her mother's passing. If this is a testament to how bound up her autobiography is with the history of her family of origin, it is also evidence of how constrained the production of a narrative of her own is by Hemangini's suffering and pathos. Whether or not Janaki would have seen her "own" story as a valuable literary, historical, or even "nationalist" subject is a matter for speculation. Because she was largely English- and later Cambridge-educated, she would presumably have come into contact with Western literary traditions that privileged the self, though she makes no allusion to the impact of such exposure in her text.[106] Nevertheless, part 3, which begins right after her mother's death and inaugurates the section of the "Family History" that is properly Janaki's, starts with a chapter entitled "Early Married Life: Park Street; again, 1908"—the year of her wedding. As Janaki's insertion of the word "again" suggests, this chapter is a bit of a false start, since it recounts the happy events of her courtship and social life prior to Hemangini's death—including her involvement as honorary secretary of the Calcutta branch of the National Indian Association, whose monthly meetings were occasionally held at Park Street.[107] The overlap of her new life with P. M. and her mother's death help to account for this recursive strategy, as Janaki exhibits her struggle both to reconcile the joy of those days with the fact of her mother's continued sorrow and to represent the difficulty of moving beyond the shadows of Park Street into her own story.

When Janaki does take up her own story she makes a familiar return to the narrative of the conjugal house, allowing its architecture, interiors, and grounds to tell the story:

> Our first house after our marriage was No. 66 Lower Circular Road, up a lane almost opposite St. James' Church. The approach was bad and the neighbourhood somewhat slummy, but the house itself was quite liveable (a cousin of mine . . . called the house "a Lotus on a dung-heap"!). It was two storied with two rooms on each floor; the downstairs rooms were rather damp but could be used as dining room and dressing room, and there was a tiny office room and a verandah. Upstairs there was a drawing room and bedroom and a long verandah with a tin roof, which was too hot to be used in the summer though pleasant enough in winter, and a small open balcony facing south that was a great resort on a summer evening. We had a pony called "Baby Boy" and a trap, and also the small brougham from 6 Park Street, but this was not very useful at first, as we had no coachman![108]

Soon after the birth of their daughter Tara, the Majumdars moved again, this time to No. 1 Elysium Row, in "the very nicest part of Calcutta, just beyond the Cathedral, and a few minutes walk from the Maidan."[109] P. M. was making better money by then, and this was reflected in the larger house and property, which are again brought to life in some detail.

Much if not most of part 3 is given over to what Janaki calls "life

in Elysium Row" and, eventually, to the home the Majumdars built in
Ballygunge after World War I—but not until a brief obituary of No. 6
Park Street has been provided.

> We had found that it would be better to sell 6 Park Street as no mem-
> ber of the family could afford to keep such a large establishment, and
> it was bought by a Marwari merchant and let out in flats. The house
> (now no. 24) is still there, but the garden was acquired by a motor car
> firm and a large garage built facing the street so the house is no longer
> visible from the road. . . . The neighborhood also has completely
> changed from a residential area into a very busy shopping centre, and
> none of us have ever regretted the sale of no. 6.[110]

If this seems a rather unceremonious and even unsentimental way to
mark the end of a generation, it also bears witness to Janaki's conviction that "home" is still recognizable even when its structures have
been transformed and, in this case, even when its address has been
renumbered and its access blocked from view. For Janaki the place
remains historically significant because it points to what home was
but no longer is: testimony to the family's progress, to the movement
of history, and to her own historical consciousness. Here it becomes
evident that Janaki's purpose in revisiting Park Street (and, by extension, in writing the "Family History" which has helped to preserve
it) is to keep the *desire* for home alive precisely because she recog-
nizes that home is ultimately impossible to inhabit except through
memory. For it is, in turn, the project of remembering that makes
the *house* into (a) *home.* This conviction helps to explain why she
wrote the "Family History" in the first place: to compensate for the
material loss, and the invisibility in history, of familiar familial
homes.[111] Indeed, the narrative of families on-the-move and family
dwellings bought and sold stands in stark contrast to the text itself,
which aims to provide her children's children with an enduring, permanent legacy. In this sense "Family History" is more than an archive, or even a simple reminder of what home looked like. It
becomes a family heirloom—that highly prized commodity that
transmits memory while legitimating a collective, middle-class past *as*
"History."

For all its emphasis on interiors and "private" homes, Janaki's
narrative is, finally, the work of a prominent Indian daughter trying
to establish a place for her family's past in history, if not in public.[112]
The question of address is surely significant here: the "Family History" takes the tacks it does precisely because she wrote it for the
family, never imagining that it would enter the public sphere.[113] It

should be noted that there were two other publications that bor-
rowed from "Family History." Both were pamphlets, one privately
printed in 1974, the other published in Calcutta probably around
the same time but with minimal circulation.[114] These notwithstanding, Janaki's two-hundred-page handwritten manuscript remains, for
all intents and purposes, the primary archive for all subsequent Bonnerjee family histories. The fact that she wrote it in 1935 suggests the
kinds of political pressures that might have propelled her to create
an archive for the extended family. The fiftieth anniversary of the
founding of the INC brought her father's political career again before the public eye as the trajectory of the independence movement
was scrutinized and reevaluated. As she observed early on in the
narrative, "reading the accounts of the Jubilee in the press makes
one realise what a lot of water has flowed under the bridge since
1885!"[115] In fact, Janaki committed her "Family History" to paper at
a historical moment when the Gandhian movement was entering a
new phase. It was precisely at this time that Gandhi began to pursue
strategies that were increasingly independent of a Congress that little resembled the band W. C. Bonnerjee had led half a century before.[116] Majumdar did not intend her text as a critique of Gandhi,
whose ideas she pronounced "sound," but rather as a reminder of
what different incarnations nationalism had had in the past, and, of
course, how invested her family was in those representations.[117]

In an era of mass political demonstrations that often involved
the very public participation of women, Janaki's "Family History"
foregrounds the contributions of one unsung heroine who made
W. C. Bonnerjee's professional success possible by her very private
sacrifices. In this respect, it contributes to the narratives of Indian
women's self-sacrifice that were both produced by the Gandhian moment and, of course, antecedent to it as well.[118] And yet it was not
only at the level of high politics that major shifts were occurring—
shifts that gave different valences to house and home and the kinds
of values they were believed to archive. As Sudeshna Banerjee has illustrated, the rhetoric of disciplined domesticity that had emerged
in Victorian Bengal and had characterized the Indian nationalist
quest for the recognition of the upper-caste Hindu home both in
and as modernity had disintegrated considerably by the 1930s. By
then, she argues, the image of the house as a repository of the redemptive power of the indigenous bourgeoisie was under siege—in
part because of real financial constraints placed on the material
prosperity of Bengali households, postwar and postdepression, in
part because of the cult of unattached, masculine "youth unrest" that

manifested itself in both the romance of the gypsy and, of course, in the cult of Gandhi.[119] With the ideological moorings of the Victorian *bhadralok* home no longer secure, "the search for an alternative justification for middle-class existence remained unresolved, with . . . [that] class indecisive as to where it should be invented—whether in the home or outside it."[120]

Janaki's idealization of Hemangini is undoubtedly tied to these contemporary currents, as well as to the ways they intersected with critiques of Hindu marriage "and its repressive, patriarchal notions of compatibility"—evidence of which was to be found not just in the campaigns against the Sarda Act of 1929 but throughout vernacular and English print culture in the 1920s and 1930s as well.[121] What makes Hemangini so pivotal to the "Family History" when we interpret it as a cultural product of the 1930s is that she can be read as a kind of antiheroine: the quiet, subservient domesticated Indian woman whose propriety can never be questioned—unlike some of the other women "in public" in this period. To borrow from Kamala Visweswaran, Janaki enables Hemangini's work to count: she makes it function as a certain kind of nationalist "speech," albeit one that harks back to earlier nationalist versions.[122] Thus, even though the "Family History" is structured around a recurrent tension between the public man who represents professional success and national identity versus the woman/mother who embodies personal suffering and sorrow, Hemangini's pathos ends up producing the far more powerful statement about nationalism-in-the-making. In short, Janaki did not actually need to foreground W. C. Bonnerjee, since Hemangini does the work of embodying the values of "Indian nationalism" that Janaki wishes to represent even better than he could have.[123]

By constructing Hemangini as evidence of the kinds of profound social and cultural transformations that can occur in the recesses of domestic space, Majumdar made visible how conservative of patriarchal ideals those transformations could be. She may well have shared the "civilizational ambivalence" that characterized the careers of nineteenth-century Indian social reformers—those men who "helped to reinvent traditional India by making women guarantors of the transformed home, with the responsibility to protect the integrity of the men who trafficked in the deracinated discourses of the nationalist world."[124] In this sense, Janaki identified with the legacy of her father, even as she subjected his domestic disciplinary regimes to critique. As a truly "modern" woman—Cambridge educated, married for love, comfortably cosmopolitan, and anglophilic—she was, after all, the more successful, less vexed product of those regimes herself, though perhaps also guilt-ridden about her mother's suffering and her own and her siblings' role in it.

Hemangini's pathos as Janaki imagined it arguably throws her own story into shadow. In many ways, her marriage to P. M. and the birth of her children end up being as subordinated to her mother's story as they are to her father's. At the same time, the "Family History" performs a service for Janaki as a "nationalist's daughter" that we cannot afford to overlook. Because she devotes so much of her memoir to recounting how her mother must have felt, the "Family History" becomes a vehicle through which Janaki is able to imagine and preserve a very private interior space—her mother's emotional life—that few contemporaries would have had had access to. It is an archival resource, and a rare one at that—for her grandchildren and their children, and in turn for us. Even if that interior ends up being more Majumdar's fantasy than anything else, this is a maneuver of no small significance, given the fact that "imperialism, nationalism and women's movements have collaborated in hollowing out all specificity for Indian women"—making them emblems without interiors, subjects without subjectivities.[125] Janaki's history materializes a certain kind of gendered bourgeois national subject for scrutiny and appreciation—a highly privatized subject that might have been comforting to remember and to claim at a historical moment when the public image of the Indian nationalist woman was less undifferentiated and less indubitably respectable.

Hemangini emerges as a modernizing model within the constraints of the nationalist bourgeois (and patriarchal) project.[126] Like Anandibai Joshee, her more famous contemporary, she represents "the obedient wife of an allegedly visionary husband rather than . . . an independent agent with a will of her own."[127] But Janaki's memoir works as much to serve the family's history in the nation's memory as it does to satisfy a daughter's curiosity about her mother's past; indeed, in political terms, it makes those two sentimental projects one and the same. To argue this is not to suggest, as Fredric Jameson has, that all colonial writing can be reduced to nationalist allegory, but rather that the nation has a particular kind of purchase on the domestic.[128] This is especially true in Janaki's case, where a daughter is trying to release home from the nation's grasp precisely in order to preserve its history on her own terms—that is, through the maternal figure. I would argue that Janaki recognized the combination of coercion and affection that W. C. used to produce this modern mother-as-modernity. Whether she understood that dynamic as also characteristic of her father's brand of nationalism is an intriguing question.[129] Hers is, in the end, a rich and complexly "domestic" archive that demonstrates how intimately connected the personal, the familial, and the political were for the first several generations of Indian women writing in both English and vernacular languages.[130] It also—and perhaps above all—makes Janaki visible as the discerning modern, if not nationalist, bourgeois subject. If Hemangini's story is a counterarchive to the hegemonic narrative of diasporic Bengali nationalism, it is embedded in, and works against, the biography of Janaki herself.

For all its subplots and narrative counterpoints, Majumdar's "Family History" is a remarkably self-possessed text. It bears none of the marks of Rassundari Devi's *Amar Jiban* (published in 1874), with its "hesitant moves" and its scrupulously devotional commitments.[131] Indeed, for all the complex political and familial reasons detailed heretofore, the "Family History" is as much Janaki's story as it is Hemangini's: a kind of modernist version of Ramabai Ranade's *Himself* (1910), one that replaces the husband–girl bride dyad with the mother-daughter one and transforms the family history into an archive from which the gendered conditions of nationalist formations in the context of colonial modernity can be read.[132] With its roots in the household, the "Family History" (or "Hemangini's story") is, above all, a highly situated knowledge produced through an elaborate and finally bourgeois architectural imaginary that remodels as it remembers, leaving the "original" always in doubt. Because of the history of her own peregrinations and the transitory nature of her own experience of home, Janaki's memoir offers home as a survivor *of history* only if it is built and rebuilt through memory—in large part because no "storey" is given, but requires the active and continual work of the imagination for its meaning. At the same time, the fact that her "Family History" has not been published until now leaves the site of "History" itself ambiguous, even as it reinscribes the "Family" as a private, elusive space that is valorized as the right and proper subject of nationalist nostalgia.[133] Lest Janaki's narrative be dismissed for its often conservative effects, it is worth remembering that her determination to furnish a domestic genealogy of Indian nationalism was not without risk.[134] As she remarked with some unease at the very beginning of her narrative,

> The following is an attempt to jot down the main facts of the family history of both the Majumdar and Bonnerjee families, so that our children and great grandchildren may not be entirely ignorant of the his-

tory of their forbears. No apology is required for making this attempt;
so many changes have taken place and are still taking place in India
and the whole world since the time when this family history begins,
with the birth of my father-in-law in 1822, that it becomes almost
a duty to try to look back at things as they were then, while records
are still available, and people [are] still alive who can remember the
past.[135]

Although duty may have motivated her, anxieties about the dangers
attendant on public exposure and self-representation remained. If
imagining home is as political an act as imagining the nation, Janaki
Majumdar's "Family History" attempts to manage the political implications of the past by putting her own narratives of home within
reach of national memory, yet just outside the grasp of a fully public
history.[136]

Chapter Three

TOURISM IN THE ARCHIVES

Colonial Modernity and the Zenana in Cornelia Sorabji's Memoirs

[Purdah] causes such social and national waste that it is not even necessary to elaborate on it here. Now the time has come to focus one's thoughts with a great deal of sharpness on this issue. Discussion must now take place on what is the real extent of loss in giving . . . appropriate freedom to women and on how much advantage has actually been gained from such imprisonment.

—Nazar Sajjad Hyder (1894–1967)

I want the culture of all lands to be blown about my house as freely as possible. But I refuse to be blown off my feet by any. I refuse to live in other people's houses as an interloper, a beggar, or a slave.

—M. K. Gandhi, quoted in Jawaharlal Nehru,
The Discovery of India

In a speech to the Royal Empire Society in October 1932, Cornelia Sorabji declared that "the great struggle of the future will be between the modern and the old-fashioned woman."[1] For those in India and Britain who were familiar with her public career, Sorabji's declaration would have come as no great surprise. Since her appointment as Lady Assistant to the Court of Wards in 1904, she had earned a reputation as an advocate for "the old-fashioned" woman—which for her meant the inhabitant of the zenana, or the women's quarters of the elite "Indian" home. Although the zenana (physical site of seclusion, or women's quarters) was not coterminous either with purdah (the practice of seclusion, including the wearing of the burqa) or with the "Indian" home *tout court*, it had emerged nonetheless as an emblem of "traditional India" by the 1930s. *Purdahnashin* (secluded women who might be Hindu or Muslim but were in any case always high caste or upper class) were equally crucial to the terms of imperialist and anti-colonial debate by the time Sorabji addressed the Royal Empire Society—not least because prominent nationalist women like Nazar Sajjad Hyder (quoted in the first epigraph)[2] rejected purdah during the interwar years as a species of imprisonment and an impediment to female emancipation. As with debates about conjugality, reformist critiques of purdah did not originate in this period. But they were galvanized into a concerted attack on purdah as groups like the Women's India Association and the Muslim Ladies Association gained legislative victories and political ground in the first three decades of the twentieth century.[3] In the struggle to which Sorabji referred, the zenana was not simply the domestic face of political debate between imperialists and nationalists. As sati had been a century earlier, the zenana—and the purdahnashin with it—was one of the chief ideological sites through which power was sought, negotiated, and contested in the two decades before Indian independence.[4]

Cornelia Sorabji was at the heart of debates about the role that the zenana, and by extension the precincts of house and home, should play in shaping modern Indian culture. A Parsi Christian who had trained as a barrister at Oxford in 1889–92, Sorabji devoted her life to two related projects: improving conditions for purdahnashin and publicizing those conditions to reform-minded audiences in Britain and India. She used her legal skills and her official connections to investigate the homes and detail the lives of hundreds of "secluded" women in the first three decades of the twentieth century. The archive she left behind is rich and varied, comprising India Office records, memoirs, and contemplative books and essays. Taken

together, these amount to an ethnography of twentieth-century purdahnashin and especially of the space of the zenana—a space that
for Sorabji represented not just "the beginning and the end of
Progress" but also the salvation of India in the face of modernity
and one of its political manifestations, the nationalist movement.[5]
Sorabji was determined to preserve the interiors of the Indian home
from the depredations of nationalist and feminist reformers because
she had her own modernist visions of what it could and should be.
For her, the zenana was valuable above all as an antinationalist
model for the modern Indian woman. She was well positioned to undertake this ideological project. In part because of her tremendous
capacity for self-promotion, and in part because of the market value
of an Indian woman who could commodify the zenana in critical but
also appreciative terms, Sorabji was recognized as the foremost authority on the zenana of her day among a certain literate, India-
minded public in both metropole and colony. Indeed, as newspaper
reviews of her publications consistently suggest, she was considered
an extraordinarily reliable interpreter of the "hidden world" of purdah, offering "true pictures of Indian home life" and "giv[ing] her
readers a glimpse of the life of those who live inside and the disabili-
ties that their seclusion entails."[6] According to the *British Weekly*, re-
viewing her 1934 autobiography, *India Calling*, Sorabji "opens a door
and lets us see a world that is known to very few."[7] For those who
were interested in what she called "The Inside" of the high-caste
Hindu or Muslim home, Sorabji was celebrated as its most authoritative guide.

Sorabji's fame as a zenana expert did not mean that her views
were uncontroversial. An antifeminist by her own definition, she had
long been an ardent and vociferous antinationalist as well.[8] In the
1920s she gained a reputation for criticizing Gandhi and his followers because they advocated political reforms that she claimed were
out of touch with the majority of Indians beyond the "progressive"
elite.[9] She was often at the heart of very public, even transnational,
controversies like the one that Katherine Mayo's book *Mother India*
generated in Britain, India, and the United States in the late 1920s
over the connections between child-marriage and Indian capacity
for self-rule.[10] In Mayo's view, child-marriage and the phenomenon
of child-motherhood that often eventuated from it raised questions
about Indians' fitness for self-government. It was a position that
Sorabji openly shared. Her identification with *Mother India* alienated
her from Indian nationalists and feminists and aligned her not just
with Mayo but with Mayo's unapologetically proimperialist opinions

more generally. Never shy about defending her controversial, antinationalist arguments in public, Sorabji capitalized on the publicity generated by Mayo to advance her own arguments about the sacral character of zenana life and the indispensability of purdah for preserving Indian identity in the context of modernity. Though as I suggested in chapter 1, purdah and the zenana are by no means interchangeable (one is a practice, the other a space), Sorabji's public work contributed to what was often a blurring of the two in the ideologically charged, politically tumultuous interwar period—a blurring to which the Katherine Mayo debate arguably contributed in the British as well as the international press. So determined was Sorabji to make the connections between *Mother India* and "her" purdahnashin that the *Bombay Chronicle* reported that Sorabji was in danger of "outmayoing Mayo" in her Royal Empire Society speech and that "hisses greet[ed] Miss Sorabji" in response to her characterizations of Indian women.[11]

As the collections at the India Office Library testify, Sorabji was frequently embroiled in controversies to which the public was not privy—as, for example, when she tried to persuade Lord Salisbury and Samuel Hoare, then secretary of state for India, to investigate terrorist cells in Bengal in 1933, much to their annoyance.[12] It was an obsession that would persist well into the 1940s, earning her a reputation as an "unruly subject" that has proven difficult to dislodge even half a century on.[13] These sharp-tongued engagements with officialdom notwithstanding, Sorabji's salvo at the Royal Empire Society is more than just a provocation. Nor should it be read merely as a pointed example of how crucial the figure of woman (whether the purdahnashin or Sorabji herself) was to the kinds of gendered political struggles that characterized colonial modernity. What compels our attention is Sorabji's claim that the contest between the modern woman and the purdahnashin belonged to the future, when in fact it had been the basis of debates about modernity in India for at least a hundred years—debates in which she herself had served as a publicly recognized leader for some time by 1932. Here, as elsewhere, Sorabji was determined to stage the past as the future, and to do so by representing the zenana and its inhabitants as vestiges of history-in-the-present that had the redemptive power to solve the crises generated by the collision between imperial power and the claims of nationalist reform. If such maneuvers highlight her role as an apologist for British imperialism, they also reveal a set of ideological relationships that speak to issues beyond her particular subjectivity. They illuminate the larger domain of colonial modernity and the overlapping systems of surveillance and knowledge-production it authorized as well. By insisting on the purdahnashin as survivors of history, Sorabji turned the zenana into a museum, staked her claim as its authoritative tour guide, and transformed it from an archive into a souvenir for consumption by a variety of imperial and colonial publics.

Cornelia Sorabji was born in Poona to Christian missionary parents who were converts from Zoroastrianism. The history of her family as well as her own biography are bound up inextricably with these hybrid origins. From the time she studied law at Oxford in the 1880s and 1890s, Sorabji struggled to reconcile her identity as a Parsi Christian with her identification as a secular professional woman seeking legitimacy as one of the first female lawyers in colonial India.[14] Her conviction about the role her family had played in shaping the woman she became and the career paths she had chosen is evident from the books she wrote about her parents' remarkable lives as Christian missionaries and her sister Susie's distinguished career as an educational reformer.[15] Given the combination of Sorabji's fervent Anglicanism and her family's equally passionate dedication to the Christian mission, it is not inaccurate to characterize these works as hagiographical; they are suggestive of a reverence for family life that was to infuse her lifework and may account for her belief in the redemptive power of house and home. The family motto—"we . . . [are] in the world to serve others"—became her professional credo, the cornerstone of her commitment to the cause of purdahnashin. In both her private correspondence and her public memoirs, Sorabji viewed her family history as the nurturing ground for her own professional ambition and credited her mother especially with directing her toward the law. The imprint that Franscina Sorabji left on her fifth child was inspirational at more than just an emotional level: it marked out patterns of work and of narrative that were to have a long-lasting effect on Cornelia's representations of zenana women to both herself and her reading public. In an example she gave in *India Calling*, Cornelia recalled a Hindu widow who sought Franscina's help because she suspected that the man charged with managing her property was swindling her. This story arguably became the template for the kinds of tales that Sorabji told throughout the 1920s and 1930s about the ill-fated purdahnashin under her supervision as legal advisor to the Court of Wards.[16]

Sorabji's career path was forged in the crucible of Christian family life in Poona, but it was equally shaped by the pressures of secular reform and professionalization that her legal training at Oxford and her own ambition for doing "useful work" in the world brought upon her.[17] Earning a Bachelor of Civil Law degree at Oxford was undoubtedly a tremendous academic accomplishment, but what practical work it equipped her to do was less obvious. She struggled in the 1890s as much to earn her living as to ascertain what exactly she had been trained *for* in a British imperial context, since her gender barred her from the kind of practice she had been groomed for. This is not to say that Sorabji was at a loss about what to do. Even before she left Oxford she had in mind a career as a "lady legal commissioner," and in her travels back and forth between Britain and India before 1900 she floated the idea of applying that post specifically to purdahnashin in public talks and private conversations with government officials whom she knew.[18] The Court of Wards to which she was eventually appointed was a site of adjudication for widowed women and their minor children seeking the disbursement of property, maintenance monies, and other family-related legal matters. The idea that a female government officer should be attached to it as a legal advisor was, if not her own, then certainly the result of the pressure Sorabji was determined to put on the India Office through her own persistent appeals and the influence of the friends in high places she had managed to secure during and after her time at Oxford. In 1903 she testified to India's secretary of state in London about the need for "a new profession for women." A question was put in the House of Commons in the same year about the condition of Indian women in the Court of Wards.[19] The fact that Sorabji's plan for action coincided with an intensification of discussion about the origins and practices of purdah in the vernacular women's press suggests how important the zenana was at the turn of the century as a symbol of "Indian" culture for a variety of competing ideological factions.[20] The position that resulted from these efforts was "Lady Assistant to the Court of Wards of Bengal and Eastern Bengal and Assam" in 1904. [21]

Although Sorabji was deeply invested in her role as a legal practitioner, in her capacity as official advisor to the Court of Wards she was first and foremost an ethnographer for the colonial state. And while she received much attention during her lifetime as a pioneering woman lawyer, she ought rightly to be remembered as the first Indian woman to be salaried as a native informant for the Government of India.[22] This was a job with a long history in British India, where there was an intimate relationship between knowledge production and governmentality that has been well studied.[23] Knowledge collection, like tax revenue collection, was crucial for the maintenance of colonial rule, in large measure because information about the colonized had its own kind of political and cultural capital, signaling recognition on the part of the Raj that rule on the ground in India could not proceed without either an appreciation of "local knowledges" or the collaboration of local elites. Knowledge meant surveillance, and surveillance was tied to the voluminous paperwork of a colonial bureaucracy dedicated to producing. As the financial commissioner of the Punjab remarked in 1860: "the annual papers are meant to be a photograph of the actual state of the community."[24] Well into the twentieth century, "rule by record" and "rule by report" remained protocols of colonial administration, even if the panoptical hopes of Victorian colonial administrators could not necessarily be realized. As Richard Suarez-Smith has noted, the knowledge system that underpinned colonial power had as its aim a transnational consensus about the terms and conditions of colonial rule: "to 'know' Indian society was to know what was good for it, and it was the function of . . . reports to enable the middle classes, both in India and England, not just the government officials, to participate indirectly in the experience of rule and in the broad outlines of knowledge about the ruled."[25]

As the author of annual reports enumerating her Court of Wards activities from 1904 to 1922, Cornelia Sorabji actively participated in this tradition of collaborative colonial rule through the standardization of knowledge about "native" women. Each report contained statistics of how many estates were visited, what kinds of work was undertaken, what expenses were incurred. Taken together they represent almost two decades of "evidence" about purdahnashin lives, cast in the distinctive discourse of the colonial modern: statistics.[26] Such statistics were intimately bound up with her own career aspirations and her desire for financial security; among the purposes of detailing the scope and reach of her work was to press for a better salary, more traveling money, and, above all, a government pension upon retirement. They also served to bring into view a domain of indigenous life that was but imperfectly known, and that had a shallow and uneven official archive.[27] Viewed collectively, Sorabji's reports amount to an official snapshot—a statistical "family history," if you will—of hundreds of zenanas across India. "Seeing for the state" enabled Sorabji to produce a remarkable archive of what she referred to as "a hitherto unexplored country"—that country being "the Orthodox Hindu community" through its innermost domains, the zenanas.[28]

The structural properties of the reports are worth examining in some detail, not least because they prefigure—in much the same way that Franscina Sorabji's earlier encounter with the vulnerable Hindu widow had—the narrative forms that Sorabji's more public pronouncements on the zenana would take.[29] Typically the reports moved from general surveillance to a particular focus: from a bird's-eye view of the year's work (part A) to detailed accounts of the estates and the purdahnashin under surveillance (part B). In the report of 1919–20, for example, Sorabji dealt with education, health and sanitation, and the pressures of overwork; she made suggestions about specific families and cases; and she ended with summaries of the developments in each estate over the past year. The latter ranged from mundane accounts of sickness, house repair, and recalcitrant ranis to vignettes that capture the drama of family intrigue, sibling rivalry, and parent-child conflict.[30] Occasionally, they were nameless, as when she called the widow on the Panhati estate "the old lady." More typically she gave their full names and produced short or long genealogies that might include their natal origins, the circumstances of their marriage, or the terms they had negotiated with the government for their allowances.[31] Although the confines of the zenana were of primary interest, Sorabji's reports testified incidentally to the many ways that local and even global politics crossed the purdahnashin's threshold, as when she got involved with the case of Nogendra Nath Sen Gupta, a son from the Kali Tara Sen Gupta estate who was accused of terrorism in 1907–8, or when she organized lantern talks for purdahnashin during World War I to inform them of events affecting the fate of the British empire. As Sorabji argued in her annual report for 1914–15, the women were as concerned "as if their homes were in London itself."[32] Though by no means a figment of her imagination, the zenana was also not "the boundary-wall . . . shut out from the breeze-swept moors of True Progress" that many contemporaries believed it to be.[33]

For Sorabji, who shared the general antinationalist conviction that "there has never been . . . a consolidated India until Britain secured this for us," surveillance for the state was a self-evidently imperial enterprise—one that was well served by the kinds of "documentary evidence" she collected in her annual reports.[34] In her view, two chief conclusions emerged from this evidence: first, that the zenana was the exemplary Indian home and, as such, represented the heart and soul of "true" India; and second, that "progressive" reformers who lacked such intimate knowledge were in no position to speak for or prescribe reforms for the "little ladies" in her care.[35]

"Emancipated" Hindus, she claimed, did not have the right "data" from which to make these kinds of decisions about reforms for women, unlike "those of us who live among the orthodox."[36] Clearly twentieth-century political contests in India left their mark on these conclusions. A staunch antinationalist and anti-Gandhian, Sorabji viewed the zenana as a political football and was determined that the evidence she collected about it serve as a counter to organized Indian nationalism whenever possible. Indeed, she saw herself as indispensable to the task of correcting nationalist assertions about the end of the zenana, the dissolution of purdah, and the resistance of purdahnashin to their seclusion. And so she routinely insisted on the "special knowledge" that her position—as a woman and as a lawyer—allowed her to relay to the British government in India.

Like all objects of the ethnographic gaze, therefore, "the zenana" that was archived in Sorabji's reports bore the imprint of her self-interest, and was refracted through the double lens of her political and her professional interests. As a result it appeared most often as an unruly, undisciplined space, beset by unscrupulous local men and naive widows. She cast a number of purdahnashin as "dodgers" and "intriguers" and saw it as her duty to intercept their schemes to get "unsupervised control of a sick-budget allowance" and the like.[37] In this sense Sorabji functioned as a loyal colonial servant, demonstrating that she was as interested in securing economies for the colonial state as she was in stabilizing British imperial power writ large—precisely because she understood these to be coterminous projects. Her research on the zenana was motivated by the conviction that its dwellers were politically useful to a colonial regime under siege by nationalist agitators. "There is no conservative," she contended, "like your purdahnashin."[38] What she created for the colonial state was a formidable archive of zenana life, as well as an unwitting account of her own political, personal, and professional agendas. Needless to say, the zenana that emerges from her Court of Wards activities cannot and should not be viewed as authentic, despite and of course because of Sorabji's insistence that it was so. In addition to surfacing as a vanished monument of a bygone era in Sorabji's annual reports, the zenana ends up as almost incidental to her quest for power and influence as an English-educated Indian woman trying to stake a reformist claim in the context of what she viewed as a dangerously progressive nationalist agenda in India.

One particularly vivid example of this quest for reform authority from the hundreds of mini-ethnographies contained in the reports will have to suffice. The case of the maharani of Bettial preoccupied

Sorabji in 1911 because the maharani was in such dire straits when she was summoned to her household. According to Sorabji, she was *non compos mentis* as well as violent, striking the English nurses from the Minto Nursing Association who were charged with overseeing her daily care. Convinced that the maharani was upset in part because her purdah was not being respected—she was attended by an English male physician, Dr. Caddy—Sorabji made the reinstatement of her seclusion her chief objective in her capacity as legal advisor to the Court of Wards, under whose jurisdiction the maharani fell. This met with resistance from the English doctor, who had prescribed force-feeding for the maharani. Determined to enforce his "medical" regime, he approached her waiting room, but every time he did so the maharani fled into her bedroom and closed the door. Sorabji whole-heartedly approved of this, suggesting that the doctor carry out all his instructions to the maharani this way, "so that she might sit in Purdah behind the half door," as was evidently her practice when Board of Revenue officials come to speak with her.[39] At this juncture Sorabji wrote to the member of the Board of Revenue in charge of the Bettial estate, who insisted that the doctor be allowed to follow his own protocols. The story that ensued was dramatic: the maharani strenuously resisted the force-feeding, causing her nose-ring to bleed and sending Sorabji back to the Board officer to request that only the nurses and not the doctor be allowed to pin the maharani's hands down and administer the tube—again, in order to maintain purdah. Sorabji also told him that Hindu women were used to fasting and that the maharani "is [being] treated as if she had the habits of an Englishwoman."[40]

Sorabji did not press the government to put a stop to the forcible feeding. Perhaps she felt that she had no recourse against the rulings of the Board; perhaps she sympathized with the forcible feeding treatments then being used against suffragettes in Britain, to whom she was implacably opposed.[41] Significantly, she chose to make use of the Bettial estate case as an occasion for defining her own authority over the zenana more clearly. As she told the Board officer:

> The policy of the Court of Wards has been that those not used to Indian custom cannot have complete authority in the zenana. This is one reason why I was refused a European assistant even though she would have worked both with me and under my direction. Yet—we leave Maharani entirely to an English doctor and nurses, none of whom have ever nursed an orthodox Hindu patient of Maharani's standing.[42]

After much to-ing and fro-ing, the Board of Revenue directed her to take over the maharani's household, which she did with relish.[43]

Whether or not the men to whom these reports were directed paid any attention to them is an important question. Sorabji had a reputation as a busybody *and* an excessively verbose correspondent that was both warranted and unfair. She was persistent in her belief that she was an authority on all manner of subjects beyond the Court of Wards and equally relentless in pursuit of official replies to her briefs, letters, and queries. Her determination to get higher pay and a status equal to her credentials in the colonial bureaucracy paid off: she got her pension and was able to retire from government service in 1922, at the age of fifty-six.[44] Two colonial bureaucrats with whom she was in correspondence, Board officers MacGregor and Stephens, actively mocked her paranoia and misinformation on terrorism, with MacGregor asking her: "Is this a return to your earlier role of 'Teller of Tales'?"—referring to reviews of her published work that credited her with being an excellent storyteller.[45] Officials dodged and then rejected her recommendations that she get an assistant to help her with the work or that her position be made permanent after she retired. Neither of these "dreams" of hers eventuated.[46]

Regardless of these failures, Sorabji's zenana ethnography reveals much about the historical conditions of imperial rule and the intersection of zenana life with it. We can deduce something about the physical geography of the estate zenana, and about the kinds of incursions male representatives of the state (doctors and Board officials) made into it, both routinely and in times of crisis. As a discursive strategy, her focus on the zenana as a microcosm of colonial governance, a kind of domestic miniature, has what Nestor Garcia Canclini calls a "monumentalizing effect": it brings us closer and more intimately to the zenana itself and, in the process, allows us to apprehend it in a single, magnified gaze.[47] Given how little the Board of Revenue probably knew about its charges in the Court of Wards, Sorabji's role in magnifying the zenana was arguably crucial to the regulatory capacity of the colonial state. Such an interpretation reminds us that Sorabji's ethnographies were powerfully allegorical, performing claims to "positive science" by drawing attention to the zenana's storied character, its capacity to represent a variety of worlds in miniature.[48] And if we read against Sorabji's characterizations, as the Board officers might well have done, it is possible to interpret the maharani as a resistant subject, trying to thwart the violation of her body through forcible feeding in ways that are starkly coincident with metropolitan feminist forms of political action.

I am not especially interested in seeing the maharani as a "displaced suffragette"—because of the way such a reading privileges the political history of the metropole as the center of feminist modernity—not to mention the categorical violence it does to the complexities of women's engagements with power, whether resistant or conformist. More telling are the traces of purdahnashin savviness that Sorabji documents even and especially when she aims to cast zenana women as intriguers at worst and as helpless illiterates at best. In her annual reports and in countless legal briefs, draft opinions, and notes she wrote in connection with her Court of Wards work, we get glimpses of the canniness of several purdahnashin— many of whom communicated with Sorabji through documents they dictated to their estate managers in the vernacular that were then translated into English by clerks in Sorabji's employ. The rani of the Banailli estate at Bhagpur, Srimati Chandrabati Koer, wrote to Sorabji, for example, explaining why she needed to hire an assistant manager to oversee the dispensation of her regular charitable donations to local schools and shrines. "I have no intention of spending this amount thoughtlessly," she told Sorabji,

> or of letting it be filched from me by hangers-on, as I believe is the kindly fear for me of the authorities. A Hindu childless widow has few reasons to make her desire life: but at least she can make her life of service to others through the wise administration of her income. And I intend to inquire personally into such objects of utility and charity as are worthy of support: and after making due provision, as I must do month by month, for the needs of myself and my immediate family, [I will] devote my income to said objects.[49]

Koer ended by insisting that she would oversee the manager herself, and that while she would take the advice of the Board commissioner when appropriate, "I should appreciate the capacity to make selection and allotment myself."[50] It is difficult to know what hand Sorabji had, if any, in the translation of this letter into English; at any rate it was written with the presumption that Sorabji would be the intermediary between Koer and the commissioner, Mr. Hallett. When Hallett replied, however, he conveyed his response directly to Koer via letter, and she in turn informed Sorabji about the Board's reluctance to grant her request. "We have to take a bold front," she wrote to Sorabji, "and oppose this kind of loot. My money seems to be all at the disposal of the sweet will of the officials."[51] Koer's critique of a predatory colonial state went unremarked by Sorabji. But as in the Bettial account, we see Sorabji's unwavering commitment to the preservation of purdah, the work of mediation she did between purdahnashin and the Raj, and the ways in she tried to claim exclusive authority about the purdahnashin to the Board of Revenue. Equally clear in the Banailli case is how that authority was circumvented by Koer and Hallett both.

Taken together, the Bettial and Banailli cases suggest how determined Sorabji was to try to parlay intimate, household knowledge into official knowledge, both in her dealings with the Board at the time of the incidents and in her representations to the government in her annual reports and legal briefs. Sorabji's determination to transform domestic knowledge into matters of state is not unusual. It was characteristic of white women reformers in this period from San Francisco to London to Sydney—and even of some Indian women working to gain a foothold for women's suffrage and feminist priorities in nationalist politics.[52] If she was trying to rescue zenana inhabitants and purdah women from accusations of uncontrolled sexual passion, there is little evidence of it.[53] What makes her remarkable is that unlike her contemporaries, many of whom identified with imperial power but struggled to distance themselves from it—and in contrast to her Indian counterparts, who took an increasingly anticolonial stand in this period—Sorabji believed that domestic knowledge could and should be the basis for new modes of political rule in a colonial state struggling to come to terms with a variety of nationalist challenges. Disciplining the domestic—bringing the zenana under the surveillance of the state and, more directly, under her own supervision—was a constitutive feature of her model for imperial governance. In this sense she tried to seize the zenana back from elite male Indian nationalists such as W. C. Bonnerjee, for whom the family romance of home had provided much ideological and political ammunition against imperial rule.[54] As her correspondence with Koer illustrates, in some cases at least, she was also trying to wrest the domain of the household from purdahnashin who were willing and able to exercise control over their own destinies. For Sorabji this reclamation, however partial and contested, always involved proving the loyalty of purdahnashin to the Raj and, at the very least, shoring up imperial power on the ground. Appealing to imperial ideologies of progress and presuming as she always did the ultimate benevolence of the colonial state, she reminded her superiors that "every question comes back to the woman in India, and back particularly to the illiterate woman of the zenana. Until this is faced and solved, very little real social progress can be made."[55]

The narratives that Sorabji produced about the Bettial and Banailli estates were not unique among her purdahnashin tales, at least not in terms of the kinds of ideological purposes to which Sorabji put the zenana and her own official position as well. In 1920 she opened her annual report with the observation that "this year's record has beaten all previous years, and has proved this office more than ever a 'clearing house' for the needs of Orthodox Indian Purdahnashins." She went on to say that "it is to be remembered that this Office is now in domestic as well as business, educational and friendly charge of wards' zenanas . . . enumeration of its duties is impossible, its possibilities are without boundary."[56] Sorabji's triumphalism was no doubt warranted: in the same report she logged over twenty-six thousand miles traveling to purdahnashin and demonstrated that in the course of less than two decades she had built her clientele to include 126 estates, made up of "622 women and children in my large official family."[57] Not only was the zenana brought to the sightline and under the purview of the colonial state through an unprecedented archival presence, but Sorabji had also managed to extend the boundaries of her "office" (both literal, in the sense of her post, and figurative, in the sense of her work space) so that it encompassed a domestic sphere "without boundary." Sorabji's own peripatetic life meant that while she was busy figuring India as the zenana and the zenana as *the* domestic form that was most politically useful for the Raj, she was rarely at home herself. While touring for the Court of Wards she quite literally carried her office with her, and even after her retirement she lived in hotel after hotel, inhabiting rooms where she would "shut off my bed and dressing table, and . . . [make] an 'Office' of the main part of the room. This helps me to house . . . [my] files etc. and saves me Chambers' rent."[58]

It is tempting to read Sorabji's embrace of the cause of zenana women and her concomitant homelessness as an ironic counterpoint to her life story. This is especially so because of the rhetoric of self-sacrifice that undergirds her accounts of work for the Court of Wards. Not only was every space turned into a (domesticated) workplace; but, as she commented wistfully in her diary as she labored to darn her stockings in one of her many hotel rooms, "one can be domestic in a house as one never can in a hotel."[59] Moreover, as she argued in a brief to the Board of Revenue in an attempt to secure a higher salary after seven years on the job, it was precisely because of her success in extending the limits of the domestic that "domesticity" threatened to take over her whole life: "I . . . work . . . often night and day. I . . . am never, so to speak, off duty."[60] Salaried work had literally become like women's traditional household work, ruling her life temporally as well as spatially and subjecting her to a variation of the middle-class housewife's all-consuming domestic drudgery.

And yet to leave all this to the domain of irony would be to miss the fundamentally perverse nature of her identification with purdah-nashin. For the coincidence of home and homelessness that Sorabji herself insisted on is actually symptomatic of the doubling of her own professional agenda with what she claimed were the interests of zenana women. Such a doubling, which was the presumptive rhetorical ground from which she fashioned her arguments about the zenana for three decades, is evidence of how thoroughly the career of this "New Woman" was dependent on the figure of the "old-fashioned" zenana inhabitant—and how reliant it was in turn on a kind of gendered imperial historicity: one that plots the woman of the present (and the future) on the grid of the woman of the past.[61] That Sorabji herself appreciated this fundamental dependence can be seen in the distinction she insisted on in her autobiography between her work as "a roving and privileged Practitioner of the Law" and the immobility of the purdahnashin in the precincts of the zenana.[62] What guaranteed their status as artifacts was precisely the fact of enclosure and the isolation and timelessness it apparently imposed on them. In Sorabji's hands these were phenomena that made them seem like inhabitants of a country within a country, and Sorabji herself a modern traveler constantly stumbling into souvenirs of a past as yet untouched by modernity.

The glimpses of zenana life recorded throughout her 1934 autobiography, *India Calling*, produced this contrast repeatedly by following a standard procedure: they telescoped Sorabji's arrival, her approach to the walled courtyard, her exploration of the inner quarters, her conversation with the rani or other inhabitants, and her analysis of the customs, practices, and conditions of life on the "Inside." Not only did this cast her as the traveler and them as the secluded ones; it established the purdahnashin primarily as a destination as well.[63] Sorabji often recounted the forms of transportation available to her for getting to zenanas, as when she visited the maharani of Baroda: "I moved from point to point . . . by train, riding an elephant, in palanquins, camel carts, in old-fashioned barouches . . . [and] in a 'coach and four.'" In this way she was able to dramatize the geographical isolation of zenana women and signal the mixture of urban and rural, traditional and modern conveyances to which she had access as a professional woman. The extent to which this characterization depended on the relative ignorance of readers about the specificities of elite Indian women's actual situations is significant here: in fact the maharani of Baroda traveled extensively in Europe and by the early twentieth century appeared in public photographs without a veil.[64]

Once inside, Sorabji produced elaborate verbal pictures of zenana life that conjured up the sparseness of the furnishings, the closeness of the quarters, and the intimacy of an all-female space. But it was the physical interiors of the zenana complex that captivated Sorabji's roving eye, and to which she devoted the most attention in the scenes she re-created. On her visit to the maharani of Baroda, she focused on the bath, the bedroom, and the dressing rooms, mapping the layout and elaborating the accoutrements (basins, dressing-table, saris, and jewelry) that could be seen there. Evocative and precise, the catalogue of objects is not merely descriptive but is designed to specify the material practices of Hindu femininity in its most intimate spaces:

> Saris in use were hung over long pegs attached to the walls; the overflow was kept in chests—rather like the chests of the eighteenth century found in old cottages in Cumberland. The dressing-table was—a portable box! There was a (bad) looking-glass in the lid, and there were compartments for the oils the women used for their hair, and for the red powder (sindur) with which they painted the parting down the middle of their heads, and with which they put the red dot on their foreheads after puja. The line signifies, I am a wife: the dot, I am dedicated to my Lord (husband). One woman told me it was to her a daily renewal of her vows of service to her Lord when she placed on her forehead the mark first put there upon her wedding-day. . . . Among the Progressives in these latter days it has lost all meaning, and is only a cosmetic.[65]

Sorabji deemed the only mirror in the dressing-room "bad," thereby guaranteeing that her account served as the only reliable technology through which the interior was made visible to readers. Of equal significance is her insistence that the scene she recounted is of days gone by, when authentic Hindu femininity could be counted on, in contrast to the "progressive" (read here: feminist) habits of her Hindu women contemporaries, who in her view preferred the aesthetic to the symbolic and in any case were incapable of fully appreciating traditional customs and their meanings. Rarely do Sorabji's engagements with modernity address the tropes of consumer culture common to the West, but here her reference to cosmetics resonates with European discourses that linked the modern woman with gloss, artifice, and superficiality.[66]

Perhaps because she understood that the capacity to reflect on the meaning of one's own life or practices was thought to be a sign of modern consciousness (and by extension, of cultural superiority) in the context of colonialism, Sorabji cast the zenana inhabitants she made available for scrutiny as pre- and perhaps even antimodern.[67] In the passage just quoted she suggested that she was able to recognize at least one thing that her clients could not: namely, that the objects they used for their daily toilette were both out of place and out of time. In addition to the zenana itself, the chests of drawers are made visible as echoes of an earlier era (English rural life in the eighteenth century)—in a deliberate and characteristic display of Sorabji's anglophilic sensibilities and of her cosmopolitanism as well.[68] In fact, Sorabji's cosmopolitan vision routinely breaks the surface of *India Calling*, thereby revealing her determination to be seen as the bearer of "traditional [read here: Hindu women's] India" to the threshold of modernity itself: the reader's sightline. Although photographs are sprinkled throughout the text, they only capture outdoor scenes—children playing, guards at the zenana gate, temple scenes. The closest we get to the purdahnashin themselves is through images of their conveyances: an ox-cart ("for the rich") and a *dhuli* ("for the poor"). This contradiction between drawing us in and keeping us at bay—that is, at the threshold of the zenana interior—is typical of Sorabji's rhetorical mode in the autobiography. It effectively highlights our dependence on her as the purveyor of an otherwise distant and unreachable world. The fact that a number of the most detailed zenana visits in the autobiography recall Sorabji's experiences at the turn of the century further underscores the distance in time and space these women are made to represent, as well as Sorabji's own indispensability as a witness to their primitive isolation both in and as history.

The case of the woman Sorabji called "the Squirrel-Lady" (because she allowed squirrels to climb all over her, believing she had been one in a previous life) is an instructive example of the kind of imperial historicity on which Sorabji relied to persuade her readers about her claims to special knowledge. At her client's insistence, and despite Sorabji's skepticism about the success of the case, Sorabji tried to negotiate a rent settlement for this woman from her estranged step-grandson, who proceeded to try to palliate the old woman by sending her a new garment and urging her to come and meet him and settle the matter in person. The "Squirrel-Lady's" waiting-woman, "skilled in the intrigues of the Palaces," warned against the meeting, and when Sorabji had the garment analyzed chemically it was determined that it had been threaded with a poison designed to kill. Sorabji was impressed by the fact that the Squirrel-Lady bought annuities for the waiting-woman and her husband from the arrears she eventually won, but she ended by terming the whole event "mediaeval" and speculating that in death the old woman had returned to the squirrels she had been so fond of in life. In this sense, the characters who emerge in *India Calling* are actually caricatures of either the simple or the cunning female—versions of contemporary Western and orientalist representations of the Hindu woman dating back to the eighteenth century. Whether she understood it fully or not, Sorabji's claims to the status of modern professional woman (with her knowledge of toxicology and her orientalist convictions) were clearly rooted in antimodern models that the archive of the zenana cast up in a variety of forms. Thus, the rhetorical maneuvers Sorabji performs in *India Calling* do more than imagine Hindu women in their settings. They help to align Sorabji herself with the modern, secular, and male colonial/legal establishment while stabilizing secluded women as the pathetic objects of modern technologies of surveillance inside the zenana itself.

Although Sorabji's visits were not limited to Hindu homes, her concern for the future of the zenana did resonate with communalizing discourses in 1920s Bengal, at least, about "the dying Hindu."[69] Like a tourist who surveys the landscape for sights of vanishing authenticity, she constructed the zenana as a kind of heritage center and her own work as the place to which readers could go to witness this vanishing monument of "Indian" civilization. The image of the female tourist, with its connotations of amateurism, was one she was at pains to reconcile with the professional status that, in turn, set her recognizably apart from her purdahnashin clients. It is nonetheless difficult to ignore the touristic qualities of *India Calling*, especially if we recognize that "tourism paradigmatically involves the collection of signs"—the zenana being the ultimate signifier of a "collectible" traditional India.[70] Given the fact that her work for the Court of Wards was referred to in her annual reports as "tours," Sorabji is in many ways exemplary of the overlap between the administrative gaze and the tourist gaze to which John Urry, a leading scholar of tourism, has drawn our attention.[71] Against the monotony and fixity of the zenana life she described in her autobiography, Sorabji ranged far and wide across India, visiting purdahnashin from Katthiawar to Bengal and, in the process, produced images of purdah households that emerge as a kind of "enclavic tourist space" by the end of *India Calling*.[72] She cast these images as part of a larger narrative in which the burden of work in and for the zenana was mitigated by the pleasures not just of travel but of relating the journeys to appreciative audiences. In a number of instances, getting to the zenana was difficult, dangerous, and sometimes exciting, involving treacherous terrain, floods, and camping out in all kinds of weather between destinations.[73] Even the availability of "a Raj motorcar" was no guarantee, as roads were often impassable and the effort so exhausting that, as Sorabji put it on one journey, "I felt that the end might come at any moment."

While it is true that these stories—subtitled "travels and thrills" in one chapter and always culminating in a zenana visit—illustrated Sorabji's vulnerability to the twin perils of the rural landscape and the elements, they also shored up her claims to cosmopolitanism because she always triumphed. What's more, she always returned to civilization to tell the tale. In one such narrative, she was sitting outside her tent drinking tea when an armed bandit tried to scale a nearby wall and approach her. He lost his footing (after she warned him to be careful!) and she was saved. Sorabji reported that though she was a "defenceless woman . . . experiences like those . . . invigorated me" and opined that "hazards are invitations to a more joyous life." The fact that Sorabji recounted this incident years later at a Washington, D.C., dinner party further underscored her cosmopolitanism—not least because that account was followed immediately by the observation that "it is not this way, however, that the orthodox Hindu looks at death. His indifference to death is indisputable; but it is not the 'hurry-up-and-pack-it-all-in-while-you-may' attitude of my Western tale."[74]

These tales from *India Calling* gloss over the ongoing arguments Sorabji had with India Office officials about the terms of her employment, and specifically the discussions she had with Board of Revenue officers about the reimbursement of her traveling costs.[75] The "Raj motor car" was hardly the glamorous provision of a grateful colonial government to its hard-working servant but rather an ongoing point of debate that takes up quite literally dozens of pages of correspondence in the Sorabji manuscript collection.[76] This discrepancy does not mean that the archive that houses the correspondence (the India Office Library) is more original or authentic than the autobiography (because the latter has been published and edited). As evidence, both the India Office Library holdings and the autobiography are fundamentally self-representational—in ways that draw, revealingly, on Sorabji's skills as a lawyer. In her letters to the Board, Sorabji pleads a case for her own professional authority and its corollary, her financial worth; in *India Calling* she is making a case to her reading public about the centrality of purdahnashin (and by extension, of her work) to the future of India. To be sure, the annual reports she submitted in connection with her work for the Court of Wards were the staging ground for much of her later published writing about the zenana and purdahnashin, in the periodical press as well as in memoirs. Her diaries and letters are, in turn, the backstage of those official reports—sites where the experiences written up later in the annual reports take on the immediacy of a different kind of reportage, all the more interesting as Sorabji often wrote letters with her diary right next to her.

This overlap of genres raises questions about the multiple and fragmented pieces of "the Cornelia Sorabji archive," its generic complexities, and its angular relationship to facile categories of public and private, institutional and personal. Reading across all the archival sites without privileging one over the other—without, in other words, seeing the materials in the "state" archive as more reliable than her published work—is one way of interrogating the imperial historicity that not only undergirds Sorabji's representational techniques but also resides at the heart of much "modern" disciplinary practice.[77] It is a way of refusing to see the Cornelia Sorabji of 1904 as a primitive model of her self of the early 1930s, a way of refusing to lay the grid of that evolutionary model onto the counternarratives of colonial modernity she produced. Such an anti-imperial, indeed antihistoricist, reading is especially crucial since the articles, essays, and books that Sorabji published and that entered the transnational public sphere were praised not simply for their insights into the zenana world but also as being the equivalent of "half-a-dozen blue books rolled into one."[78] Sorabji's authority as a reliable archivist/ethnographer/tourist depended precisely on this blurring of genres.

Across each of these discrepant yet interconnected archival domains, the doubling of modern/zenana woman that initially secured her the job of legal advisor to the Court of Wards consistently shaped Sorabji's vision of the purdahnashin as the remnant of a bygone era and herself as the all-knowing, wise counselor trying to do her job under the most primitive of circumstances. On one level, Sorabji's investments in remembering the zenana woman of the turn of the century as the quaint and harmless remnant of a more placid time may seem benign enough. Even the self-interest she exhibited in representing "the Hindu woman" as a zenana resident and, in turn, as evidence of the need for a certain kind of reformist intervention can be read as symptomatic of the kind of professional exigencies experienced by many women of the wartime and postwar generation who found themselves in the position of justifying their career pursuits to a variety of audiences and constituencies. In a context where representation was presumably a critical component of her legal duties and her claims to professionalism, it was undoubtedly crucial for her to demonstrate her capacity to observe and then to represent purdahnashin precisely as dependent clients. At the same time, I want to suggest that Sorabji made such representations widely available to a reading public beyond the official archive of the India Office by transforming the zenana interior into a souvenir: no mere artifact of the past but an object manufactured expressly for consumption by contemporary critics of the brand of colonial modernity that had taken hold among mostly middle-class Indians.

Sorabji's repeated recourse to the simple if misguided zenana woman of the past to elaborate her own social reform mission had decidedly political purposes as well. For the return to the zenana offered her an opportunity to unmask what she believed to be a modernity-gone-badly-wrong at the heart of contemporary nationalist projects in 1930s India, especially where women were concerned. Indeed, her quest to make "the *purdahnashin* in her setting" visible became an opportunity for antinationalist nostalgia, as the volatile events of the 1930s repeatedly returned Sorabji not just to the peace and calm of the zenana courtyard but to earlier historical moments, namely the turn of the century, when the nationalist movement had not yet mobilized on a mass scale and when images of the Indian woman had different (though no less ideologically charged) valences. Sorabji's accounts of purdah women in *India Calling* are intended to serve as a counter to the versions of "the modern woman" that were on offer, and increasingly visible, in 1930s nationalist politics, even as her stories tend to strand women like the Squirrel Lady "outside" history.

The political stakes of Sorabji's interventions were, admittedly, incredibly high by the time she was writing her autobiography in the early 1930s. At the same historical moment that Janaki Majumdar was situating the long-suffering heroism of her mother at the center of her "Family History" and Sorabji was hoping to center the zenana woman at the heart of her own counternarrative of colonial modernity, advocates of Gandhian nationalism were drawing women out of the home and into the streets in an attempt to reshape the standards of respectable femininity. Women were being arrested and put into jail and were turning, in several much-celebrated cases, toward less peaceful protests than street demonstrations or the salt march.[79] Much to Sorabji's chagrin, Gandhi was rapidly gaining an international reputation; when she traveled to America in 1929–30 and 1931–32 she devoted as much energy to combating what she viewed as misunderstandings of Gandhi's programs as she did to promoting the cause of purdahnashin.[80] Perhaps most galling of all for Sorabji, Indian feminists, who had used the occasion of the Mayo debates to articulate a much clearer platform about the relationship of women to Indian nationalism, were increasingly forces to be reckoned with in emergent debates about the form and character of an "Indian" colonial modernity. More specifically, they used the 1929 Sarda Act, which raised the minimum age of marriage to fourteen for girls, as an opportunity to publicly debate what the nature of Indian women's role in politics and the family should be under colonialism.[81] Sorabji was extremely dismissive of the Indian feminist movement, in part because she believed that the women involved had been influenced by British and even "Bolshevik propaganda," but also because she saw it as her chief ideological competition for the figure of "the Indian woman."[82] In her diaries and private correspondence she derided Sarojini Naidu, Madeleine Slade, and other "Progressive Women," calling feminism "a puffball—not an edible mushroom" and declaring that "the woman question has always been, since organized, an anti-British (and now) Terrorist movement."[83] When she spoke of the "misdirected patriotism of the extremist" she directed her remarks as much to feminists as to followers of Gandhi, marking herself as the champion of purdahnashin but also as a decidedly antinationalist and antifeminist public figure. When she complained that "the masses and the enlightened are traveling at an uneven pace," she cast herself as the representative of a majority of "Indian" women for whom the zenana was the true—and, as she would have it, the proud—"enemy of Progress in India."[84] The fact that she focused on the most privileged zenanas in India (those purdahnashin who were proprietresses of often quite significant estates) did not figure in her calculus, an oversight in keeping with her lifelong investment in elite societies in both Britain and India.

The account Sorabji published entitled "A Bengali Revolutionary" in the British periodical *The Nineteenth Century and After* in 1933 helps to frame the more immediate political context in which she wrote her autobiography and to shed light on the ways that her commemorations of the past were not merely self-interested but advanced an agenda that was as antinationalist as it was antimodernist.

The point of departure for this article was the recent wave of terrorism in Bengal in which "women confederates . . . prove[d] a useful and unsuspected asset to the machinery of revolt."[85] Significantly, Sorabji's piece turns immediately back to 1907 and the protests surrounding the partition of Bengal—as much to suggest the long history of terrorism connected with Indian nationalism there as to emphasize Bengali nationalism's Hindu bias.[86] In that year a woman who claimed to be responsible for terrorist acts was brought to Sorabji, in her capacity as legal advisor to the Court of Wards, by the commissioner of police in Calcutta. The British authorities, claiming to "have no war with women," professed to be able to do nothing with her and asked for Sorabji's help. From her first observation of the woman, Sorabji decided on a plan:

> as my eyes fell upon her hands lying on the table opposite me, I noticed that the nails were dyed with henna, and realising the import of that fact, I was thinking to myself, "She is not a Hindu, or she has been masquerading as a Moslem," or "she is a woman of the streets"—when she put her hands behind her back and burst into fluent Bengali. "A Moslem friend of mine did that to my nails," said she.[87]

As Parama Roy and Michael Silvestri have both documented, disguise had been a common feature of both terrorist activity and British intelligence work in colonial India since the nineteenth century.[88] Keen to demonstrate her unerring capacity to sniff out a pretender, especially one masquerading as an authentic Hindu woman, Sorabji judged this woman "dangerous" and decided that the best place for her was her own house. Having been told that she was a zenana inhabitant (though certain that she was lying), Sorabji set her up on the lower floor of her home and treated her as if she were a purdahnashin, vowing to respect her as "an Orthodox Hindu of the highest caste . . . and while you are my guest I promise you that nothing to which you might as a Hindu object shall come in at my gate or be cooked in my own kitchen." In addition to informing the servants about what the woman was to be fed, Sorabji ordered them to secure her in the house and limit all communication with the outside world. "For the rest," Sorabji explained, "I treated her as I should an illiterate *Purdahnashin,* showed her pictures and talked to her in the vernacular . . . her self-imposed inhibitions prevented my asking her to share my meals—that would have outcasted an Orthodox Hindu, or to share my life or my friends—impossible to a secluded dweller of 'the inside.'"[89] The woman in question was evidently frustrated by these limitations on her movement and tried repeatedly to get possession of the household copy of the *Statesman*, "betraying" her knowledge of English and thus revealing the impossibility of her supposed status *and* undermining Sorabji's attempts to read her illiteracy as evidence of her primitiveness.[90] In order to break her story, Sorabji held a "party of my Wards—genuine Orthodox women of Raj families." Purdah parties and clubs had been common across India since 1900, and as the century progressed they came increasingly under the purview of the Muslim Ladies' Conference and later, the All-India Muslim Ladies' Conference.[91] None of these political realities make their way into Sorabji's account. Instead, she took this opportunity to reassure her readers of her special knowledge of and relationship to purdahnashin, emphasizing how carefully she protected their seclusion by erecting "tent-walls from the doors of the carriage . . . through the hall and all the way to my drawing-room." She also insisted on her importance in the local community by underscoring that "they loved these outings, the only ones allowed them, and allowed them only because they call me 'Aunt-Mother' and were my official children."[92] After the purdah party, Sorabji claimed that the woman broke down because she was tired of being enclosed like an "orthodox Hindu."

Though Sorabji never identified her by name, the woman turned out to be an agent of the local terrorist organization working out of the Maniktolla Garden area of Calcutta—one of many hundreds of women galvanized by the partition of Bengal in 1905 to support secret societies by providing food and shelter to revolutionaries, carrying messages, and hiding weapons.[93] Despite her disapproval, Sorabji could not resist reproducing her story. Here it is difficult *not* to read the woman terrorist as Sorabji's double *and* her opposite: as she is represented in the essay, she emerges as the mobile modern woman, not just in the employ of the rebels but enlisted specifically to travel all over India and to lecture zenanas about the necessity of revolution. As her story unfolds, the woman intimates that the purdahnashin were not as docile or unworldly as Sorabji liked to presume. "'Yes,'—[she said] defiantly—'we made bombs to kill you while you and your friends were having tea parties for us . . . we laughed a great deal at that.'"[94] If this report was unsettling to Sorabji, she had the last word, for the woman claimed that what precipitated her confession was Sorabji's determination to treat her like a purdahnashin:

> You know how you have treated me. I could never communicate with anyone, not even with my friends. I was smothered with kindness, on

the wrong assumptions. Day after day I saw English officials come to your house whom I longed to attack. To-day all those *Purdahnashins* with whom I longed to make friends poured into the house. I got nowhere near them. It was too much. You were treating me like a child. I felt that I could not stand it one minute longer—I who nearly made a fresh mutiny."[95]

Sorabji's triumphal conclusion was: "So it was vanity that had betrayed her after all!"

This facile ascription—together with Sorabji's account of how she turned over the woman's confession to the commissioner of police—indicates how thorough her identification with the British government in India was, as well as how crucial her reductive representations of "the Hindu woman" were to her ideological collaboration with British rule. Her embrace of what Christopher Pinney calls the "detective paradigm" in this case further suggests her determination to mimic the strategies of visual control characteristic of colonial modernity *in situ*—and to produce a combination of detective story and tourist guide of the perils of domesticity itself.[96] Finally, her decision to place the woman under her own version of "house arrest" makes clear how readily she could adapt her preoccupation with the pedagogical function of the zenana to what she perceived of as the necessities of colonial rule in crisis. Such political canniness makes it impossible to read Sorabji as innocent about the revolutionary potential of the purdahnashin. In fact, she volunteers that she was aware of how the zenana was used to collect money for "the bomb-makers" and that she herself, as a local intermediary with both zenana women and Lord Minto's government, had been warned against letting unknowns into the women's quarters.[97] Moreover, the whole account in *The Nineteenth Century and After* is driven by the rivalry between herself and the unnamed woman revolutionary for access to purdahnashin and their political allegiance—a rivalry so politically charged that Sorabji felt compelled to turn the modern nationalist woman into a zenana inhabitant precisely in order to thwart her access to the same secluded women she counted on as her clients and her "children."

That she does so by bringing the zenana itself into the interiors of her own home, and focusing her surveillance techniques on those same spaces, suggests how intimate a struggle over Hindu women's bodies this contest was—as well as how tenuous Sorabji's attempts to (re)domesticate the purdahnashin might have been in the context of the political battles of this period. It also reflects her conviction that the home could and should be the center of political life in

India and that purdah itself could be a site of social service and evolutionary reform. As early as 1917 she had argued that

> it is there [in the zenana that] we must begin—not, I think, by opening
> zenana doors, and doing away with the custom of Purdah; but by edu-
> cating there, behind those closed doors, patiently, gently, moving inch
> by inch, keeping finally all that is beautiful, being equally firm about all
> that is wrong and that does not belong to Orthodox Hinduism in its
> purest original sense.[98]

Although Hindu orthodox women were arguably her biggest preoccupation, it was Muslim women who dominated her accounts of purdah parties, who organized the Purdah Fairs she participated in, and
who spoke in the "public" of the purdah subcommittee meetings
such as those that operated in the Bengal League of Social Service
for Women.[99] Sorabji was, predictably, quite disapproving of those
Begums who chose a less conventional political route, reserving particular disdain for Begum Shah Nawaz and her sister-in-law Mrs. Asaf
Ali, the latter whom she described in 1933 as "a rabid Congress
worker and just out of jail."[100]

In a very real sense, then, the purdahnashin was an example of
what Sally Alexander has called "the metonymic signs of femininity
particular to a generation," regardless of her specific political allegiances.[101] In this context, Sorabji's determination to represent the
zenana women she details in *India Calling* as counters to "Progres-
sives" and "Extremists," isolated from worldly events and disinterested in contemporary politics, must be seen not just as an attempt
to shore up her own credibility as an authority on the zenana woman
but also as a highly politicized fantasy about what her role—and
theirs—should be in modern India. This fantasy emerged at a moment of political crisis in the early 1930s when women's role in terrorist activity was intensifying. Some of those who were wounded in
failed terrorist plots, like one Preeti Waddadar, committed suicide by
taking potassium in order to avoid imprisonment—thereby creating
a whole new category of woman martyr for the cause.[102] But it was
also a fantasy that valorized the hierarchies that British imperial rule
had long imposed on Hindu-Muslim polities and, ironically, actively
reproduced the brahmanical vision of India that dominated nationalist politics in the pre-1947 period. In addition to being the legal
guardian of disenfranchised elite women, Sorabji imagined herself
as their guide through the perils of contemporary nationalism and,
very possibly, their savior from it as well.

Perhaps most significantly, the story of the "Bomb lady" that appeared in *The Nineteenth Century and After* had been in circulation in public at least since 1924, when it formed part of an article Sorabji wrote for the journal *Asia* entitled "'Indian Women of 'The Outside': The Emancipated Who, with No Book of Rules, Have Attained New Spheres of Freedom." As its title suggests, it was a derisive look at what Sorabji viewed as the fraudulence of the "modern Indian woman" as against traditionalists like Mrs. Ramabai Ranade and a variety of other women "social service workers" pictured in the article. The version of the "Bomb-lady" tale she mobilizes here is both an attempt to discredit terrorism and an effort to trace connections between the woman's "dramatic individuality" and those (like the All-India Women's Conference) who were pursuing "English equal-citizenship crusades" in India.[103] But the story related in *Asia* is much attenuated compared to the 1933 version; it is scarcely more than an elaboration of the notes she had scribbled in her diary when the event happened in 1907 and is wholly subordinated to a larger tirade against "the progressive Indian lady" who is committed to "this era of destruction, of razing-to-the-ground, of rebuilding."[104] Her re-scripting of the Bomb-lady narrative as its own didactic tale in and for 1933 was geared toward a metropolitan market growing increasingly uneasy about the directions the nationalist movement was taking. As evidence unearthed not once but twice from Sorabji's "archive," it offered a guided tour of the innermost regions of Indian politics, casting up the Bomb-lady herself as a souvenir of the past and as a premonition of what might be as the struggle for Indian self-government unfolded in the interwar years.

Although she was clearly anti-Congress and anti-Gandhi in this period, it is worth noting that Sorabji was not without nationalist sentiments of her own. She was not above linking emancipation from purdah to Indian progress, as her 1930 article in the London *Times* testifies: citing the franchise for women in all the provinces of British India, she verged on boasting when she declared: "thus it happen[s] that in one or two instances we got ahead of England."[105] Her objections to the ubiquity of terrorism and of nationalist activity in general in the 1930s stemmed as much from her conviction that it was not indigenous (i.e., that it was part of worldwide communist activities emanating from Paris, Berlin, and Moscow) as from the hostilities she harbored toward Congress leaders for their anti-British activities. In her mind these were not always distinguishable and, therefore, even "mainstream" nationalism represented an external assault on the British empire that was neither purely nor legitimately "Indian."[106] In the 1933 periodical essay, as in the 1934 autobiography, her response to such manifestations of modernity was to return to a less complicated historical moment (namely, 1907) when the possibility of continuities with the past seemed more realistic, and when conspirators masquerading as orthodox Hindu women could be seen for what they were and suitably dealt with—through privatized, individualist, and semilegal solutions. In so doing she insisted on inserting "her" purdahnashin into history even as she tried to secure her own role as arbiter of what counted as legitimate political action in both the past and the present. This is especially evident if we understand Sorabji's narrative in *The Nineteenth Century and After* as an attempt to trivialize the anti-partition movement, and if we read her representation of the Bengali woman terrorist as a figure of fun offered up for the amusement of the (British) reading public in service of a larger critique of what kinds of nationalist protest ought to be taken seriously in the context of 1930s politics. These are interpretations borne out by her insistence that the pranks carried out by the rebels to get into the zenana were nothing more than "childish," compared presumably to the official business that brought her to "her" purdahnashin.[107]

As Sorabji remarked wryly in "Indian Women of 'The Outside,'" "in the year 1907, women were the best missionaries that anarchy had in India."[108] Like Indian feminists and the nationalists with whom they sympathized, the "Bomb lady" was threatening to Sorabji because she was in danger of appropriating the clientele whom Sorabji most coveted as her own. In 1929 Isabel Hartog had reported in the *Contemporary Review* that the All-India Women's Conference had brought purdah women to their meetings in Poona (1927), Delhi (1928), and Patna (1929). She argued that "the number of women who come out of purdah increases year by year" and that therefore it was reasonable to conclude that purdah was "relaxing."[109] This was just one in a long tradition of such arguments, dating from the end of the nineteenth century, that prophesied the end of purdah—though Hartog had powerful contemporary evidence: the Begum Sultan Jahan of Bhopal had left seclusion, signaling a break, at least among elites, with the outward signs of tradition in ways that were alarming both critics of nationalism and its advocates.[110] Not incidentally, Hartog's representations elided the fact that this Begum of Bhopal had had a long history (since almost the turn of the century) of travel and political work, so that her "eruption" into public view at the end of the 1920s must be seen as part of a larger imperial project of dramatizing purdah and its critics in ways that were not always totally historically accurate.[111] The zeal with which Sorabji sought to commemorate the zenana as the site of "real India" and of the "authentic" is an index not just of how elusive they had both become by the mid-1930s as unproblematic subjects of either modernity or tradition but also of how subject they were to misinterpretation from a variety of quarters.

Nowhere is the anxiety prompted by these spectacles more clear in Sorabji's writings than in her professional memoir, *India Recalled*, published in 1936. Despite the fact that feminist historians have questioned the extent to which Gandhian nationalism challenged, rather than effectively reorganized, gender norms in the various campaigns and agitations of this period, many contemporaries believed they were witnessing the emergence of a radically new, and at times questionably respectable, "Indian woman"—especially in the person of those Hindu women who left the confines of home to protest in the streets and in salt marches under the banner of *Bande Mataram*.[112] Between the rise of terrorist activity in Bengal and the apparently increasing prominence of women and feminists in the public and private deliberations of Gandhian nationalists in 1934–35, the evidentiary value of the zenana was greater than ever. Sorabji's quest to fix the purdahnashin in their ever-changing settings is a direct response to what she perceived as an intensification of the political crisis in India. As such, examining the narrative strategies she uses is crucial for appreciating how she inscribed this crisis in her text.

India Recalled opens with an even more marked commitment to the ethnographic perspective than she had espoused in the autobiography—in part because the stakes of scientific objectivity and accuracy about the enduring value of the zenana as an enculturating and (conservative) pedagogical site were so great in the face of increasing popular evidence to the contrary. While claiming that her book was not a "learned disquisition," she also insisted that "this is not fiction, but a record of living India" prompted by Westerners' curious questions about "how secluded Indian women live."[113] Even more intriguing is her invocation of the camera as the medium best suited for capturing the images she wished to preserve. She called the book "a film of living pictures . . . [that] tell their own story"— thus evoking the technology of looking common to her writings in this period and signaling a more disembodied and more expressly modernist authority than before.[114] The reasons for this "eye in the door" approach are both personal and political: on the one hand, Sorabji's own sight was failing; on the other she was highly conscious of the fact that Gandhi used film as a means of propaganda, and she herself had taken to another "modern" technology—radio—as a means of countering nationalist "propaganda."[115] The cinematic approach to *India Recalled* is indebted to both of these phenomena; it is also an innovative idiom in which to articulate the commitment she had to subjecting the zenana and its landscapes to surveillance as the purveyor of state-sponsored colonial ethnographies to a more general reading public. Picking up on her filmic intentions, the *Illustrated Weekly of India* called Sorabji "a skilled and graphic writer" and *India Recalled* "a work of revelation."[116]

As in *India Calling*, Sorabji insisted on the juxtaposition of the modern and the traditional in order to ally herself with her subjects *and* create a recognizable distance from them—for, as she informed her readers, "storytelling is a traditional past-time with us; and we speak in parables as do other races."[117] But while the mixture of modern lens and traditional story established her privileged point of view at the intersection of past and present, it also conveyed a revealing sense of urgency that these "pictures" of zenana life had to be captured in whatever medium possible before the occupants escaped through "that open Zenana door."[118] The cinematic stance taken up early on is maintained throughout the text, continuing Sorabji's commitment to making zenana life visually accessible as well as spatially concrete for the reader. Indeed, the episodes recounted in *India Recalled* have a snapshot quality first announced in the photograph that appears opposite the title page (entitled "Outcastes at the Temple Door") and sustained throughout by a dozen illustrations—many of which position the viewer at the threshold of a "Hindu" ceremony or scene. In contrast to the autobiography, however, the photographs in *India Recalled* end up being the most telescoped feature of the text. For what begins with the promise of a photo essay on zenana life quickly turns into a more generalized view of the joint-family system in Bengal, with freeze-frames of ceremonies like marriage and Ganesh worship, local festivals, pilgrimages, household duties, and prayers. The zenana itself goes in and out of focus as the subject of the narrative, which opens continually out from inner quarters onto a variety of landscapes. As narrator, Sorabji herself rarely proceeds inward from the outside, as was typical in *India Calling*, but more often than not wanders across properties and estates and vast tracts of countryside—in pursuit of her legal business, to be sure, but also in search of an authenticity that apparently eludes her now within the confines of the zenana itself. Nor is it the desire to be appreciated as a modern woman explorer that drives her. Instead she zigzags across the pages, eschewing carefully crafted verbal images of interiors and inner sanctums for the more sweeping views made possible by the technology of the camera she has introduced at the start.

One notable effect of this panoramic approach is the depersonalization of the memoir: Sorabji disappears from view, but so do individual women—there is no "Squirrel-Lady" or maharani to particularize zenana life. By the end of the book, purdahnashin are scarcely even recognizable as the motivation for the project, as aggregates like "Village India" and "Sadhuins" (holy women) displace them, erasing them almost completely.[119] On the rare occasions when individuals do stand out, their attachment to seclusion is seen to be eroding, as in the case of Giribala, a young widow whom Sorabji visited as part of her Court of Wards business in Bengal. Though Sorabji's legal interventions on her behalf constitute the core of her story, it is Giribala's frustration with the loneliness and "neglect of human contacts" in the zenana that frames the tale.[120] As she tells it, Giribala "had a great and secret surprise which she sprung upon me. She had acquired a Singer's sewing machine, and had made loose covers for her chairs, because she had found my room in its summer chintzes."[121] One of the first mass-marketed "consumer durables," the sewing machine had also been touted from the start as an agent of civilization and a sign of the modern.[122] As with the zenana women of Sorabji's annual reports, Giribala's story demonstrates not just how ineluctably modernity had made its way into the zenana but also how constitutive the emblems of modernity were for the very trope of the zenana itself. Whether or not Sorabji intended to signal the precarious vulnerability of the purdahnashins' world or not, she had to admit that signs of the modern and of "progress" were to be seen pressing up against the very walls of the zenana. As she wrote in connection with Giribala's situation, "the emancipation of women . . . [was] seeping through the closed door of the Zenana, when restless young things, their blood stirred by quite other causes, felt its hot breath upon their cheeks."[123]

Sorabji's commitment to tracking "the interaction of the swiftly moving and the static," together with her conviction that purdah was not dead in India, motivated each of her memoirs, even as what was "static" was in the process of changing over the course of the decade in which she wrote both memoirs.[124] The race against time that impels the narrative forward in *India Recalled* allows us to see with particular vividness how determined Sorabji was to fix zenana women as pathetic yet romantic subjects trapped at the crossroads of then and now—thereby securing them as objects of the accelerating, nostalgic desire for the traditional woman that is among the many contradictions at the ideological heart of modernity, colonial or otherwise. The vulnerability of purdahnashin to the temptations and corruptions of modern life dramatizes the equally precarious nature of Sorabji's authority over what could even count as "the zenana," especially when something as emblematic of modern consumer culture as the Singer sewing machine could be seen to have made its way into the innermost quarters of *purdah* life. As a consequence, she ended up consolidating herself as "the active, newly autonomous, and self-defining subject" against which the traditional figure of the orthodox Hindu woman might be measured and appreciated, largely by means of her own remarkably cinematic vision.[125] Despite her professed admiration for the pristine quality of zenana life and its isolation from the trappings of the modern world, it was Sorabji herself who prompted and even enabled the pathway to modernity that purdah women like Giribala sought: for it was *her* sitting room that the young widow aspired to imitate, and *her* chintz pillows she used as the model for aestheticizing daily life in the zenana. What appear as paradoxes—ironies, even, given Sorabji's attachment to the isolated, authentic, recoverable, zenana woman of the recent past—are, in fact, symptoms of her own ambivalence toward "the modern woman" as she was being imagined and remade in the Indian context, as well as evidence of the kinds of "split allegiances" that any engagement with, let alone articulation of, femininity produced under colonial modernity.[126]

Sorabji was self-conscious enough about the visibility of these split allegiances to monitor reviews of her books with as scrupulous an eye as she did the zenana estates and, at least in the case of *India Recalled*, to tailor the book itself to what she perceived was both its marketability and its optimum political effect. She dithered about adding a chapter critiquing "Progressive" women lest the suffragettes pounce on her. She worried about the way her editor at Ninbet, Mr. Liddendale, made her rewrite her prose and made her add "more vignettes" so that the book would have more of a "Portraits of Woman" feel to it.[127] Sorabji did fight to keep some of her unique way of phrasing things in the book, though she appears to have given up on the title "This way—India!" in favor of Liddendale's preference, *India Recalled*.[128] As with *India Calling*, Sorabji treated the book like a scholarly production, checking references at the British Library and in general taking her reputation as an authority on the zenana very seriously.[129] More so than during the writing of *India Calling*, however, Sorabji was highly self-conscious about the need to assemble an archive of her collected works. As she wrote *India Recalled* she corresponded with her friend Lady Elena Richmond (a Somerville college chum) in England, instructing her to bundle all Sorabji's letters to her so that she might use them as a resource when finishing the book. Although in the end she didn't consult these— "there seems to be eno[ugh] material in what I have in my memories and my diaries to justify the book"—what she did do was to use the occasion of *India Recalled* to effectively create the beginning of the India Office Library's collection of her workbooks, letters, diaries, and vast newspaper clipping collection.[130]

In fact Sorabji had long kept a "diary of cuttings," to which she referred often in her letters to Richmond and to which Richmond also actively contributed.[131] When she was in London finishing up details of the book in the late summer of 1936, she instructed Richmond, "I'm leaving the bundle of letters in the Flat in a box marked to be sent to you in case of my death. So you will ask—else they will get burned. No time to take them now."[132] She also had some of her things removed from storage and spent an afternoon organizing them, during which things were evidently both "destroyed and sorted."[133] If these letters document the founding moments of Sorabji's official archive—one that would be deposited in that last, vast vestige of colonial bureaucracy, the India Office Library, by her friend Lady Richmond—they also commemorate Sorabji's determination to control the terms on which she would enter "history" as a subject. Rarely does an individual have the opportunity to participate in the creation of her own archive or to try to calcify the fragments of her biography to such a degree; even rarer is the opportunity to see the very processes of archival consolidation, and the will to knowledge-control they symbolize, so deliberately discussed in the "archive" itself. Had she been asked about it, Sorabji would no doubt have chalked it up to her own exceptionalism, a conviction she had held since her days at Oxford and that, arguably, motivated her life's work until her death at the age of eighty-eight in 1954.

In part because of her lifelong claims about her own uniqueness, it is tempting to locate Sorabji alongside other modern/modernist women of the interwar period—Frida Kahlo, Zora Neale Hurston, Leonora Carrington—who also struggled with the "insider/outsider" dilemma as they sought affiliation with a variety of modernist cultural formations.[134] Equally instructive is the possibility that she might be read, after Abdul JanMohammed, as a "border intellectual," caught in two cultures but at home in neither and hence compelled to create utopian possibilities in—and in Sorabji's case, out of—the past.[135] In terms of her representational practices, she perhaps most resembles her modernist contemporary the Indian artist Amrita Sher-Gil, whose "quasi-nationalist, quasi-realist paintings of rural folk" were matched by a preference for "high" art references, just as Sorabji's narratives about the antimodern Hindu woman are marked by a clear identification with things British, imperial, and cosmopolitan.[136] As Sher-Gil did in the art world, Sorabji made an "irreversible social space" for herself in the domains of law and social reform, holding fast to a certain male model of disinterested professionalism and producing an indubitably "orientalist imaginary" in the process.[137] More provocative still is the comparison with Pearl S. Buck, whose novels about 1930s China share the ethnographic perspective of Sorabji's work and remind us that the India-Britain axis is by no means the only one along which it is possible to read the fragmented histories of a gendered colonial modernity across the globe.[138]

This scripting and rescripting of self through a set or series of "Others" is symptomatic of any number of elite, educated women struggling to stake a claim for themselves in and for modernity in the context of colonialism.[139] What Sorabji's corpus allows us to appreciate are some of the competing versions of modernity that were on offer in the context of nationalist politics, even as her work, both ideological and practical, tends to homogenize the zenana dweller as a figure inevitably "outside" history. As I have shown, the very act of representing the purdahnashin to an English-speaking public—whether that was comprised of authorities of the colonial state or participants in a transnational sphere constituted by imperial power—threatened to make Sorabji a decidedly modern subject both in spite of, and because of, her own paradoxical relationship to "the Indian woman." To reprise Raymond Williams, Sorabji cast the zenana woman as the "archaic" (that which belongs to the past) when in fact purdahnashin were "residual" (formed in the past but still active in cultural processes). In her determination to excavate what was pure and precious about "traditional" femininities, she constantly revealed her deep investment in being seen as the discerning professional woman—an identity that was clearly aligned with the secular, the modern, and the masculine. She was what Williams would call an "emergent" historical figure: fully involved in producing new meanings and values, new practices and social relations—those belonging to the "modern woman" whom she alternately feared and scorned.[140] Sorabji's insistence on the zenana as the sign of authentic India is undoubtedly a hallmark of her unique political commitments, and her narratives about it stand as an example of the kinds of "little knowledges" that colonial modernity aimed to eclipse, in India as elsewhere.[141] The archive she left behind offers us an opportunity to read the zenana as a dynamic and above all *material* subject through which competing memories of "Indian women" have been articulated—a "narrative matrix," as James Young has argued elsewhere, from which a variety of contradictory histories must be imagined.[142] And despite her preoccupation with the domestic traditions that that archive memorialized, we can—and should—still read her as neither traditional or subaltern. Those traditions are, rather, an example of what David Lloyd has called the "nonmodern": subjects that emerge "out of kilter with modernity but nonetheless in dynamic relationship to it."[143]

To consign her work to "women's history"—or worse, to write it off as unrepresentative of mainstream political trends of the period because of her staunch antiprogressive positions—would, however, be to do a disservice to the complexities engendered by the crises of colonial modernity to which Sorabji was a witness, and in which she was something of an agent, in twentieth-century India. Rather than interpreting the archival traces Sorabji left only as proof of her peculiar politics or contradictions, I want to read them as evidence of colonialism's often unpredictable intersections with modernity, their mutually constitutive tropes, and, above all, their multiple and unanticipated genealogies.[144] Like the zenana, India itself was routinely characterized by Westerners as having "a superabundance of the past in the present."[145] In this sense it was not unlike the Indian village, which was of course one of the persistent signifiers of Gandhian nationalism: something to be surveyed, studied, marveled at and, ultimately, dwelled in because of the excesses of the past it embodied as much as for the redemptive power for the present and the future that it promised.[146] If the village and the zenana were therefore infinitely susceptible to reinvention, it was their appropriation as exhibitionary sites—house museums, if you will—that gave them purchase in the nationalist and imperialist imagination alike. Provincializing India, it would seem, was as much a modernist impulse in the context of colonialism as the necessity of provincializing Europe appears to be in the postcolonial moment: not a shadow or derivative process by any means but one that was constitutive of the very signs under which history was gendered, disciplines were practiced, and memory was brought into being by and for modernity under the historical pressures of colonial hegemony. Since India qua India (whether as zenana or village) has itself been one of the most spectacular museums in the world, we should not be surprised that it generated a global market for its souvenirs and an imaginative archive that was shared by nationalists and imperialists alike. This common predisposition for the colonial miniature in the context of the imperial gigantic should give us pause.[147] At the very least, it suggests that Sorabji's determination to preserve "her" purdahnashin in the domain of memory was not out of step with the times at all. It signals, instead, the uneven and unlooked-for terrains of colonial modernity itself.

Chapter Four

A GIRLHOOD AMONG GHOSTS

House, Home, and History in Attia Hosain's *Sunlight on a Broken Column*

[Chacko] explained to them that history was like an
old house at night. With all the lamps lit. And ancestors whispering inside. "To understand history,"
[he] said, "we have to go inside and listen to what
they're saying. And look at the books and pictures
on the walls. And smell the smells."
—Arundhati Roy, *The God of Small Things*

As the first generation of partition survivors reaches its twilight half a century after the cataclysm, new histories of 1947 challenge not simply the official record of events but the very possibility of housing the past in anything like conventional history. The work of oral testimonies and the narratives of ordinary men and women, combined with a refusal by authors like Ritu Menon, Kamla Bhasin, and Urvashi Butalia to submit to traditional claims of historical objectivity, put the nation—with its reliance on specific, usually sanitized scripts of the past—on notice.[1] Oral histories place the concept of a reliable archive at risk, compelling us to confront, especially in the person of the reluctant or resistant rememberer, the distortions, depredations, and often willful amnesia of all "repositories," speaking subjects included. As Amrit Srinivasan has observed, "as an ordinary member of society speaking from private memory and experience, the survivor . . . provides a corrective to the understanding of history as an exclusively specialist activity."[2] That the "simple, brutal political geography" of partition, which drove so many from their homes and forced millions to reconstruct their lives in new homelands, should result in the democratization, and the destabilization, of what Arundhati Roy calls "the History House" is a particularly poignant verdict on the past.[3] The pluralization of partition narratives—however belated—has unique political urgency because both experiences and accounts of contemporary "communal" violence in South Asia are often produced through reference to official histories of partition.[4] It offers a rare and politically important opportunity for scrutinizing the various forms and fictions through which memory has been articulated and can therefore be reimagined as a site, a dwelling-place, of legitimate historical practice.

The memory of place, and specifically of the physical layout and material culture of home, is a common feature of partition narratives—a phenomenon that reminds us of how intimately connected spatial relations are to social relations, as well as of how influential architectural idioms can be of the practice of remembering. Even when the image of home fades, its interiors are vivid in memory, as this excerpt from Intizar Husain's short story "The Stairway" illustrates:

> To me even our old house looks like a dream. Climbing up in the half-lit landing you had this strange sensation of walking in a tunnel; one bend leading to another, the second to a third, as if all your life you would be zig-zagging along a never-ending series of twists and turns, with stairs folding into infinity, but then, unexpectedly, the

bright open roof appeared and you felt you were entering an alto-
gether unknown country.[5]

For many, of course, the memory of home was as terrifying as the
memory of flight. In the story "A New Home" by Kartar Singh Duggal, the house is the prison that the family dare not leave at the
height of the riots in and around Lahore.[6] In Jyotirmoyee Devi's
novel *The River Churning*—which opens with the single, poignant
line "Sutara Dutta returned home"—the neighborhood locations
and interior spaces of house and home are consequential to the terror that she conjures through memory.[7] For Saadat Hasan Manto,
best known for his Urdu writings on partition, "home" in the wake of
1947 was an asylum, and not just in a metaphorical sense, as his story
"Toba Tek Singh" describes in excruciating detail.[8]

The compulsion to remember through home can be found even
among historians of partition, as can be seen in the narrative that
opens Urvashi Butalia's partition history *The Other Side of Silence* and
arguably sets the stage for the rest of the text. Butalia's uncle Rana
stayed back when the rest of the family fled to India; he insisted that
his mother remain with him in the house in Lahore; and eventually
he married a Muslim woman, converted, and changed his name.
When Butalia goes to Lahore in search of her uncle four decades
later, she finds that the house—"a rather decrepit old house in a
suburb"—is at the very center of her family's struggle for remembering and forgetting. Not only is the house the lingering symbol of a
family's flight and a son's betrayal, it figures in each part of the testimonies she has collected in her family as a centrifugal presence—
including Butalia's own. "Tell us," her relatives demand when she returns to Delhi, "tell us what the house looks like, is the guava tree
still there, what's happened to the game of chopar, who lives at the
back now[?]" And her abiding memory of her arrival on the threshold of the house in Lahore for the first time is as follows:

> Vaguely I remember looking at the floor for inspiration, and noticing
> that engraved in it was the game of chopar that my mother had told us
> about—it was something, she said, that my grandfather had made es-
> pecially for his wife, my grandmother . . . door bolts were drawn
> and I was invited in.[9]

This liminal detail becomes pressed into the service of memory, in
part because Butalia understands the significance of the house
("that big, rambling haveli") in her family's history.[10] Significantly,
when she talks about her experience of arriving in Lahore, that ac-

count merges almost seamlessly into her tale of approaching the
house for the first time:

> What I was not prepared for . . . was the strong emotional pull that
> came with the crossing. I felt—there is no other word for it—a sense of
> having come home. And I kept asking myself why. I was born five years
> after Partition. What did I know of the history of pain and anguish that
> had dogged the lives of my parents and grandparents? Why should this
> place, which I had never seen before, seem more like home than
> Delhi, where I had lived practically all my life?
>
> What was this strange trajectory of histories and stories that had
> made it seem so important for me to come here? Standing there, in
> the verandah of my uncle's house, I remember thinking, perhaps for
> the first time, that this was unexpected. When I had begun my search, I
> wasn't sure what I would find. But I wasn't prepared for what I did find.

Here, "the crossing" into Pakistan is parallel to, if not synonymous
with, crossing the threshold of the ancestral home. Each border-
crossing is fraught in different ways: she has difficulty getting a visa
into Pakistan, an experience that dramatizes her status as a citizen of
India and marks her clearly as a "national" subject; and because her
uncle converted to Islam, the family home is now a Muslim household, with all the implications for religious purity and impurity, for
"inside" and "out."

Eventually Butalia's mother and sisters return themselves, and
Rana gives them "a proper tour of the house." They are able to "go
back into their old rooms, to find their favorite trees, to remember
their parents and other siblings"—to revisit the past, in other words,
by inhabiting its physical structures.[11] Butalia is remarkably frank
about her ambivalence in the face of all this. Her characteristic hon-
esty allows us to appreciate that even if her encounter with the violence of history is secondhand, the family house stands at the very
heart of that encounter—ghostly interiors, whispering ancestors,
and all. For partition's witnesses, as for those who act as witnesses for
them, the stakes of such memoryscapes are especially high. For survivors the process of *creating* a place *for* memory involves *reconstructing* a place *from* memory. And, indeed, many seem unabashed and
even unapologetic about the fact that their "historical" understanding relies precisely on the merging of factual and fictive "materials"
for its sustaining power. If what scholars have argued about the
mnemonics of space and place is true, then the actual practice of remembering may create more "storage space" for knowledge and
memory—a space that should be seen not just as individual or private property but also as the grounds of a critical "national" his-

tory.[12] While it is unverifiable in the case of partition survivors, this claim about the expansive effect of such techniques may offer some explanation for the persistence of spatial descriptions in oral narratives, even and especially where those narratives compress or occlude the space of home so that it leaves a scarcely legible trace.

I do not mean to suggest that there is some kind of universal impulse that produces "house memories" either randomly or discriminatorily, or that home is necessarily the destination of all memory. Nor does every single partition narrative have images of home at its center, for clearly many such accounts are as concerned with the relentless movement of displacement, the breathless panic of escape, the sheer terror of running for one's life. Middle- and upper-class status, with its correlative symbolic and material investments in private property, is certainly more likely to produce memories centered on house and home. And yet it can hardly be surprising that circumstances of forcible expatriation and civil war would be likely to produce vivid memories of home, or that the architecture of domestic arrangements should loom large in even casual remembrances of such upheaval and disruption. In order to understand the cultural and political meanings of memory in moments of crisis such as partition, the discursive forms that they took must be seen as more than merely incidental. These are in fact the very *matériel* of memory, especially where remembering is a kind of defensive posture, designed as much to keep the past in place as to bring it forth into the present—and especially when the conventional historical archive has so little to offer us by way of insight into women's experiences of partition.[13] If memory is as much an art as a social or cultural practice, then an examination of its architectural idioms offers one way of getting at the complex relationship of material culture to aesthetic practice and, in turn, of aesthetics to the historical imagination.[14]

Partition fiction is a particularly vivid example of the art of memory-work, as well as an archive whose possibilities have yet to be fully explored. It is perhaps not surprising that the recovery of oral histories of partition has coincided with a turn to fiction as a site of historical evidence in the last ten years. As Homi Bhabha has argued, "literature haunts history's more public face, forcing it to reflect on itself in the displacing, even distorting, image of art."[15] One of partition's leading historians, Mushirul Hasan, goes so far as to contend that drawing on fiction as an archive of partition experiences offers an opportunity to access "multiple versions of the truth" about the events of 1947, yielding an intimacy—and a political immediacy—that is not possible through any other discursive practice.[16] For

Hasan, Attia Hosain's *Sunlight on a Broken Column* (1961) is one of
the most compelling archives of Muslim experience before, during,
and after partition. In his estimation, the stories she tells in the book
"are seemingly 'fictional'" but are also "in fact fairly accurate representations of the political ferment that split middle class and
landowning families along ideological lines." Most significant for my
purposes, Hasan is willing to give them the status of "historical texts"
because they

> illuminate certain aspects of the liberation struggle which are only
> dimly covered in records and private papers. They bring out the ten-
> sions, conflicts and contradictions in movements perceived as mono-
> lithic, autonomous and linear. They introduce nuanced discourse in
> an area of research dominated by highly magisterial generalisations.[17]

And yet for all his determination to recover *Sunlight* as a legitimate archive, Hasan casts the novel as evidence of implicitly small
histories—family histories—that supplement the extant magisterial
histories, nuancing dominant discourses about partition without
necessarily challenging the politics of traditional archival readings or
interrogating the gendered status of memory and its relationship to
history itself.

Sunlight is by no means the only "partition" novel that can be
counterread as a history.[18] In fact, the tension between the "official"
archive and the "fiction" of partition stories has engendered a
heated debate in the field of 1947 history.[19] Unlike some, I am less
interested in testing the "reality" of scholarly findings against the
"fiction" of novels or other genres of writing than I am in examining
the tropes that women writers in particular used to figure their apprehensions of history. Under the pressure of this commitment, *Sunlight on a Broken Column* becomes more than simply a domestic fiction or the familial face of partition. The novel can be understood,
in the first instance, as an attempt to account for the past by producing the history of one family dwelling—literally *materializing* one
community's experience of terror and political violence. It may also
be read as an effort to lay claim to home as a legitimate, persuasive,
and ultimately irrefutable partition archive: evidence of the desire to
dwell in history when house and home have become uninhabitable.
The novel is, in short, a historical argument about the impossibility
of dwelling comfortably at home in the wake of the unspeakable violence of the past.[20]

At the center of Hosain's narrative is Laila's family's home, called
Ashiana (or, the nest). It is the "arched, carved, latticed, pillared,
sprawling house" to which she is fundamentally, yet uncomfortably, attached.[21] Originally her grandfather's, the house passes upon his
death to her aunt and uncle, with whom she lives, since her parents
are both dead. Though this is the house in which she was born, Laila's
orphan status makes her as much an observer of the house as an inhabitant; her relationship to its rhythms and her ultimately failed attempts to accustom herself to its culture make her a kind of migrant
to, and in, it as well.[22] For although she is on good terms with her relatives and even considers the house her home, Laila offers us a view of
it that is alternately encyclopedic and abbreviated—moving from the
courtyard to the verandah to the drawing room to the mirrors on the
walls and back again with an eye for detail that highlights her peripatetic vision and anticipates her permanent exile from Ashiana at
the end of the novel. As with Janaki Majumdar's "Family History," the
entire narrative depends on our glimpses of the interiors of the
house, their connection to one another, the kinds of constraints they
place on Laila's mobility, and her vexed relationship to a certain version of domesticity. Like all private spaces, Ashiana's are never simply
or self-evidently interior but are continually open onto the public, the
national, and the historical, helping not just to reflect these domains
but to produce them as well.

In this text, however, unlike Majumdar's, there is no mother with
whom Laila can identify or disidentify. Ashiana stands in for the
maternal figure, furnishing her, quite literally, with models of domesticity that she eventually rejects by choosing her own marriage
partner and buying herself a small cottage in the hills—effectively
renouncing her past attachments, if not her family history. This is
perhaps because, unlike the house in the Bonnerjee "Family History," the home in *Sunlight* is destroyed by an act of civil war—by the
effects of state-sponsored violence that coincide precisely with the
moment of Laila's controversial marriage choice. It would be easy to
see the interior of Ashiana as a refraction of Laila's emotional life, its
corridors, passageways, and winding halls as her route to freedom,
and its demise as the end of her childhood innocence. Ashiana
clearly shapes the very terms through which she apprehends the
conjuncture of politics and history at partition; and in the end she
is haunted by the very interiors through which she is compelled
to imagine, and remember, the past. And yet *Sunlight* is not self-

evidently a bildungsroman. It is not teleological, as novels of development invariably are; quite the contrary. Ashiana exhibits degeneration rather than youthful growth: it is disintegrating well before partition—a process Laila is uniquely positioned to appreciate because of her peculiar angle of vision as the orphaned daughter of the house.

This is not to say that *Sunlight* is a renunciation of politics. Rather, the political desires that the narrative valorizes are not "progressive" in a Nehruvian sense. If anything, Laila refuse to imagine the kind of emancipatory future heralded by the champions of the post-1947 order because she is skeptical of the possibilities of a post-partition, postcolonial modernity for elite women of her generation.[23] In this respect, *Sunlight* is an example of what Claudia Tate has called a "domestic allegory of political desire"—especially when read against both the culture of elite Muslim reformers from which Hosain came and the cultural histories of partition that are gradually emerging fifty years after independence.[24] Most important, the centrality of Ashiana to the story is matched by its structural vulnerability, enabling it to stand not just as a nostalgic symbol of what was but as a silent and accusatory witness in the present: a testimony, in other words, to the ways that "private memory is constantly assaulted by the revisionary movement of history."[25]

Born in 1913, Attia Hosain grew up in the heart of reformist *taluqdari* (landowning) culture in Oudh, in the United Provinces of British India. Like many elite Muslim men in the late nineteenth century, her Cambridge-educated father, Shahid Hosain Kidwai, was active in the political and national movements of the twentieth century. As did many progressive men of his generation, he considered the education of girls to be crucial to both their marriageability and to the cultural capital of the family. Though he died when she was just eleven, his influence on Attia was considerable. He sent her to the La Martinière School for Girls in Lucknow, named after the French merchant-soldier Claude Martin and housed in the Kurshid Manzil—one of the many "Indo-European palaces" that graced the city into the twentieth century.[26] The concentric circles of Mughal and European culture that Hosain's school physically embodied are metaphors for the urbanity of the colonial Lucknow of Hosain's childhood, as well as a template for the hybridized lifestyle—"part-European dilettante, part-Indian courtier"—that made it an enduringly cosmopolitan cityscape.[27]

Kidwai arranged for his daughter to be taught Urdu and Arabic

at home and encouraged her never to lose touch with their ancestral village. His concern for her education, as well as his extensive
personal library, turned her into an avid reader: someone who, by
her own admission, grew up "unsupervised" on the English classics, which helps account for Laila's love of books, described in *Sunlight* as "garlands of gold."[28] According to Hosain's daughter, her
mother's personal collection included authors ranging from Dickens
and Brontë to one of Cornelia Sorabji's publications.[29] Unlike many
educated Muslim women of just one generation earlier, Hosain was
not what Gail Minault has described as a "secluded scholar," living in
"hermetically sealed respectability."[30] In her introduction to the
1989 Penguin edition of Hosain's short stories, *Phoenix Fled*, the novelist Anita Desai describes Hosain's upbringing as "sheltered, rather
than secluded." Her religious education was "liberal," and she and
her sisters did not wear the burqa, though the family car did have
silk curtains on the windows.[31] When it came to higher education,
Hosain was a pioneer: she attended Isabella Thoburn College in
Lucknow and in 1933 became the first woman from a *taluqdar* family
to graduate from college—a fact that did not prevent her from re-
senting the fact that her brother was sent to Cambridge and she was
not.[32] A contemporary observer of the college remarked:

> The school was strictly purdah, surrounded by a high wall, with an old
> woman keeping guard at the gate. If by chance the gate is opened and
> a man—even a coolie—passes, there is general uproar, even six-year-
> olds running and screaming, "Purdah, purdah" as they hide their
> faces.[33]

This was a memory Hosain would later translate directly into a scene
in *Sunlight* (see hereafter). Given the fact that her father was connected to contemporary nationalist leaders (his great friend was
Motilal Nehru, Jawaharlal's father), Hosain's involvement in politics
was in many respects an extension of family culture—another reminder of how artificial concepts like "public" and "private" can be,
as well as how intimately intertwined those spaces invariably are.

Hosain was influenced in the 1930s by England-returned friends
and relatives who were involved in the Communist Party and Congress socialist circles, evidence of which is to be found in *Sunlight on
a Broken Column*, where heated arguments break out between Laila's
peers about the attitudes of the Congress party and its members toward Muslims, as well as about the fate of British imperial rule.[34] The
city of Lucknow undoubtedly played a crucial role in this politicizing
process, since it was "the effective capital of the United Provinces" by

the 1920s and the headquarters of "the most important political organization in India after the Congress," the Muslim League. It was, in sum, "the political center of upper India."[35] In keeping with the long history of architectural wonders in Lucknow, its political centrality was signaled by the building of a new House for the United Provinces Legislative Council in 1921, sidelining the *de jure* capital of the province, Allahabad. Lucknow's emergence as a force to be reckoned with both culturally and politically was made possible by an exceedingly well-educated and active Hindu middle class—one that sustained three newspapers in English alone—as well as a cadre of organized Muslim political activists that dated from the end of the nineteenth century.[36] As Congress struggled to negotiate the terms on which Muslims would participate and be represented in its organization in the first years of the twentieth century, the All-India Muslim League was founded in Dacca. It moved eventually to Lucknow, where the "Young Party," under the leadership of Sayyid Wazir Hasan, helped to orchestrate the Congress-League Pact of 1916 (also known as the Lucknow Pact)—bringing Nehru, Gandhi, Tilak, and Jinnah all to Lucknow to oversee its settlement and thereby showcasing its growing significance to imperialists and nationalists alike.[37] The Young Party and its advocates did not share *taluqdari* values; those were represented, however ineffectually, in the British India Association—a quasi-political form that predated Congress and was decidedly anglophilic in its character and affiliations. What's more, men more radical than Hasan inside the party became increasingly involved in Khalifat politics, led by the *maulana* Abdul Bari, who tried to persuade Gandhi to take up that cause. As for Congress, its operations from the 1920s to the 1940s "moved into the hands of Lucknow-based leaders," so much so that by the early 1930s, the time *Sunlight* opens, Lucknow was the capital not just of "Hindustani high culture" and the United Provinces but arguably of a historically influential all-India political vision as well.[38]

Hosain was drawn into the politics of the period through Sarojini Naidu, who persuaded her to attend the All-India Women's Conference in Calcutta in 1933. According to Hosain's later reminiscences, she reported on the event for newspapers in Calcutta and Lucknow, at the same time that she was beginning to write short stories for publication.[39] As a student at Isabella Thoburn College in the early 1930s, she would have also been keenly aware of the ways that fiction was being rapidly claimed as the "literary domain of nationalist ideology" by writers of a variety of political persuasions.[40] Such claims burst onto the Lucknavi scene dramatically in 1932 with the publication of *Angare* ("Embers"), a collection of short stories by Sajjid Zahir, Rashid Jehan, Ahmed Ali, and Mahumduzzar—stories that were "a ferocious attack on society" and that set off a firestorm of outrage and protest in the local press.[41] The Urdu papers condemned their "blasphemy and atheism," *maulvis* issued fatwas, and death by stoning was suggested as the most appropriate punishment for the authors.[42] The book, written in Urdu, was banned by the United Provinces government, and all but five copies were destroyed. These were archived, three in the holdings of the Keeper of Records in New Delhi (now the National Archives of India) and the other two in London: one in the British Library and one in the India Office collections. Although the *Angare* authors maintained that they were unprepared for the outcry, they might reasonably have anticipated what could result from writing fiction satirizing "current Moslem conceptions, life and practices," including religious education and purdah, in some instances from a Marxist perspective.[43] This was not the first collection of short stories to be banned by the imperial government on the grounds that it was an incitement to sedition, but the reaction it provoked among Muslim commentators was unprecedented.[44] One of the most tangible consequences of the controversy was the formation of the Progressive Writers' Association (PWA) in 1936 by the *Angare* group.[45]

Hosain was a contemporary of Zahir, Jehan, and other progressive writers, including the short story writer Ismat Chugtai.[46] Her future husband's brother had been a classmate of Zahir at Oxford, and Jehan was married to her cousin. According to Hosain's daughter, Attia "was influenced by, and supported, their ideas."[47] Hosain's association with this circle meant that she was caught up in the post-ban enthusiasm in ways that were as political as, if not more than, her involvement with the All-India Women's Conference. The dangers of association with *Angare* sympathizers should be clear. Not only did such association imperil one's public reputation, especially if one was a woman, but the socialist overtones of *Angare* and the communist undertones of its organizational successor, the PWA, also raised the political stakes of involvement with the writers significantly. As late as the 1990s, Hosain struggled to explain her relationship to politics in the public sphere in those tumultuous times:

> My political thinking now, you have got to understand it [was] . . .
> the Thirties. The ideas came to me at the time when I was reading left-
> wing literature of any kind. My young relatives, men who had been
> brought up here [England], school here, University here, they went

back like all the intellectuals of the Thirties went back, thinking that
Russia was the answer, because at that time Communism seemed the
answer when you were fighting imperialism.[48]

Hosain attended the first meeting of the PWA in Lucknow, and
Rashid Jehan, a medical doctor, remained a longtime friend.[49] But
this did not mark a debut into politics of even the literary kind for
Hosain, whose marriage to Ali Habibullah occurred the same year as
her graduation from Isabella Thoburn—an event that also coincided
with the furor over the publication of *Angare* and its subsequent
ban.[50] By her own admission, she felt "tied and restricted in many
ways by traditional bonds of duty to the family," though she did consider herself "a fellow traveler" with the PWA in its early years.[51]

Like Laila's, Attia's marriage choice was unconventional and
controversial: she married a cousin against her mother's wishes. She
later remembered how her mother accused her of "having be-
smirched the family honour" and that her family considered her a
rebel and an anticonformist.[52] But in marrying Habibullah, Hosain
actually remained quite firmly within the *taluqdari* world of which he
also was a part. Like her father, he had been educated in England,
and his father was chancellor of Lucknow University. Both her family
of origin and her family by marriage were politically well connected:
according to Desai, her mother-in-law sat in the United Provinces As-
sembly as a representative of the Muslim League "but maintained
her independent view that Muslim leaders should remain in India,
not go to Pakistan."[53] Hosain did not share this view, taking her children (Shama Habibullah, b. 1938; Waris Hussein, b. 1940) to live in
Britain in 1947. As she told Laura Bondi, who interviewed her almost fifty years later,

> I preferred to stay in England, for there was no way I was going to Paki-
> stan. . . . The magic of India lies in the magic of its human relation-
> ships. Despite all the ugly phenomena and the poor governance, the
> human factor is still miraculously strong. The day that disappears,
> India will be a poor country.[54]

And in another interview with Nilufer Bharucha:

> I am not a Pakistani. I never wanted to be one. When Independence
> came, my husband and I were in England. We had UK passports and
> my husband was doing war repatriation work. We were asked if we
> wanted to go to Pakistan. We said no, I had two small children to bring
> up and we decided to stay on in England. I have lived in England for
> over 50 years now. But my roots are still in India.[55]

Hosain had had some experience in radio in Lucknow and later in Bombay, and once in London she worked as a BBC broadcaster, presenting her own women's program as part of the Eastern Service.[56] Though, as I will argue hereafter, *Sunlight* is a ghostly memoir of life in and around Lucknow in the decades leading up to partition, the BBC archives leave an even more ghostly trace of Attia's relationship to partition and the exile it prompted. To the best of my knowledge there are no recordings to be had of her voice, even though she did literally hundreds of broadcasts from 1948 until the 1960s, as the raft of receipts documenting her remuneration testifies. Only a handful of scripts remain. Together with the payment stubs, they indicate the tremendous range of topics she spoke on, from the cinema to Beethoven, comparative religion to art, Good Friday services to "How I First Got Started Writing."[57] There is evidence that she wrote some of her own scripts and even suggested topics for the broadcasts—like her "Passport to Friendship" piece, which was prompted by a trip to the Soviet Union in 1964.[58] Those who supervised the scripts at the BBC often amended what she had submitted so that it corresponded better to what they considered "broadcastability" in the Commonwealth and beyond, though Hosain did not always agree. When Owen Leeming of the Talks Department wrote her a memo saying that the story she wanted to read, "A Journey— . . . and Tomorrow," would not read well on air, Hosain replied:

> Thank you very much for your letter, and for returning the book. I can quite understand how different it is to like a story when one reads it— and when one hears it read. . . . I enjoyed my first experience of reading a story in English. And I was flattered to get a farmer in Gloucester who wrote a charming letter to tell me how much he enjoyed listening to the story.[59]

Savvy about what English as well as ex-colonial listeners might like, Hosain read a variety of set texts, from classics to other kinds of prose. She also did unscripted discussions, as when she participated in Mortimer Wheeler's Asian Club for the BBC's "London Calling Asia" program.[60] On at least one occasion she acted as a roving reporter, complete with tape recorder, for the Weekend Review series.[61] Her broadcasts were popular, garnering letters of praise from both listeners and BBC bureaucrats. Her contributions to a 1956 broadcast, "A Conversation on Homesickness," brought particular acclaim. Mr. Richard Daly of Dartmouth wrote the BBC to say that "I know exactly what she was trying to express. It is beyond the labels of nationality, creed, colour and all other self-projections of the human

self, that are all so petty, pathetic and cruel."[62] Possibly in response
to this kind of letter, B. C. Horton from the Talks Department told
her in memo that the Home Service was prepared to repeat the
"Homesickness" program. According to Horton this was "most unusual," and "we can all feel very pleased about it!"[63]

Hosain's contribution to "A Conversation on Homesickness"—
one of half a dozen scripts that have survived in the BBC archives—
tells us much about the frame of mind she was in as she thought
about and began writing *Sunlight*, which was composed over the
course of three years before its publication in 1961.[64] The other two
participants in the broadcast were Maria Korchinska, a Russian
harpist who had lived in England for twenty years, and Alicia Street,
an American married to a Briton who had been there for nearly the
same amount of time.[65] Both these women opened the program by
confessing that they felt no nostalgia at all for their countries of origin. Hosain, in contrast, admitted that "I envy both of you because I
feel that . . . [India is] constantly nagging at my mind, it's there all
the time, and it doesn't take very much to bring it to the surface: seeing spaces, seeing the shapes of trees, seeing fields: that is particularly what reminds me of it."[66] And later in the broadcast:

> I've been here eight years. Well, perhaps eight years is not long enough
> to become completely a part of the life of any country, and quite apart
> from that there are problems that are obviously more mine than yours
> because I cannot get so completely integrated and there is a much
> greater difference between the two lives that have to be put together.
> And that might be the reason for my nostalgia; it definitely has [a] cer-
> tain emotion that is painful. . . . I love England, and I love the expe-
> riences I [have] had here, but at the same time there is definitely a
> positive missing of the past, of what is there now, because the past and
> the present for me in relation to my nostalgia seem to be mixed up.[67]

Whether Hosain viewed the "greater difference" to which she referred as a strictly racial one is open to interpretation. Later in the
broadcast when speaking about her children's experiences in Britain
she remarked that "they have never felt any kind of discrimination
or anything like that—[but] there is still within them a difference
from all the other children. They do have a feeling of belonging and
not belonging."[68]

As the conversation progressed, Korchinksa and Street tried to
convince Hosain that eight years was not enough time to become ac-
climated to Britain. In response, Hosain waxed emotional about the

relationship between nostalgia, homesickness, and the question of belonging with respect to her own experience in Britain:

> [*Hosain:*] . . . as you know in the East we have a very strong feeling of the family, and the family is a tremendous tribe, a huge clan of people who always stick together in times of trouble. I must admit they get a bit on one's nerves at certain times because there is a lack of sense of individuality sometimes, you know. . . .
>
> *Street:* Yes, yes.
>
> *Hosain:* You know how it is with a very strong sense of the tribe always collecting. And that is something that in one way in England is very pleasant, that one's freer. But at other times, especially when one is feeling lonely, when there may be need of someone who understands, who has a greater interest in one than however kind a friend; at those moments of loneliness and those moments of sort of fear when one is perhaps not feeling too well, wanting to have responsibilities taken away from one; at those moments I feel terribly like having someone there who is part of that bigger pattern of life. . . .
>
> I wish I didn't have it but I feel I have it . . . this feeling of not having roots. You can understand that in my case it's even more difficult than in yours because suppose anybody comes from any part of Europe into this country, they do, in appearance, in conversation, in their manner, in everything, become so much a part of the life of the people you don't expect that when they're walking down the street or going anywhere, anybody will say, automatically, "Where do you come from?" expecting you to say you do not belong to the country, even to be a bit disappointed when you say that you've lived so many years in London. Well, there is that difficulty about roots. Another thing that I feel is that no matter how much I love the country, and I love the people, it is a feeling as if there was a sheet of glass between me and them. And, another thing is, no matter how much it is my home, I feel it isn't really. It's like being in a wonderful hotel where everything is beautifully done—everybody's been terribly kind—but I'm there waiting to go somewhere else—but where? I never really know.[69]

The "sheet of glass" metaphor is particularly evocative, conjuring as it does the shared imaginative space of elite imperial-colonial landscapes as well as the asymmetries of access to belonging that shaped them.[70] Hosain's experience of London as a wonderful but ultimately unsatisfactory "hotel" gives us an equally evocative sense of the transitoriness that even the most anglophilic of Indians living in Britain might feel and echoes the epitaph on W. C. Bonnerjee's gravestone half a century earlier.[71] Her reflections also suggest why Hosain may have been drawn to writing *Sunlight* at this particular historical moment, and why she privileged Ashiana, the ancestral home, as the site of its dramas. As the novelist Mulk Raj Anand commented some twenty years later, "it is likely that the nostalgia for home may have urged the novel on."[72]

That writing itself was a means of escaping the hollowness of "hotel life," of creating an alternative interior into which readers could be drawn, is equally evident from Hosain's comments near the end of the 1956 broadcast:

> When I am feeling very lonely or very outside things, when I cannot make anybody understand the complete *me* . . . it's just as if somebody came in—into the middle of a story. I have to tell them the beginning. You might have to know the end sometimes—don't know it myself—but it's halfway through that they've come in, and I have to explain . . . so much.[73]

Here Hosain poignantly anticipates Meena Alexander's later conviction about writing "as a shelter," an architectural structure that in turn houses and shields a specific set of interiorities that are as material as they are affective.[74] If *Sunlight* was borne out of a deeply personal experience of diasporic longing, the shadow of history in the form of partition was ever-present in Attia's narratives of alienation and belonging: "Events during and after Partition are to this day very painful to me," according to Hosain. "The strength of my roots is strong; it also causes pain, because it makes one a 'stranger' everywhere in the deeper area of one's mind and spirit *except where one was brought up*."[75] In light of even this minimal biographical sketch, it is difficult not to read *Sunlight* as highly autobiographical and Ashiana as a deeply personal "history house"—especially since its name is taken directly from that of Attia's own family home.

Before proceeding to the narrative itself, a word on the genre is necessary. There will be some for whom Hosain's choice of the novel signals a Westernized sensibility that throws the "Indianness" of the arguments she makes therein into doubt. As much as I regret the quest for authenticity that engagement with such concerns valorizes, they do raise questions that help to historicize Hosain's project. As the literary scholars Meenakshi Mukherjee and Jasbir Jain have both argued, the novel as a literary form has almost as long a history in India as it does in its putative "home," Britain.[76] Not only were those "Indian" forms *not* derivative, "the novel" itself must be understood as a profoundly colonial commodity: not produced first in Britain but, to be more historically accurate, in and through the colonial encounter. The novel was consolidated, in other words, as an already hybrid form—even while, as Suvir Kaul has observed, its development from an eighteenth- into a nineteenth-century phenomenon produced a "partial retraction from its colonial origins."[77] Not surprisingly, the idea that the novel is a Western original has persisted, and indeed it haunted the reception of *Sunlight* in significant ways. In his preface to the Indian edition (published by Gulab Vazirani, New Delhi, for Arnold-Heinemann in 1979), Mulk Raj Anand, probably the most cosmopolitan Indian novelist of the day, worked hard to rescue *Sunlight* from the category of autobiography and to place Hosain in, or at least next to, the canon of modernist authors—James Joyce, Virginia Woolf, and E. M. Forster among them.[78] He strove, in other words, to modernize Hosain by moving her from the realm of amateur/autobiographer to what he viewed as the exalted and more legitimate status of novelist. Parallels with Woolf are apposite, especially given the centrality of the physical spaces of home in *To the Lighthouse* (1927); equally instructive is the comparison to Elizabeth Bowen's house memoir *Bowen's Court* (1942). Such affinities raise questions about the nature and scope of colonial and postcolonial Bloomsbury, a subject that is signaled by Anand's *Conversations in Bloomsbury* (1981) and calls out for more scholarly attention. Hosain, for her part, cast her historical encounter with partition as the *biography* of a *house* because it enabled her to revisit a world that was lost, and possibly too because it allowed her to domesticate the modernist novel on her own terms. Moreover, writing a life-story of Ashiana was, I suspect, preferable to thinking about *Sunlight* as her own autobiography. As she insisted to one interviewer five years before her death, *Sunlight* is "like an autobiography, but it is not one."[79] To another she commented, "it's not purely fictional, it is factional."[80] A legitimating gesture, perhaps; and in light of the fact that the title of the novel is taken from T. S. Eliot's poem "The Hollow Men," we cannot afford to ignore Hosain's investments in being considered a modernist in her own right. Such a reading need not foreclose the possibility that *Sunlight* is also an argument about the need to rematerialize home as the site of a specific, cataclysmic history. If, as Iris Murdoch has suggested, the novel qua novel acts as a dwelling-place, Hosain's determination to house Ashiana in it makes both personal, literary, and political sense—in addition to demonstrating how each of those domains was thoroughly informed by the other.[81]

From beginning to end, the novel threads through the recesses of domestic space, so much so that the house itself is rarely backdrop but emerges as the central character.[82] Anticipating the legacy of mourning and loss occasioned by partition, *Sunlight* opens in 1932

with a presentiment of death that is announced through a change
in the usual spatial arrangements in the house: "the day my Aunt
Abida moved from the zenana into the guest room off the corridor
that led to the men's wing of the house, within call of her father's
room, we knew that Baba Jan had not much longer to live." The
deathbed drama throws the rhythms of daily life into confusion and
the interiors of the house into bold relief. Because Aunt Abida had
moved from the zenana, she tells us, "we had had our meals in her
room. Ramzano and Saliman, our personal maid-servants, carried
the dishes on large wooden trays covered with gay cloths, from the
main kitchen to the pantry of the English kitchen near the guest-
room." The choreography of the grandfather's death is subsequently
traced through the corridors and doorways of the house in part 1,
staging Laila as the nostalgic narrator and Ashiana as the recurrent idiom of history. This is not simply because Laila refracts her
memory and her past through its interiors, but because she herself
understands time as an "endless corridor" of years.[83] As is typical for
the novel as a whole, it is the house in part 1 that both absorbs the
coming cataclysm and makes it visible, tangible, to those who dwell
inside. Baba Jan's room is sequestered, so that the mystery of his
death and dying have to be glimpsed from corridors or guessed at by
the silence emanating from his room. The battles between the old
man and the dutiful daughter Abida can also only be half-heard,
"through the curtained door of the guest-room"—"that little room
of swaying shadows." For Laila, Ashiana struggles to tell the story that
no one in the rest of the house will speak: "the sick air, seeping and
spreading through the straggling house, weighed each day more op-
pressively on those who lived it."[84]

Baba Jan's lingering death shifts the routines of the household
away from the zenana, a break from tradition that signals the beginning of the dissolution of the family and its dwelling as well. Laila
offers us only images of the zenana from the outside, or from the
courtyard's edge—in part because after her grandfather's death her
Aunt Abida is not confined to it as her sisters-in-law had been, in part
because the women's quarters are so naturalized for her that they do
not merit description. I do not want to suggest that purdah is not a
theme of the novel, for it is. We are continually told whose presence
Laila's aunts remove themselves from—whom, in other words, they
reserve for purdah. These include not just men visiting the house
but some women as well, such as an ex-courtesan, Mushtari Bai, of
whom they disapprove. The literal mobility of purdah can also be
gleaned from the following scene: Laila and her cousins are walking

to a relative's house when they see a manservant in the distance. Their maidservant calls out "Purdah! Purdah!" and he turns his back as they walk by.[85] (This is the scene based on the Isabella Thoburn experience mentioned earlier.) Nor is Laila beyond putting purdah to such uses herself: when she's told that Ameer, a young man whom she has literally just bumped into and who will become her beloved, is about to come to the house, she begins to excuse herself, to the surprise of her cousin who exclaims, "Why are you going . . . ? You are not in purdah."[86] In contrast to the representations of it in Sorabji's memoirs, where it was a fixed site of authenticity and tradition in a moment of crisis, the zenana in *Sunlight* is an interior that is in many respects already history, and is not particularly lamented as such. The fact that Uncle Hamid's purdah relatives mobilize themselves to cast a public vote for him when he runs for office on the Congress ticket is powerful evidence of the kind of political, if conservative, uses to which purdah might be put. The concept of seclusion, on the other hand, can be and is purposefully mobilized—not necessarily as a foil to the modern but as a familial/familiar strategy designed to afford women control over their movements and the terms of their sociability.

It is worth reflecting further on the relative marginalization of purdah in *Sunlight*, as well as on the mobility that Hosain ascribed to it throughout the novel. Her representational choices are especially intriguing in light of the "profile" that Mulk Raj Anand wrote to accompany the first Indian edition, referred to above. The "profile" opens as follows, with Anand speaking in the first person:

> Out of the purdah part of the household, screened by a big Kashmiri walnut carved screen, emerged the profile of a young woman—apparently to see who was in the living room.
>
> Sajjad Zaheer and myself were seated on a green velvet settee in the living room of Ishaat Habibullah, the son of a big *taluqdari* family, who was Bunne's [Zaheer's] classfellow in Oxford.
>
> "Attia, come and meet Mulk, just come from London . . . and Bunnebhai is here!"
>
> Tentative at first, then brightening, the young woman came in with her right palm uplifted in the polite salaam of the Oudh aristocracy. I exclaimed: "Surely an 18th century Mughal picture of the time of the Bahu Begum!"[87]

By all accounts, Hosain respected and admired Anand, one of the most famous novelists in Bloomsbury and pre-1947 India; nor is there any reason to believe that his patronage was anything but welcome to her. At the same time it is hard not to see him casting her here as the quintessential secluded Muslim lady emerging before his (and our) eyes from the purdah part of the household—appearing first not just in profile but, quite literally, as a purdah-nashin in miniature. And she was not just in miniature, but straight from an eighteenth-century, and notably pre-British, past.

To be sure, Anand spun his own modernist fantasy about Attia-as-purdah-lady, suggesting in the "profile" that the novel was the result of his encouragement and suggestions, comparing Hosain to Virginia Woolf and *Sunlight* to E. M. Forster's *Howard's End*.[88] Each of these contentions was dependent on the Attia-as-purdahnashin who opened the "profile": the emancipated purdah lady who got inside the modernist novel and made it her own. He had much in common with Cornelia Sorabji in this regard, suggesting how constitutive the zenana, and with it the purdahnashin, was of a modernity that was transnational—on the move—as well as colonial. Given that Anand was writing his "profile" in the late 1970s as a way of translating Hosain and her work to new audiences and generations, the persistence of this trope into the late twentieth century is quite remarkable. Reading *Sunlight* against this portrait, it is conceivable that Hosain intended to offer a counterimage of purdah that complicated this persistently modernist stereotype, one with which she was undoubtedly familiar and one she might well have anticipated, given her immersion in the PWA, of which Anand was also an active member.[89] A full decade before the publication of *Sunlight*, Hosain had publicly criticized purdah as "the greatest hindrance to the political development of Indian women."[90] Her resistance to the fetishization of purdah—its domestication, if you will, which Anand mobilizes to introduce the Indian publication of *Sunlight*—enables Ashiana to occupy the central narrative spaces of the novel, distracting us time and again from the precincts of the zenana and deflecting our gaze toward the more public spaces of the house to which Laila is consistently drawn.[91]

The drawing room of Ashiana is prime among these spaces, and her description of it signals both its centrality to the house and the peripheral status of the zenana in her vision:

> Into this vast room the coloured panes of the arched doors let in not light but shadows that moved the mirrors on the walls and mantel-piece, that slithered under chairs, tables and divans, hid behind marble statues, lurked in giant porcelain vases, and nestled in the carpets. Footsteps sounded sharp on the marble floor and chased whispered echoes from the high, gilded roof. In this, the oldest portion of the house, I heard notes of strange music not distinctly separate but dif-

fused in the silence of some quiet night as perfume in the air . . . in the corridor beyond there was light. It broke into the patterns of the fretted stone that screened this last link between the walled zenana, self-contained with its lawns, courtyards and veranda'd rooms, and the outer portion of the house.[92]

Clearly Ashiana is more of an "architectural homage" to the urbane hybridity of the *taluqdari* culture from which Hosain came than it is to the zenana per se. After Baba Jan is dead and the house is redone by his daughter and her husband, Laila recalls with precise detail the contents of the "original" rooms—furnishings and decorations that she effectively equates with "the character of the house."

> New furnishings and decorations altered the rooms, changing them from friends to acquaintances. I missed the ghostliness of the drawing-room. It had had a personality, gloomy and grotesquely rich, reflecting one of Baba Jan's eccentricities.
>
> In their old age Baba Jan and his friends, the Raja of Amirpur and Thakur Babir Singh, had taken to attending auctions in much the same spirit as had once made them big-game hunters, and they displayed their trophies with a similar sense of triumph. But while they were discriminating about tigers and panthers, and antlered stags, china and crystal, ivory and jade, marble and metal, prints and paintings were crowded together regardless of beauty or genuineness.
>
> Now the room looked naked, its contents distributed between the rubbish-heap, junk-room and Hasanpur. The junk room was my aunt's delight. She couldn't bear to throw anything away. . . .
>
> The furniture too was changed. The old-fashioned straight-backed, brocade-upholstered chairs, and the marble and brass-topped tables round which they had been mathematically grouped, were exiled to Hasanpur. The rejuvenated rooms reminded me of English homes I had visited with Mrs. Martin, yet they were as different as copies of a painting from the original.[93]

The overlay of Mughal-imperial and British-imperial style is striking here, as is the anglicization of the family home after the death of its last late Victorian patriarch. Equally telling is Laila's nostalgia for "the original" Ashiana, which has the power to conjure that past in memory. Laila asks her nurse, Hakiman Bua, what the house was like when her parents were alive, and she tells her; from there, "on the light warm waves of her words I went back in search of light and love, each moment a festival." Here Hosain excels at capturing the transformative power of movement through the rooms of the house, a phenomenon that anthropologists have long recognized as part of the production and reproduction of cultural values and, in the case of the ancestral family home, as part of the experience of historical change as well.[94]

The loss of the Mughal-British imperial world evoked in the passages just quoted is ever-present through Laila's experience of the house, which serves as a constant reminder that she does not comfortably belong to the present, or at least that she now feels more stranger there than friend. Ranajit Guha has argued that belonging is, above all, a practice of being together in "shared time" by participating in "the now" of "everyday life."[95] As an outsider to Ashiana, Laila is constantly trying to keep up with "the now" of household culture—a "now" marked off by the patriarch's death, a present recognizable in the new furniture and reorganization of the rooms of the house in the wake of the new familial order. That she does so by remembering the patterns of the household through the interiors of the house might be read as evidence of the fact that recourse to shared spatial as well as temporal imaginaries is crucial for creating and maintaining a sense of belonging. But Guha may be overdetermining the desire for belonging, as well as underestimating the vexed relationship that women have to "domestic" time—the most intimate and sought-after time, yet also the most potentially imprisoning time for wives, mothers, and daughters. In Laila's case, Ashiana is a place whose strangeness is not inviting, whose "inside" is to be cautiously observed rather than joyfully entered.

This is no doubt because as she comes of age (her fifteenth birthday comes and goes unremarked on by others as Baba Jan is dying) she is able to read the signs of death that are everywhere in the house. But it is also because patterns of domesticity, and indeed of conjugality, are intertwined with those signs of death, in ways that organize Laila's experience of life at Ashiana from the start of the narrative. The question of marriage, for example, looms large for all the young women in the house, and discussions of their marriage prospects unfold as Baba Jan lies dying. From the opening pages of *Sunlight* we learn that Laila's cousin Zahra will be married off, though not without great argumentation in the house over who is suitable and why. Zahra is the good Muslim girl: she has "read the Quran, she knows her religious duties; she can sew and cook, and at the Muslim school she learned a little English, that is what young men want now." The men in the family—who have to arrange for the girls to be married—agree: uncle Mohsin approves of Zahra because she's been brought up "correctly, sensibly," and not permitted to dress "like a native Christian," as Laila evidently was accustomed to do while her parents were alive. Zahra is only too happy to concur, and she and Laila argue constantly about the necessity of marriage, not just for elite girls like them but also for wayward servant girls like Nandi, whose sexuality becomes an issue because she is preyed on by men in the house and is then forced to leave, thereby bearing the burden of male promiscuity. Her banishment is a sign of things to come, a warning about what kinds of behavior—and what kinds of desires—Ashiana can contain and what kinds it cannot, especially where women's sexuality is concerned.

If, as Susie Tharu has argued, desire is one of the "impossible subjects" in the scene of the high-caste family, Nandi is undoubtedly one of Laila's doubles in *Sunlight*, insofar as her exile from (and eventual return to) Ashiana foreshadows the protagonist's own story.[96] The trauma Nandi experiences in the wake of her unwanted sexual encounters allows Laila to explore a path to womanhood that is not readily available to her as the rebel in the family: she takes up the role of nurse and mother to the servant girl in the servant quarters—identities to which she has no access elsewhere in the house and that promise to turn her into the kind of good girl her family continually laments she is not. In this sense, Nandi is the standard bearer of "bad girl" behavior, making Laila's own tryst with Ameer more respectable in contrast, even as Nandi offers an opportunity for Laila to critique the callousness of her careless elders in an ostensibly nonpolitical register. In keeping with what Ann Stoler has written about servants in the colonial Javanese context, Nandi "speaks past, rather than back to, the colonial archive and the nostalgic memoirs" of her employers.[97] As in Janaki Majumdar's "Family History," the servants who belong to Ashiana make visible the ways in which class and caste constitute respectable girlhood and womanhood in an elite community, offering a contrapuntal note to the counternarratives of gendered colonial modernity that underwrite this bildungsroman *manqué*.[98] With the possible exception of Nandi, the servant characters in *Sunlight* are generally underdeveloped, both in an absolute sense and also as compared with the complex ideological work they are made to perform in Hosain's short story collection from 1954, *Phoenix Fled*. Here entire narrative arcs center on ayahs and kitchen servants, albeit with a touch of the same benevolent aristocratic tone that surfaces in *Sunlight*. Some are heroic, some are cruel; but to a person they make those who inhabit "the big house" seem "pale and ghostly" in comparison.[99]

As with the various generic forms that Cornelia Sorabji's writings took, it would be easy enough to read *Phoenix Fled* as the dress rehearsal for *Sunlight*: a kind of archival foundation for the "real" history that takes place in and through Ashiana—especially since reviews of the book characterized it as evidence of the promise of a writer-to-be rather than as that of a full-fledged author in the way that *Sunlight* established her.[100] This evolutionary model has in fact dogged the short story since its generic origins, as Mary Louise Pratt has ably demonstrated.[101] In Hosain's case there is an unusually neat parallel between form and fact: after the success of *Phoenix Fled* she moved from a one-room flat to "a proper house," which in turn became a kind of literary salon, reprising her own experience of Ashiana as a young woman and very possibly helping her to telescope her recollections of her childhood home in the form that *Sunlight* would eventually take.[102] At the same time, however, Hosain's relationship to the character of Nandi offers an interesting challenge to this telos. As Hosain recalled about the writing of *Sunlight* some thirty years after its publication, "there is a character in there . . . I do not remember the name . . . it is a woman . . . she was not supposed to be there. That character grew and grew and grew."[103] When pressed, she conceded that it was Nandi: someone who should probably have had her own story, but nonetheless ended up taking up more space in the novel than Hosain had anticipated, perhaps because her doubling of Laila was more powerful—and unsettling—than the author herself consciously realized.[104]

If Laila (and Hosain with her) cannot fully appreciate Nandi as her double, she clearly understands Zahra as her immediate foil, and a vexing one at that. At times she laments that she was not raised like her cousin, even as she treasures the sense of freedom that her father instilled in her before his death. Laila's bookishness and willfulness are public affairs inside the family dwelling, witnessed and commented on loudly and often by disapproving aunts and uncles. Her irreverences are quieter, more private affairs, as when she fails to offer the proper respect to the body of her dead grandfather ("I had not covered my head; I had not raised my hand in salutation, and I could not").[105] The origins of Laila's opposition to traditional marriage are never specified. The fact that she had an English governess for a time is an implied explanation, though when Mrs. Martin appears at the house to pay her respects after Baba Jan's death, Laila cringes at Martin's attempts to claim her as a protégé—perhaps especially because Martin insists on calling her by her Westernized nickname (Lily) and reminding the family that "as far as dear Lily's father, well, he was just like one of us." Whatever the reasons, Laila is adamant in her rejection of arranged marriages, telling her cousin Zahra, "I won't be paired off like an animal."[106] And after Zahra's marriage Laila observes that "she was now playing the part of the perfect modern wife as she had played the part of the dutiful purdah girl."[107] Nor is Zahra the only character for whom marriage is destiny. Across the time of the novel Laila watches as her friend Romona is married off, to a life of "luxurious incarceration," as her Aunt Abida takes a husband, and as all the young men and women in the novel pine after unrequited love or pair off in more or less accepted unions. Among the unions that do not get made is the one between Asad, Laila's distant cousin, and Zahra. Zahra's mother and uncle deem him unsuitable, mostly because of his impoverished background but also because of his radical political views. His desire for Zahra hastens her marriage to a more respectable man.

If these dramas are portents for Laila, their significance for us lies in the way Ashiana, together with other domestic spaces in the novel, shapes the contexts and the contours of such subplots. Baba Jan's death means that the household must move to the ancestral home in Hasanpur, a poor second to Ashiana and one whose interiors get virtually no descriptive attention in comparison. The trip to Hasanpur allows Laila to see a variety of houses that cannot compare to Ashiana, beginning with the ruins of the Bhimnagar Palace that she views from the curtained car on the way and ending with her cousin Zainab's grandmother's house, to which she and Zahra and Zainab flee to escape the rituals of mourning and burial in the ancestral village. The ruins of the one and the sheer poverty of the other are strange and marvelous forebodings of what Ashiana will become. But it is in the house at Hasanpur that Laila and Zahra have their most spirited argument about marriage, a conversation that begins calmly enough on a terrace in the old part of the house. This is itself a historical spot, connected to marriage and conjugality: "The brides of the household had been kept in the rooms behind this terrace, and their bridegrooms crept up the steep stairs at night, and left as stealthily before anyone was awake."[108] It is this very spot that provokes the angry exchange between Zahra and her cousin, prompting Laila to condemn the "old-fashioned" customs attached to traditional marriage as "nasty," "stupid," and "ridiculous." From there they wander into the nearby orchard that was "surrounded by a high mud wall so that it was possible for purdah women to walk in it."[109] Here, in the most secluded, outmoded space of the ancestral home, Laila admits that she envies her friend Sita's opportunity to study in England, and that she wants to "go round the world." She also tells Zahra that she hopes they stay in Hasanpur, rather than returning to Ashiana. Soon thereafter, her uncle Hamid (now the head of the family, as the oldest living son) informs her that she will indeed be able to go to college locally, and lets her know that she has a choice of staying or returning to Ashiana: "After all," he tells her, "both places are your home, literally yours, as you have a share in them."[110]

Although she elects to remain in Hasanpur, Laila's exile is brief, and it ends as part 2 of the novel begins. Now dependent on her Uncle Hamid and Aunt Saira, when they take up residence in Ashiana she must do so as well, especially if she wishes to continue her education under her uncle's auspices. Upon her return Laila experiences the family house as a kind of extended zenana, "a withdrawn world enclosed by creeper-covered walls."[111] And yet this is scarcely an enclosed space: into it intrudes nationalist politics, often, if not always, through the persistent question of unmarried women's sexuality and their conjugal destiny. To be sure, Laila's college friends talk politics among themselves. Nita is the Hindu nationalist idealist; Nadira Waheed's mother is a Muslim League sympathizer; Joan is an Anglo-Indian who defends the Raj; and Romana is a relative of Nadira whose family came from a small Muslim state. But the college also brings the nationalist movement into Ashiana's drawing room, and it is here, inside the house, that the most volatile eruptions take place. When Nadira's mother visits Aunt Saira and tells the tale of a local Muslim college girl who ran away with a Hindu boy and ended up killing herself, the elder women cast aspersions on her morality. Laila rises to her defense, which opens Saira up to criticism that Laila does not observe purdah. Saira explains, "we observe the spirit of the Quranic injunction by limiting freedom within the bounds of modesty." But the Begum Waheed reads Laila's defense of the wayward Muslim girl as evidence that Laila's own virtue is in danger. And when Laila argues in favor of marriage for love, the drawing room explodes and the ladies fall into an uproar: "the word 'love' was like a bomb to them."[112] "Inside me," Laila recalls, "a core of intolerance hardened me against the hollowness of the ideas of progress and benevolence preached by my aunt and her friends. Rebellion began to feed upon my thoughts but found no outlet."[113]

As in many coming-of-age novels, sexuality is not only a site of private contestation, it is bound up with control of the means of reproduction, both biological and national, as well.[114] Laila resists the pathways laid out for her by her elders in these terrains, yet she also consistently resists aligning that rebellion with the political unrest that swirls around her. Indeed her refusal to identify or sympathize with "public" politics of any kind, except as a critic of all its contemporary variants, further alienates her from the house and the passions that animate it. The more Laila experiences Ashiana as emotionally and psychologically constraining, the closer politics comes not just to the threshold but to the very heart of the household. In the first instance Asad, the second-class relative, gets involved in demonstrations against the viceroy's visit (it is now 1937) and is wounded in the subsequent violence. Bloodied but defiant, he takes refuge in Ashiana, where his beating at the hands of police occasions a heated debate about the injustice of British rule and the best way to combat it. More unsettling still, Nita, who was also involved in the demonstrations, dies of her wounds. The conjuncture of her death with the sale of the ruined Bhimnagar Palace next door to a self-professed Hindu nationalist brings anti-imperialist politics quite literally home: "Its spacious grounds [had] . . . always ensured the privacy of our house." Anticipating her return to the ruined Ashiana at the end of the novel, Laila "wandered through the empty rooms and across the deserted courtyard as if carrying out a sentence. The silence was not the dead quietness of unoccupied rooms; it was desolate and rich with vibrations of sounds that had been recently stilled."[115] Remarkably, Laila has little to say about politics even at this stage and is mostly made impatient by the extreme positions her friends and relatives take up, either for or against colonial rule. Above all, she is a pragmatist; when Zahra asks her if she knows that *taluqdari* families have a right to audience with the king, she replied, "I wonder if that knowledge would have helped me when the king's groom's grand-daughter called me 'nigger' at school and refused to play with me?"[116]

Laila's impatience with politics continues throughout the novel, to such a degree that her cousin Saleem's new wife Nadira (also her former college friend) accuses her of believing in nothing, of being capable of only sarcasm and criticism.[117] Before this juncture, however, the household flees to the hills for the summer months—a break from Ashiana that Laila welcomes, especially as it gives her the opportunity to get to know her cousins Kemal and Saleem, sons of Hamid and Saira just returned from ten years at school and university in England. Significantly, it is here—away from the family home —that she is able to pursue her romance with Ameer, albeit clandestinely. But her exile does not last for long, and when the family returns to Ashiana she attends university as a postgraduate student. Nationalist politics is accelerating, and as always this tells in the daily routines of the house:

A new kind of person frequented the house. Fanatic, bearded men and young zealots would come to see Saleem; rough country-dwelling landlords and their "courtiers" would visit my uncle. Saleem had, metaphorically, discarded his old school tie and my uncle his spats and gloves. Suave, sophisticated tea and dinner parties had become infrequent, and Government House receptions an interlude. Every meal at home had become as peaceful as a volcanic eruption.[118]

The focus of these eruptions is ostensibly party politics: Hamid is running for a Congress Party seat, which Saleem fiercely resents because he insists that the Congress is anti-Muslim. He has socialist leanings and accuses his father of "feudal" attitudes, while Hamid defends his role as *taluqdar*, in that he sees himself as the legitimate guardian of the rights of his peasants and tenants. It is, he claims, "a question of existence," not revolution. At the core of this debate is Saleem's relationship to the house, as the eldest son and heir: it is a legacy with which he feels uncomfortable and that is a persistent concern because of the social and political unrest breaking out around Ashiana. While he rails at his father, "I have been called a parasite and have been told that I live in this house on sufferance," his mother begs him not to leave home—a plea that presages his eventual flight to Pakistan, as well as the family's ultimate abandonment of Ashiana after partition.

Laila is, as usual, focused as much on the physical context of the discussion, on the material culture of the room, as on this politically charged domestic conversation itself:

We took our places silently at the table. On the starched white tablecloth, red roses in a silver bowl splashed their violent beauty. Light from the delicate chandelier was warm on rosewood, glittered on silver-copper, glimmered on crystal and glass, lay softly on china plates and the paintings on the ivory walls, and deepened the folds of limegreen damask curtains. Uncle Hamid's "question of existence" was very unreal.[119]

Her thoughts are not merely "elsewhere"; albeit absentmindedly, she is cataloguing the material possessions that represent what is really at stake in the struggle between father and son over politics—that is, the future of the family property and Saleem's relationship to it. Of equal concern is Ameer; and later it is from another dinner table like this, filled with talk of politics, that she slips away to meet him. He comes on her uncle's property for the first time, and they are discovered kissing together in a curtained room by Aunt Saira. Laila knows that their once-secret love affair is over. As she feels Ameer squeeze her hand in sympathy and support, she ponders the confrontation with her family that is inevitably to follow. Significantly, it is Ashiana and her once and future exile from it that she remarks on: "In the morning the sun would come and waken me in this house as it had done since I became a conscious being. Yet I had already left this home forever."[120]

With that abrupt, laconic end to part 3, we move to what Susan Stewart has called the "future-past" in part 4, in which Laila returns to the ruins of Ashiana in 1952.[121] It is fourteen years after she has fled with Ameer; he is dead, having joined the army and been taken prisoner of war; he has been killed trying to escape. They have a daughter together, Shahla, who is now, as Laila tells us, about the age she was when Baba Jan died. Traveling alone to Ashiana, Laila literally relives her childhood and adolescence as she walks back through the empty and desolate rooms of the house. Characteristically, Hosain represents Laila's return to the house through her apprehension of the familiar and unfamiliar buildings on the road to Ashiana. "Tattered settlements for refugees had erupted on once open spaces," and "ugly buildings had sprung up, conceived by ill-digested modernity and the hasty needs of a growing city." But even in its dissolution, the architecture of the neighborhood is recognizable—and loaded with political and cultural significance—on the route home:

> My eyes saw with the complex vision of my nostalgia and sadness the loved arches and domes and filials, the curve of the river, the branching of the roads, the unfamiliar names and changed lettering of the road signs, the ruined Residency on its green elevation without its flag, the proud Club that had been a palace and was now a Research Institute, the pedestal without its marble Empress and with a vagrant lying across it in deep sleep, the faded feudal mansions, the Mall with new shops and cinemas . . . old buildings with neglected frontages, the church with a new annexe to its school where children no longer sang "God Save the King," the government House flagstaff carrying the tricolor . . . the first of the three-storeyed cement block of cheap flats, built by Agarwal where the Raja of Bhimnagar's palace and garden had once been, came into view with washing hung across the balconies, and shrill voices called for the start of another day. I was nearly home.[122]

Ashiana is still standing, but it is like a ghost town: the servant who rushes out to greet Laila stares at her "incredulously," as if he had indeed seen a ghost. And for Laila,

> the silence in the house was more disturbing than the signs and smell of being uninhabited through the long summer and the season of the

rains. It was not the peaceful silence of emptiness, but as if sounds lurked everywhere, waiting for the physical presence of those who had made them audible. There was a sense of arrested movement in the few pieces of furniture that had not been removed to Hasanpur.[123]

Laila recalls that "the sun's increasing warmth began to suck up the last dew from shining leaves and silvered blades of grass . . . yet I shivered as I drove through the gates of Ashiana.[124] Aunt Saira had insisted on living at the house as long as possible, refusing to abandon the family property (which "wore the signs of neglect" and mocked even its own "erstwhile grandeur"), determined that although Saleem and his wife Nadira had left for Pakistan, "this will still be his home."[125] But eventually, as did many families, Saira and Hamid had to accept the constitutional abolition of their feudal existence. Kemal was forced to sell the house; by law all Muslims who had fled to Pakistan were declared "evacuees" and their property, now "evacuee property," was taken over by Custodians. This meant that strangers were living "in the rooms where I had once searched for my lost father and mother, where I had found refuge in the love of my aunt Habida and Hakiman Bua." The strangers were professionals like the dentist and lawyer whose names were now inscribed on the gates, and less well-off refugees whose presence there "was part of a statistical calculation in the bargaining of bureaucrats and politicians."[126]

For Laila, real-world politics—despite its cruel effects on Ashiana—is secondary to the experience of the house, which for her is now "a living symbol" in whose "decay I saw all the years of our lives as family"—and in which, apparently, she no longer feels like a stranger.[127] What follows is a macabre return to the ghostly interiors of the house, in which Laila becomes a kind of tourist in her own past, as well as a guide in the present, reconstructing for us room by room what happened to Ashiana and the family as partition loomed. And so we learn about the battle Kemal waged with his mother Saira as he tried to persuade her to let him sell Ashiana—she railing against the thievery of a secular state, he retaliating by asking her why she did not just go to Pakistan "to live with Saleem in the Muslim neo-Paradise across the border."[128] Indeed, it is the last bitter family arguments, in all their painful, passionate detail, that the return to Ashiana provokes in Laila's memory—scenes we have not been privy to, scenes that lay out the story of Hamid's election contest, of family debates over what partition would really mean, of Kemal's marriage to a non-Muslim woman, and not least of Laila's own controversial betrothal. Every chapter begins with a description of a room—Hamid's study, the sitting room, the dining room, the "gloomy pantry." It is these physical spaces, even and especially in their ruinous state, that have the power not simply to conjure the past but to retrieve it from and for memory. Laila's return to the living quarters recalls one of the last meals for which the family had gathered and at which it "had the final argument by which it was ultimately scattered":

> In the sitting-room, once so formally furnished, a few discarded dusty chairs and tables emphasized its size, and shadows flickered over its emptiness while my footsteps echoed from its marble floors to the high . . . ceiling. There were marks on the walls left by paintings and mirrors that had been moved to Hasanpur. The tall naked doors leading to the verandah and garden were bolted.
>
> This was the room that had frightened me as a child with strange noises and sudden shadows, but now there were many living ghosts to drive away imagined ones.
>
> I hurried through the dining room. The dining-table had been too large for the room in Hasanpur and looked abandoned without its attendant chairs. Around it had been enacted the ceremonial ritual of meals, and the passionate clashing of wills and theories and beliefs. When those countless words had been spoken, who had known what they presaged?[129]

Laila proceeds to reconvene the family, to recall the debate about whether Saleem should leave the house and the country, and to remember the tension between the brothers as they articulated different views on partition and what it might mean for their futures and their heritage. Less than two months later, Laila tells us, Saleem and Nadira left for Pakistan, "and it was easier for them thereafter to visit the whole wide world than the home that had once been theirs."[130] It is not too much to say that the trip back to Ashiana reveals the past as another country, from which some were, and are, permanently exiled.

Hosain anticipates Salman Rushdie's "dream of glorious return" by almost half a century, though she casts it in a much less triumphal register.[131] Laila's melancholy return to the family home is more like the rehearsal of a highly individualized, private mourning, and Ashiana a stranded object on the landscape of domestic memory.[132] Such a reading is seductive, in part because it enables us to reconcile a central contradiction in the novel—namely, the tension between Laila as the stranger-at-home in parts 1, 2, and 3 and Laila as the nostalgic-penitent daughter—someone who, as she contemplates the silent house, now "merely a piece of property," "felt their remembered pain as my own."[133] Partition, in this interpretation, brings Laila back to and into the family as nothing ever could, in a grimly, "morbidly imaginative" way.[134] I want to resist this neat denouement because I think that the structure of the novel does, and because I think the politics that it enacts suggests a less conventional and, frankly, a less heroic reading. Indeed, if we were to understand part 4 simply as the return of the prodigal daughter, we would be in danger of misapprehending both the role of house and the architecture of the novel itself. As we have consistently seen, Ashiana is more than the backdrop to the story that unfolds in *Sunlight on a Broken Column*; it has as much agency as Laila, perhaps more so, especially in its capacity to commemorate a certain past but equally as a living, breathing, struggling character with the power to inspire action, contemplation, and memory itself. The way Hosain deploys Ashiana in part 4 is arguably an amplification of the way it has functioned throughout the rest of the novel—namely as an archive, a storage space from which the past can be gleaned, can be made to come alive through the reconstruction of smells, sounds, images, voices. Like all archives, it can be used to retrieve a specific temporality, to commemorate a discrete past, and to hear whispers that are scarcely audible in other contemporary sources. What is significant is how Laila makes use of the archive and the evidence—both concrete and symbolic—it has to offer.

For despite the rhetoric of ruins that pervades the text, Laila archives Ashiana not merely romantically but rather with a political sensibility that is keen and consistent—that is, not discontinuous with the first parts of the book but of a piece with them. For although Laila is unquestionably moved by her return home, and particularly by encountering the past through its domestic interiors, she is not, finally, seduced by what remains of domestic time and space at Ashiana. Even as she uses it as an occasion for producing a narrative of partition and relies on the pathos it generates as the space out of which all stories proceed, from which all history, familial or otherwise, is ultimately told, she fully understands it as the detritus of history. And she remains critical of the role of house and home in illuminating the intersection of so-called private histories with national ones, as well as of their ability to reveal politics in its most intimate and "domestic" forms. Here, the choices her female relatives made about house and home are as telling as the fate of Ashiana itself. Recalling the violence of the early partition months, when she was on the run with her daughter by Ameer, Laila recalls "the fear of the fiery markings that branded Muslim homes" and rails at Zahra, the "good Muslim" girl who grew up to be a good Muslim wife and mother:

> Where were you, Zahra, when I sat up through the nights, watching village after village set on fire, each day nearer and nearer? Sleeping in a comfortable house, guarded by policemen and sentries? Do you know who saved me and my child? Sita, who took us to her house, in spite of putting her own life in danger with ours. And Ranjit, who came from his village, because he had heard of what was happening in the foothills and was afraid for us. He drove us back, pretending we were his family, risking discovery and death. What were you doing then? Getting your picture in the papers, distributing sweets to orphans whose fathers had been murdered and mothers raped.
>   I did not stop to listen to her cries of protest.[135]

In an important sense, this is evidence of how influenced Laila was by the socialist critique articulated in the book by Asad and to a lesser degree, Saleem. But by far the most revealing dimension of this diatribe is the accusation: "where were you, Zahra? . . . Sleeping in a comfortable house, guarded by policemen and sentries?" For Laila, the house is a sign of privilege, and in Zahra's case, of the inextricability of that privilege with her conjugal choices and her Muslim identity. It is also a sign of how imprisoning, and blinding, the facile, unthinking embrace of home and family remains for Laila at the end of the novel.

Her own choice of a modest cottage dwelling is further testimony to Laila's conviction about the potentially corrupting effect of house-life, and perhaps of her investment in remaining a stranger to anything but Ashiana in the end. Her capacity to be appreciative of the re-sources home offers as history and her unfailing skepticism about its redemptive powers make her an interesting if not unique modern heroine. She is at once cognizant of the culture of disappearance that marks partition as a particular kind of historical tragedy and resolute about drawing on that which has disappeared as an object lesson for the present. In any case, Ashiana is, at the end of the day, more than a domestic site or dwelling-place because it can no longer comfort-ably be those things, if it ever was. Well might she have agreed with Theodor Adorno, who noted that "the traditional residences we grew up in have grown intolerable; each trait of comfort in them is paid for with a betrayal of knowledge, each vestige of shelter with the musty pact of family interests."[136] For Adorno it was the conflagration of 1940s Europe that made homes uninhabitable and "the enforced conditions of emigration a wisely-chosen norm."[137] As Vinay Lal has suggested, partition must be viewed in this context, not only so that it can be appreciated as an event parallel to the Holocaust in its barbarity and evil but also so that its significance in and for modernity can be more fully appreciated.[138] In this respect, Ashiana has to be an archive in order to be tolerable—and so Laila, and Hosain with her, makes it a repository of history that is to be mined faithfully, read skeptically, and put to use for writing a history that commemorates without anesthetizing. Under these circumstances, revisiting the past is neither an exercise in nostalgia nor a romance of the exile. After all, the young Laila consistently anticipated the disintegration of house, home, and history in parts 1 through 3 of the novel; by part 4, history has finally caught up with her. What *Sunlight* suggests is that dwelling in history is best understood as an occasion for critical reflection on the impossibility of earlier incarnations of home and as an opportunity to appreciate the stories it has to tell as an archive, in whatever state of disarray or devastation.

As in the case of Sorabji, it would be a mistake to view *Sunlight* merely as Attia's story. Scholars of Lucknow and environs have tended to see it as an area relatively untouched by the violence and upheaval characteristic of 1947—embodying a "communal harmony [that] survived the trauma of Partition."[139] As an alternative archive of partition, *Sunlight* reshapes the landscape of the historical imagination, offering a modest corrective to local and in turn to national history. That it does so by obscuring the actual violence of partition and focusing instead on its architectural ravages speaks as much to the unnarratability of 1947 as it does to Hosain's determination to bring the pressure of family history to bear on the stories the nation tells itself about its origins. Though Ashiana remains standing at the end of *Sunlight*, a survivor in and of history, the novel is not the only archive through which the ancestral home has been preserved for the present. Attia's daughter Shama, a filmmaker in Bombay, made a film of the house in the 1990s, complete with a voice-over by Hosain herself. Whether self-consciously or not, the film, called *Ashiana*, reproduces the tunneled interiority that characterizes Hosain's representations of the house in her novel. The camera moves lovingly from outside to inside, panning servants' faces, moving down corridors and into rooms, capturing fireplaces and cobwebs and montages of sepia-toned family photos that appear to be snapshots from the nineteenth century. Like Laila's return to Ashiana, this is not a "paean of praise for the old culture"; but like *Sunlight*, it *is* "full of an inherited instinctive love for it."[140] A text that makes public the inner recesses of domestic space and situates them on the landscape of contemporary politics, *Ashiana* was shown at a variety of film festivals after its completion, yet it remains accessible chiefly through the family—not exactly privately held in the way Majumdar's "Family History" has been yet not totally "public" either. Even more tantalizing is the archive that remains unavailable to historians, myself included. When I visited Attia's son Waris in London in the summer of 2000, he asked me if I knew about the diaries his mother had kept from the 1930s until her death in 1997. I said his sister Shama had mentioned them, and that they were in her possession in Bombay. Oh no, he said; she has only the copies—the originals are right here. And he gestured toward what looked like a steamer trunk in the middle of his living room, which had a padlock on it. Naturally I asked if I could be allowed to see them, but after consultations with Shama it was decided that the children weren't ready to let anyone read the diaries, as their mother was so recently gone, and they had not had a chance to read through them themselves.

When the Italian scholar Laura Bondi interviewed Hosain in her London flat in 1997, she had a similar encounter with the "house archive," noting that Hosain "still keeps a great part of her belongings in boxes and cases" and that many of her earlier short stories (some published and some not), were "lying somewhere around in boxes."[141] Bondi attributed this tendency to Hosain's lifelong skepticism about her capacity as a writer—something that is confirmed in Nilufer Bharucha's posthumously published interview with Attia.[142] Her account of Attia's relationship to her own archive has, in turn, a humbling effect in the present: an example of the truly unfinished business of history, it is a reminder of the ultimate opacity of all archives, even those we think we have access to, those we think we have "discovered," read, given meaning to. Like the trunk in Waris Hussein's living room, it is the locked door which our "blind and groping key does not yet fit."[143] Despite the histories that Hosain's diaries may yet yield, the domestic interiors and the architectural imaginary that structure *Sunlight* do offer us a remarkable, if incomplete, archive of what it could mean to be a daughter, and an orphaned daughter, both of and in history. With its curtained rooms, its winding verandahs, its murmurs and whispers, Ashiana houses Laila's story both for us and for Attia, invoking—while resisting—the romance of ruins. If *Sunlight on a Broken Column* may be said to anticipate the convictions of contemporary historians of partition who are eager to explore new and heretofore undervalued sources of that past, then Hosain's novel is what all critical history might aspire to be: carefully, quietly, and modestly prophetic.

EPILOGUE

Archive Fever and
the Panopticon of History

In a feverish stillness, the intimate recesses of the
domestic space become sites for history's most intri-
cate visions.

— Homi Bhabha, "The World in the Home"

It cannot be entirely surprising that, during an extended historical moment characterized by pronouncements about "the end of history"[1] and the "death of history,"[2] the traditional archive is being rehabilitated as the originary site of "real" history and the last bastion of "real" historical knowledge and authority. Anyone who doubts this has only to turn to various volumes in the recent *Oxford History of the British Empire* series (1998–99), where the official archive—those repositories created by the state both for the collection of data and for the production of knowledge by the rulers about the ruled—assumes pride of place against the incursions of cultural theorists, feminist critics, and postmodernism more generally. That archive is, in turn, deemed the right and proper purview of "fiercely empirical historians"—in part because at issue for scholars of empire, as for many practitioners of the discipline, is the enduring question of history's capacity for determining the truth about the past.[3] The pressures that postcolonialism in all its complexity has placed on imperial history are in part responsible for this rearguard action, in which a revival of the "true" archive is entailed. But while those pressures may be peculiar to imperial historians, they are by no means unique to them, in Britain or elsewhere. Debates about history versus truth, fact versus fiction, empiricism versus theory are all corollaries of this contretemps over the archive. They have raged everywhere at century's end, from undergraduate classrooms to the trials of Holocaust deniers to the tribunals of the Truth and Reconciliation Commission in South Africa to the very public revelations of plagiarism among prominent, popular historians in the United States. The presumptive boundaries of "the archive," and especially its "concrete" location inside the nation, have been crucial to the security of the nation-state since the onset of modern processes of archive rationalization, and they remain so in these very contemporary contexts as well. At issue in the project of interrogating archival evidence—what counts, what doesn't, where it is housed, who possesses it, and who lays claim to it as a political resource—is not theory, but the very power of historical explanation itself.[4] At risk is the presumption that history is simply the study of the past, rather than the study of the past and its "living active existence" in the present.[5] And at stake is nothing less than History's capacity to determine whether the "'real-real story' can ever be fully grasped," let alone told, in the face of often catastrophic violence and the stories that emanate therefrom.[6]

Although this is not precisely what Jacques Derrida had in mind when he coined the term "archive fever," his phrase nonetheless captures the anxieties about the contamination of both archival history and disciplinary empiricism that have undergirded debates about the future of History in the last two decades of the twentieth century.[7] What makes a historically positivist project like History vulnerable in this context is precisely the democratization—some would say, the vulgarization—of "the archive" that has followed from the intersections of mass production, consumer culture, and postmodern modes of analysis in the post-1968 period. It is not simply a matter of oral testimony—or comic books, or pottery, or chat rooms—disrupting traditional standards of archival evidence. It is equally the problem of archival proliferation, especially in the wake of the new information technology: that "windless region of hyperspace" that offers new possibilities for a poetics of the archive and new frontiers for History as well.[8] As it turns out, Arundhati Roy's "history house" is not just many mansions: its crumbling edifices are inhabited by all manner of people as well—some more recognizable as "subjects" than others. At a time when the practice of professional history appears to have so little grip on the contemporary imagination—when History of the academic variety is thought to be so persistently irrelevant to the average person's experiences, identities, desires—it seems fitting that we are, effectively, all archivists now.[9]

No less noteworthy is the fact that as the possibilities for legitimate investigative sites multiply, historians of the British empire and British colonialism have been worrying about the security of their own archival battlements.[10] In this respect they are in step with critics of the cultural turn more generally—in step with those, that is, who have articulated their anxiety about the erosion of the traditional archive by accusing practitioners of cultural history and cultural studies of going "too far" on too little, especially where the evidentiary nature of their claims is concerned.[11] In these determinations, extra-"archival" sources end up looking like a subspecies of evidence because they cannot pass the test of verifiability, and those who use them are implicated in what some fear to be the end of History as we know it. Such critiques are often accompanied by a call for a return to the archive—conventionally understood as an institutional site in a faraway place that requires hotel accommodation and a grueling nine-to-five workday.[12] It is here that the hands-on, hard work of history evidently takes place and that historians get their professional credibility—by breaking into a sweat, if not a fever.[13]

Of course, it is possible to respect and even valorize the traditional archive on the one hand and to be cognizant of its horizons, wary of its distortions, skeptical of its truth-claims, and critical of its collaboration with state apparatuses on the other. These are, arguably, the assumptions under which most professional historians work as we head into the twenty-first century. Meanwhile, convictions about the nature of the "real" archive persist in instructive forms. Nicholas Dirks, a South Asianist who is both a historian and an anthropologist, argues that the colonial archive goes "well beyond an assemblage of texts, a depository of and for history." But he also contends that

> The archive is a discursive formation in the totalizing sense that it reflects the categories and operations of the state itself, in this case of the colonial state. The state produces, adjudicates, organizes and maintains the discourses that become available as the "primary" texts of history.[14]

Dirks's larger purpose is, and has long been, to query the textualization of Indian history and with it, of India itself. Yet there is the trace of a reinscription of the panoptical possibilities of the official archive, and a touch of the seduction of the total archive here as well. Even if we concede that he is caricaturing the imperial vision of the colonial archive, it still remains for us to ask why it has proven so difficult to imagine the official archive as something other than a panoptical institution. Is it because such archives were themselves born out of a determination to survey, an outgrowth of states convinced of their all-seeing and all-knowing capabilities? Or is it because so much academic thinking remains tethered, unwittingly or not, to earlier claims about disciplinary omniscience and its relationship to truth? Such claims remain crucial to professional legitimacy, at least in the Anglo-American historical scene. The "archive hound" may no longer be an exclusively white, male, and middle-class model, but it still has tremendous purchase as the standard against which many historians measure the quality of historical research, award prizes, choose job candidates, and create powerful narratives about the work of their fellow historians.[15] In this sense, guardians of the official archive—however delusional they may be—remain as convinced of its panoptical possibilities as they do of its capacity to legitimate those who submit to its feverish gaze.

The panopticon is originally a Benthamite ideal: a blueprint for the modern prison and later the workhouse. Thanks to the work of Michel Foucault, it has become a metaphor for technologies of modern power: a model where the prison, the asylum and, above all, the hospital embody the same will to omnipotence, and to disciplinary formation, that the archive also does.[16] Security against interlopers—whether disease or the eye of the nonexpert public—was a foundational principle of all these institutions. This is a salutary reminder of the historical coincidence of the institutional origins of medicine and history: while one emerged as the custodian of the body, the other became the custodian of the archive. It underscores, as well, the historical relationship between sight and surveillance, between vision and colonial modernities of all kinds.[17] That historians of empire, and of the British empire in particular, are among the most vociferous defenders of archive history and its bodies of evidence is surely significant. Their particular strain of "archive fever" is brought on by what they see as the sickness, or at the very least the poisonous influence, of a variety of challenges to History in the late twentieth century—with cultural studies, feminist theory, and postcolonialism chief among the carriers of contagion. Contributors to the later volumes of *Oxford History of the British Empire* are again a case in point. There, the trilogy of race-class-gender pales in comparison with the triumvirate of Said-Bhabha-Spivak, each of whom comes in for relentless excoriation. This dynamic trio emerges as a corrupter of young minds and historical practice in a series of denunciations that approximate delirium, if not feverishness as well. Well beyond the confines of the Oxford project, Said and Co. are beaten most often with the big History stick—not simply because they fail to contextualize, but more precisely because they do not cleave to conventional definitions of what an archive is or where it might be found.[18] Scholars like Said and Spivak have not dispensed with the archive.[19] More unsettling by far to traditions of imperial history (especially in Britain), they have insisted on it as the unstable ground of imperial desire and colonial power—in ways that undermine the hegemonic claims of the Raj rather than servicing it. It is this critique of the colonial archive that represents a break with colonial history. And it is this alleged perversion of archival logic to which imperial historians respond with such heat and passion. In the end, the *Oxford History* and even some of its critics cast the archive as the sick man of postcolonial history—hardly dead but dissected into unrecognizability and memorialized as the victim of a veritable academic epidemic.[20]

Such evaluations are, perhaps, paranoid at best. But they constitute one of the contexts in which British imperial and colonial history has been conceptualized and written in the fin de siècle. In asking who counts as a historical subject and what counts as an archive, this book has attempted to foreground these disciplinary questions, which are often embedded in other discussions of investigative method and theoretical disposition, so that the impact of colonialism and of the gendered presumptions of colonial modernity on current debates can be more fully appreciated. It has also tried to suggest what is at issue in archiving house and home for, and as, history. At stake in the first instance is a recognition of the challenge that histories of house and home pose to the truth-fantasy of the total archive that undergirded British colonialism and, until quite recently, histories of Indian nationalism as well.[21] Although it was consistently invoked as an emblem, if not *the* emblem, of both colonial and nationalist modernities, domesticity and its spatial arrangements have long been considered outside of the traditional archive and, therefore, outside of history *tout court*—except when mobilized by the patriarchal colonial state or male nationalist reformers. The writings of Majumdar, Sorabji, and Hosain quite deliberately brought the precincts of house and home into view from the vantage point(s) of "the Indian woman," subjecting them to history's gaze in order to address the constraints of nationalist discourse and modernist reform practice on elite Indian women's experience of family, domesticity, and "national" belonging. What they produced in the process was—and is—a set of fragmented historical accounts that reflect back to imperial and nationalist histories the partiality of their vision and the half-truths of their claims about domesticity, the nation, and political desire. As we have seen, they did so using different genres of writing, for different audiences and for different political purposes. All three believed that house and home belonged in, rather than to, history—in ways that were not sufficiently recognized in their lifetimes, and in ways that did not capture the middle ground they occupied between the civilizing imperial mission and reformed nationalist patriarchalism. What they share in the end is an ideological location that Alison Light has called "conservative modernity": a radically unhinged political position that they staked as a place in history by archiving the material culture of house and home for posterity.[22]

The intersection of their peripatetic lives with crises of imperial and nationalist history in late colonial India led them to appreciate the partiality of official history, to recognize the archival value of home, and to evoke its interiors, both material and symbolic, with particular vividness. Inevitably, their mobility left its imprint on the archives they created. In Majumdar's case, the text of the "Family History" migrated from India to America, a transnational trajectory that she herself did not undertake but one that shaped the lives of the children and grandchildren for whom she wrote her story. Hosain chose the novel and, to a lesser degree, the radio to preserve her memories about home and, in the process, to make fiction serve the needs of her own postcolonial histories in London, in India— and in the spaces in between—after 1947. Although *Sunlight on a Broken Column* stands as her most enduring archive, those elusive, unarchived BBC broadcasts are in many ways far more telling. Sorabji, the most politically conservative of the three, calcified her vast personal archive and brought it directly under the gaze of the state in the India Office Library. Her published memoirs allow us to see the selectivity that went into that official archiving process, even as she secured an overdetermined image of the orthodox zenana and its purdahnashin for an eccentric antinationalist history. Indeed, juxtaposing her "public" work with the India Office materials reveals the limits of the state archive, its inability to tell the full story about its own origins, and, ultimately, the failure of its claims to a panoptical vision.

As with the "Family History" and *Sunlight on a Broken Column*, much of what counts as history for Sorabji exceeded the then-official archive—compelling us, in turn, to expand its terrain by recognizing domesticity and its interiors as legitimate archives, and archives themselves as sites with many of the "permeable qualities of the household."[23] Most significantly, by casting their work as history, the women under consideration here have made it difficult, if not impossible, to read their writing as transparently personal, sociological, or "fictional" knowledge—categories through which many women, and especially colonized women, have been called to testify at the bar of history in scholarship, in college classrooms, and in "modernity" at large.[24] By foregrounding the inner recesses of house and home as critical sites of history, they remind us that historians must be as concerned with space as they are with time. And they must account for the "enlarged space of the domestic" if they are to capture the intricacies and ironies of history.[25] It would be easy enough to conclude that archiving the domestic in this way produces a more accurate, more "truthful" history than we have had before. Indeed, one of the major premises of women's and feminist history has been that the inclusion of heretofore excluded subjects makes for a more true, more just, more "historical" history. This is a maneuver I want strenuously to resist, because following that line of argument would require us to submit to a redemptive view of history that, in the end, does not do much to get us beyond the panoptical presumptions of the traditional discipline. Triumphalism about the capacity of history—including feminist history—to see all its subjects effectively reproduces the discourse of surveillance and total vision that underwrote colonial modernity and its political manifestations, history prime among them. Embracing it would require us to participate in the hubris of the panopticon rather than face the ultimate fragmentation and ghostliness of all archives: the final unknowability of home and history in their totalities.

The women in this book may have believed that rematerializing house and home would complete an otherwise unfinished history of late colonial India. But we can see, if only by glimpsing, what their architectural imagination lost down the corridor of years as well as what it captured—with servants' lives the most dramatic and perhaps paradigmatic example of what can never be fully recovered. The evidence of "house-life" is as partial and, finally, as lost to us as that which history has typically tried to make visible, though differently so. If the history of the archive is the story of loss, this need not mean the end of History, though it begins to explain why some historians are so eager to place archives under "protective custody."[26] As the histories that Majumdar, Sorabji, and Hosain offer us testify, loss itself is nothing more or less than *the* subject of history, in whatever form it takes. In the end, their work allows us to appreciate the radical possibilities that domesticity has to offer history, should it wish to remake itself in the face of challenges posed to it by the conditions of postcoloniality, rather than succumb to the logic of archive fever and the partial truths of its diagnosticians.

Notes

Chapter 1

1. See Donna Birdwell-Pheasant and Denise Lawrence-Zúñiga, eds., *House Life: Space, Place and Family in Europe* (New York: Berg, 1999); Irina Glushkova and Anne Feldhaus, eds., *House and Home in Maharashtra* (Delhi: Oxford University Press, 1998); and Joelle Bahloul, *The Architecture of Memory: A Jewish-Muslim Household in Colonial Algeria 1937–1962* (Cambridge: Cambridge University Press, 1996).

2. See Gaston Bachelard, *The Poetics of Space* (1964; Boston: Beacon Press, 1994), chaps. 1 and 2, especially pp. 72–73.

3. Quotation is Kumkum Sangari, "Relating Histories: Definitions of Literacy, Literature, Gender in Early Nineteenth Century Calcutta and England," in Svati Joshi, ed., *Rethinking English: Essays in Literature, Language, History* (New Delhi: Trianka, 1993), p. 264.

4. See Achille Mbembe and Janet Roitman, "Figures of the Subject in Times of Crisis," in Patricia Yaeger, ed., *The Geography of Identity* (Ann Arbor: University of Michigan Press, 1996), pp. 153–86.

5. See Lata Mani, *Contentious Traditions: The Debate on Sati in Colonial India* (Berkeley: University of California Press, 1998), p. 4.

6. Jacques Derrida, *Archive Fever* (Chicago: University of Chicago Press, 1995), p. 2.

7. Quotation is Kumkum Sangari, "The Politics of the Possible," in T. Niranjana, P. Sudhir, and V. Dhareshwar, eds., *Interrogating Modernity: Culture and Colonialism in India* (Calcutta: Seagull, 1991), p. 32.

8. Kwame Anthony Appiah, *In My Father's House: Africa in the Philosophy of Culture* (New York: Oxford University Press, 1992); V. S. Naipaul, *A House for Mr. Biswas* (Harmondsworth, England: Penguin Books, 1969); see also the discussion of Michael Ondaatje's family home in his memoir *Running in the Family*, in Sangeeta Ray, "Memory, Identity, Patriarchy: Projecting a Past in the Memoirs of Sara Suleri and Michael Ondaatje," *Modern Fiction Studies* 38 (winter 1993), pp. 42–43.

9. Ileana Rodriguez, *House, Garden, Nation: Space, Gender and Ethnicity in Postcolonial Latin American Literatures by Women* (Durham, N.C.: Duke University Press, 1994); Catherine Wiley and Fiona R. Barnes, eds., *Homemaking: Women*

Writers and the Poetics of Home (New York: Garland, 1996); and Mickey Pearlman, ed., *A Place Called Home: Twenty Writing Women Remember* (New York: St. Martin's Press, 1996).

10. See Lori Askeland, "Remodeling the Model Home in *Uncle Tom's Cabin* and *Beloved*," in Michael Moon and Cathy N. Davidson, eds., *Subjects and Citizens: Nation, Race and Gender from Oroonoko to Anita Hill* (Durham, N.C.: Duke University Press, 1995), pp. 395–416, and Toni Morrison, *Beloved* (New York: Knopf, 1987).

11. Cornelia Sorabji, "Social Relations—England and India," in *Pan-Anglican Papers: Being Problems for Consideration at the Pan-Anglican Congress, 1908* (London: Society for Promoting Christian Knowledge, 1908).

12. Janaki Nair, "Uncovering the Zenana: Visions of Indian Womanhood in Englishwomen's Writings, 1813–1940," *Journal of Women's History* 2 (spring 1990): 8–34.

13. Mrinalini Sinha, *Colonial Masculinity: The 'Manly Englishman' and the "Effeminate Bengali' in the Late Nineteenth Century* (Manchester, England: Manchester University Press, 1995); Partha Chatterjee, "The Nationalist Resolution of the Woman Question," in Kumkum Sangari and Sudesh Vaid, eds., *Recasting Women: Essays in Colonial History* (Delhi: Kali for Women, 1989), pp. 233–53; Dipesh Chakrabarty, "The Difference-Deferral of (A) Colonial Modernity: Public Debates on Domesticity in British Bengal," *History Workshop Journal* 36 (1993): 1–33; Mani, *Contentious Traditions.*

14. Chatterjee, "Nationalist Resolution," pp. 233–53.

15. Ibid. For a direct critique of this see Himani Bannerji, Shahrzad Mojab, and Judith Whitehead, eds., *Of Property and Propriety: The Role of Gender and Class in Imperialism and Nationalism* (Toronto: University of Toronto Press, 2001).

16. Sanjay Seth, "Rewriting Histories of Nationalism: The Politics of 'Moderate Nationalism' in India, 1870–1905," *America Historical Review* 104, 1 (February 1999): 95–116.

17. Margaret Cousins, the Irish feminist, had the initial idea and convinced Montagu and Chelmsford in collaboration with Indian women from the Indian Women's University. See Geraldine Forbes, *The New Cambridge History of India: Women in Modern India* (Cambridge: Cambridge University Press, 1996), pp. 92–94; Barbara Ramusack, "Catalysts or Helpers? British Feminists, Indian Women's Rights and Indian Independence," in Gail Minault, ed., *The Extended Family: Women and Political Participation in India and Pakistan* (Missouri: South Asia Books, 1981), p. 127; and Radha Kumar, *The History of Doing* (London: Verso, 1994).

18. Forbes, *Women in Modern India*, p. 101.

19. See "Moslem Education—Conference of Purdah Ladies," *Calcutta Statesman*, August 15, 1925, p. 15. See also Gail Minault, "Sisterhood or Separatism? The All-India Muslim Ladies' Conference and the Nationalist Movement," in Gail Minault, ed., *The Extended Family: Women and Political Participation in India and Pakistan* (Delhi: Chanaka, 1981), pp. 83–108; and Azra Asghar Ali, *The Emergence of Feminism among Indian Muslim Women, 1920–1947* (Oxford: Oxford University Press, 2000).

20. "Mrs. Naidu—'To Set India's House in Order,'" *Calcutta Statesman*, October 4, 1925, p. 10.

21. Quotation is Shail Mayaram, *Resisting Regimes: Myths, Memory and the Shaping of a Muslim Identity* (Delhi: Oxford University Press, 1997), p. 6.

22. Tanika Sarkar, *Hindu Wife, Hindu Nation: Community, Religion and Cultural Nationalism* (Delhi: Permanent Black, 2001).

23. See Bipin Chandra Pal, "Modern Bengal—Social Transformation," Calcutta *Statesman*, November 14, 1926, p. 8.

24. Mary Hancock, "Gendering the Modern: Women and Home Science in British India," in Antoinette Burton, *Gender, Sexuality and Colonial Modernities*, pp. 148–60.

25. Mrinalini Sinha, ed. *Mother India* (Delhi: Kali for Women, 1998; Ann Arbor: University of Michigan Press, 2000); and her "The Lineage of the 'Indian' Modern: Rhetoric, Agency, and the Sarda Act in Late Colonial India," in Burton, *Gender, Sexuality and Colonial Modernities* (London: Routledge, 1999), pp. 207–21; "Suffragism and Internationalism: The Enfranchisement of British and Indian Women under an Imperial State," *Indian Economic and Social History Review* 36 (October–December 1999): 461–84; reprinted in Ian Fletcher, Philippa Levine, and Laura Mayhall, eds., *Women's Suffrage in the British Empire: Citizenship, Race, and Nation* (London: Routledge, 2000), pp. 224–39; and "Refashioning Mother India: Feminism and Nationalism in Late-Colonial India," *Feminist Studies* 28, 3 (fall 2000): 623–44. See also Catherine Candy, "The Inscrutable Irish-Indian Feminist Management of Anglo-American Hegemony," *Journal of Colonialism and Colonial History* 2, 1 (spring 2001); available at http://muse.jhu.edu/jcch.

26. "Purdah Disappears from Villages," Calcutta *Statesman*, January 20, 1931, p. 10; "Purdah Must Go!" Calcutta *Statesman*, May 10, 1931, p. 19.

27. For one of the earliest accounts of this phenomenon see Gail Minault, "The Extended Family as Metaphor and the Expansion of Women's Realm," in Gail Minault, ed., *The Extended Family: Women and Political Participation in India and Pakistan* (Columbia, Mo.: South Asia Books, 1981), especially pp. 10–12. Minault also discusses the ways women active in the Khalifat movement capitalized on the extension of household roles to enter the political sphere.

28. Uma Rao, "Women in the Frontline: The Case of U.P.," in Leela Kasturi and Vina Mazumdar, eds., *Women and Indian Nationalism* (New Delhi: Vikas, 1994), 38. For the same metaphor in a different cultural context see K. Lynn Stoner, *From the House to the Streets: The Cuban Woman's Movement for Legal Reform, 1898–1940* (Durham, N.C.: Duke University Press, 1991).

29. For a comprehensive account see Dagmar Engels, *Beyond Purdah? Women in Bengal 1890–1939* (Delhi: Oxford University Press, 1996), especially chap. 1, "Purdah and Politics."

30. Ishanee Mukherjee, "Women and Armed Revolution in Late Colonial Bengal: An Integrated Study of Changing Role Patterns," in Kasturi and Mazumdar, *Women and Indian Nationalism*, p. 53–63.

31. See Bharati Ray, "Calcutta Women in the Swadeshi Movement (1903–1910): The Nature and Implications of Participation," in Pradip Sinha, ed., *The Urban Experience: Calcutta* (Calcutta: Riddhi, 1987), pp. 168–81; and Indira Chowdhury, *The Frail Hero and Virile History: Gender and the Politics of Culture in Colonial Bengal* (Delhi: Oxford University Press, 1998).

32. Lisa Trivedi, "Spinning the 'Nation': Swadeshi Politics, Material Culture and the Making of the Indian Nation, 1915–1930" (Ph.D. diss., University of California, Davis, 1999), provided courtesy of the author.

33. Forbes, *Women in Modern India*, p. 121.

34. Ibid., p. 61.

35. Geraldine Forbes, ed., *Memoirs of an Indian Woman* by Shudha Mazumdar (New York: Sharpe, 1989); Uma Chakravarti, *Rewriting History: The Life and Times of Pandita Ramabai* (Delhi: Kali for Women, 1998); Tanika Sarkar, *Words to Win: The Making of Amar Jiban: A Modern Autobiography* (New Delhi: Kali for Women, 1999); and Geraldine Forbes and Tapan Raychaudhuri, eds., *From Child Widow to Lady Doctor: The Memoirs of Dr. Haimabati Sen* (New Delhi: Roli Books, 2000).

36. See Bahloul, *The Architecture of Memory*, p. 28.

37. See Anuradha Dingwaney Needham, "Multiple Forms of (National) Belonging: Attia Hosain's *Sunlight on a Broken Column*," *Modern Fiction Studies* 39, 1 (1993): 93–112.

38. See Marianne Hirsch, "The Novel of Formation as Genre: Between Great Expectations and Lost Illusions," *Genre* 12 (fall 1979): 293–311; and Susan Fraiman, *Unbecoming Women: British Women Writers and the Novel of Development* (New York: Columbia University Press, 1993).

39. "A Girlhood among Ghosts," my chapter title, is the subtitle of Maxine Hong Kingston's novel *The Woman Warrior* (New York: Knopf, 1976).

40. See Ackbar Abbas, *Hong Kong: Culture and the Politics of Disappearance* (Minneapolis: University of Minnesota Press, 1997), p. 23.

41. Janet Frame, *An Autobiography* (New York: Braziller, 1991), p. 9.

42. Quotation is Uma Narayan, *Dislocating Cultures: Identities, Traditions, and Third World Feminism* (New York: Routledge, 1997), p. 23.

43. I am grateful to David Prochaska for pressing me on this point, and to Jed Esty for offering me a productive way of articulating it. See also Georg Lukács, *The Historical Novel* (London: Merlin Press, 1962).

44. See Ann L. Stoler, "Casting for the Colonial: Unstoried Memory Work," presented at the Anthropology Colloquium, Johns Hopkins University, November 1998. I am grateful to Lara Kriegel for this reference. See also Stoler and Karen Strassler, "Castings for the Colonial: Memory Work in 'New Order' Java," *Comparative Studies in Society and History* (2000): 4–48; and, for late colonial Bengal, Swapna Mitra Banerjee, *Middle Class Women and Domestics in Colonial Calcutta, 1900–1947* (Ph.D. diss., Temple University, 1998).

45. Here I draw on Vivek Dhareshwar, "Caste and the Secular Self," *Journal of Arts and Ideas* 25–26 (December 1993): 115–26.

46. Rosemary Marangoly George, "Recycling: Long Routes to and from Domestic Fixes," in her edited collection, *Burning Down the House: Recycling Domesticity* (Boulder, Colo.: Westview Press, 1998), p. 3.

47. See Inderpal Grewal, *Home and Harem: Nation, Gender, Empire and the Cultures of Travel* (Durham, N.C.: Duke University Press, 1996). For debates about this see Amit Chaudhuri, "Beyond the Language of the Raj," *Times Literary Supplement*, August 8, 1997, pp. 17–18; Salman Rushdie, "Damme, This Is the Oriental Scene for You!" *New Yorker*, June 23 and 30, 1997, pp. 50–61; G. N. Devy, "Indian Literature in English Translation: An Introduction," *Journal of Commonwealth Literature* 28 (1993): 123–38; R. Parthasarathy, "The Exile as Writer: on Being an Indian Writer in English," *Journal of Commonwealth Literature* 24 (1988): 1–11; N. Krishnaswamy and Archana S. Burde, eds., *The Politics of Indians' English: Linguistic Colonialism and the Expanding English Empire* (Delhi: Oxford University Press, 1998).

48. See Ranjana Harish, *Indian Women's Autobiographies* (New Delhi: Arnold, 1993); Malavika Karlekar, *Voices from Within: Early Personal Narratives of Bengali Women* (Delhi: Oxford University Press, 1993); Susie Tharu and K. Lalita, eds., *Women Writing in India 600 B.C. to the Present*, vols. 1 and 2 (New York: Feminist Press, 1991); Himani Bannerji, "Fashioning a Self: Gender, Class and Moral Education for and by Women in Colonial Bengal," in Kate Rousmanière et al., eds., *Discipline, Moral Regulation and Schooling: A Social History* (New York: Garland, 1997), pp. 183–218; and Srabashi Ghosh, "Changes in Bengali Social Life as Recorded in Autobiographies by Women," *Economic and Political Weekly* 21, 43 (October 25, 1986): WS 88–96. For mostly men's narratives see Judith Walsh, *Growing up in British India: Indian Autobiographers on Childhood and Education under the Raj* (London: Holmes and Meier, 1983).

49. See Kamala S. Dongerkery, *On the Wings of Time (An Autobiography)* (Bombay: Bharatiya Vidya Bhavan, 1968); Rama Mehta, *Inside the Haveli* (New Delhi: Arnold-Heinemann, 1977); and Savitri Devi Nanda, *The City of Two Gateways: The Autobiography of an Indian Girl* (London: George Allen Unwin, 1950).

50. See Kusumavati Deshpande's translation, *Ranade: His Wife's Reminiscences*, from Ramabai Ranade's Marathi original, *Amchya Ayuskahtil Kahi Athvanni* (Delhi: Ministry of Information and Broadcasting, 1963); Muthulakshmi Reddy, *Autobiography* (Madras: n.p., 1964); and Lakshmibai Tilak, *I Follow After: An Autobiography* (serialized 1934–37; first English translation 1950) (Delhi: Oxford University Press, 1998), especially p. 3.

51. Kamala Chattopadhyay, *Inner Recesses, Outer Spaces: Memoirs* (New Delhi: Navrange, 1988); and Romola Chatterjee, *Courtyards of My Childhood: A Memoir* (New Delhi: Kali for Women, 1996).

52. Mary J. Carruthers, *The Book of Memory: A Study of Memory in Medieval Culture* (Cambridge: Cambridge University Press, 1990); and Jonathan Spence, *The Memory Palace of Matteo Ricci* (New York: Penguin, 1985).

53. Shaila Bhandare, *Memory in Indian Epistemology, Its Nature and Status* (Delhi: Indian Books Centre, 1993). Here Bhandare uses "Indian" though the texts she treats are exclusively Hindu. See also Kumkum Roy, "The King's Household: Structure and Space in the Sastric Tradition," in Kumkum Sangari and Uma Chakravarti, eds., *From Myths to Markets: Essays on Gender* (New Delhi: Manohar, 1999), pp. 18–28.

54. Sonia Amin, "Childhood and Role Models in the Andar Mahal: Muslim Women in the Private Sphere in Colonial Bengal," in Kumari Jayawardena and Malathi de Alwis, eds., *Embodied Violence: Communalising Women's Sexuality in South Asia* (London: Zed Books, 1996), pp. 71–88; Bannerji, "Fashioning a Self"; Dipesh Chakrabarty, *Provincializing Europe: Postcolonial Thought and Historical Difference* (Princeton, N.J.: Princeton University Press, 2000), chap. 8.

55. Quotation is Bannerji, "Fashioning a Self," p. 198.

56. Meera Kosambi, "The Home as Social Universe: Women's Personal Narratives in Nineteenth-Century Maharashtra," in Glushkova and Feldhaus, eds., *House and Home in Maharashtra*, pp. 82–101.

57. Gautam Bhatia, *Silent Spaces: And Other Stories of Architecture* (New Delhi: Penguin, 1994), pp. 5–6.

58. Bonnie Smith, *The Gender of History: Men, Women and Historical Practice* (Cambridge, Mass.: Harvard University Press, 2000); Devoney Looser, *British Women Writers and the Writing of History, 1670–1820* (Baltimore: Johns Hopkins

University Press, 2000). For a noteworthy essay on bringing literature and history together to illuminate colonial discourses see David Prochaska, "History as Literature, Literature as History: Cagayous of Algiers," *America Historical Review* 101, 3 (June 1996): 671–711.

59. Alan Sekula, "The Body and the Archive," *October* 39, 3 (1986): 3–64.

60. Leonore Davidoff and Catherine Hall, *Family Fortunes* (Chicago: University of Chicago Press, 1987).

61. Christina Crosby, *The Ends of History: Victorians and the "Woman Question"* (New York: Routledge, 1991), p. 1.

62. The quotation is from Saidiya V. Hartman, *Scenes of Subjection: Terror, Slavery, and Self-Making in Nineteenth-Century America* (New York: Oxford University Press, 1997), p. 12; she is defending the use of oral histories of African Americans in Works Progress Administration narratives as legitimate (if not transparent) historical evidence.

63. Suhrita Saha, "Book Review: Tales of a Broken Land," review of *The Partitions of Memory: The Afterlife of the Division of India*, by Suvir Kaul (Delhi: Permanent Black, 2001), *Telegraph*, May 25, 2001.

64. C. W. Watson, *Of Self and Nation: Autobiography and the Representation of Modern Indonesia* (Honolulu: University of Hawaii, 2000), p. 11.

65. See, for example, a variety of engagements with Jan Vansina's pioneering work on oral history in West Africa: Elizabeth Tonkin, *Narrating Our Pasts: The Social Construction of Oral History* (Cambridge: Cambridge University Press, 1992), pp. 83–96; Ajay Skaria, *Hybrid Histories: Forests, Frontiers and Wildness in Western India* (Delhi: Oxford University Press, 1999), pp. 1–5; Martha Howell and Walter Prevenier, *From Reliable Sources: An Introduction to Historical Methods* (Ithaca, N.Y.: Cornell University Press, 2001), p. 26; and Jennifer Cole, *Forget Colonialism? Sacrifice and the Art of Memory in Madagascar* (Berkeley: University of California Press, 2001), p. 105.

66. Luise White, *Speaking with Vampires: Rumor and History in Colonial Africa* (Berkeley: University of California Press, 2000), p. 6.

67. Eric Van Young, "The New Cultural History Comes to Old Mexico," *Hispanic American Historical Review* 79, 2 (1999): 219.

68. Peter Fritzsche's comprehensive review essay, "The Case of Modern Memory," reveals no such concerns about the truth status of memory in western and eastern Europe, the chief sites of his investigation; *Journal of Modern History* 73 (March 2001): 87–117. Nor does Hue-Tam Ho Tai in her otherwise critical take on European memory scholarship, "Remembered Realms: Pierre Nora and French National Memory," *American Historical Review* 106, 3 (June 2001): 906 ss.

69. Howell and Prevenier, *From Reliable Sources*, pp. 34–42.

70. Mary Poovey, *A History of the Modern Fact: Problems of Knowledge in the Sciences of Wealth and Society* (Chicago: University of Chicago Press, 1998); Philippa Levine, *The Amateur and the Professional* (Cambridge: Cambridge University Press, 1986).

71. Pierre Nora, "Between Memory and History: Les Lieux de Mémoire," *Representations* 26 (spring 1989): 13.

72. Nicholas Dirks, "History as a Sign of the Modern," *Public Culture* 2, 2 (spring 1990); Chakrabarty, *Provincializing Europe*; Skaria, *Hybrid Histories*, p. 6; Le Goff quotation is p. 8. As the pre-text for much of this see Jean François Lyotard, "The Sign of History," in Derek Attridge, Geoff Bennington, and

Robert Young, eds., *Post-structuralism and the Question of History* (Cambridge: Cambridge University Press, 1987), pp. 162–80.

73. Thanks to Fiona Paisley for pressing this point upon me.

74. See for example Alice and Staughton Lynd, eds., *Rank and File: Personal Histories by Working-Class Organizers* (Boston: Beacon Press, 1973); Roy Rosenzweig, "Oral History and the Old Left," in *International Labor and Working Class History* 24 (1983): 27–38; Personal Narratives Group, eds., *Interpreting Women's Lives: Feminist Theory and Personal Narratives* (Bloomington: Indiana University Press, 1989); Elizabeth Roberts, *A Woman's Place: An Oral History of Working Class Women 1890–1940* (Oxford: Blackwell, 1984); Luisa Passerini, *Fascism in Popular Memory* (Cambridge: Cambridge University Press, 1987).

75. Quotation in Jeff Sharlet, "Should Historians Take the Fiction-Writing Test?" *Chronicle of Higher Education*, May 12, 2000, p. A21.

76. Natalie Zemon Davis, *Fiction in the Archives: Pardon Tales and Their Tellers in Sixteenth-Century France* (Palo Alto, Calif.: Stanford University Press, 1987).

77. Shahid Amin, *Event, Metaphor, Memory: Chauri Chaura, 1922–1992* (Berkeley: University of California Press, 1995).

78. Peter Heehs, "Shaped Like Themselves," review of *Creating Histories: Oral Narratives and the Politics of History-Making*, by Wendy Singer, *History and Theory* 39, 3 (2000): 417–28.

79. Tanika Sarkar, *Words to Win: The Making of Amar Jiban: A Modern Autobiography* (New Delhi: Kali for Women, 1999), p. ix.

80. Ibid.

81. E-mail communication with Urvashi Butalia, May 27, 2000. See also her "An Archive with a Difference: Partition Letters," in Suvir Kaul, ed., *The Partitions of Memory: The Afterlife of the Division of India* (Delhi: Permanent Black, 2001).

82. Urvashi Butalia, *The Other Side of Silence: Voices from the Partition of India* (Delhi: Oxford University Press, 1998), and Ritu Menon and Kamla Bhasin, *Borders and Boundaries: Women in India's Partition* (New Brunswick, N.J.: Rutgers University Press, 1998).

83. This is also a feature of Skaria's work, though he is not concerned with gender per se; see *Hybrid Histories*, especially the introduction, which encourages readers to read chapters out of sequence and discusses the limits of professional history-reading for accessing the past.

84. This is Barbara Melosh's phrase. See her "Historical Memory in Fiction: The Civil Rights Movement in Three Novels," *Radical History Review* 40 (1988): 64–76.

85. See Rumina Seth, "Contesting Identities: Involvement and Resistance of Women in the Indian National Movement," *Journal of Gender Studies* 5, 3 (1996): 305–15. Her case study is of Raja Rao's 1938 novel *Kanthapura.*

86. Nicholas B. Dirks, "The Crimes of Colonialism: Anthropology and the Textualization of India," in Peter Pels and Oscar Salemink, eds., *Colonial Subjects: Essays in the Practical History of Anthropology* (Ann Arbor: University of Michigan Press, 1999), p. 176. I am grateful to Jean Allman for enabling me to see this point.

87. I am grateful to Jamie Warren for helping me appreciate this conceptual possibility, and to Edward Soja's book, *Thirdspace: Journeys to Los Angeles and Other Real-and-Imagined Places* (London: Blackwell, 1996), for providing one way of thinking through it.

88. Susan Mann, *Precious Records: Women in China's Long Eighteenth Century* (Palo Alto, Calif.: Stanford University Press, 1997).

89. Roberto Gonzalez Echevarría, *Myth and Archive: A Theory of Latin American Narrative* (Cambridge: Cambridge University Press, 1990), pp. 3, 34.

90. Roger Chartier, "The World as Representation" (originally published 1989), in Jacques Revel and Lynn Hunt, eds., *Histories: French Constructions of the Past* (New York: New Press, 1995), pp. 544–58; Gabrielle M. Spiegel, *The Past as Text: The Theory and Practice of Medieval Historiography* (Baltimore: Johns Hopkins University Press, 1997); and Homi K. Bhabha, ed., *Nation and Narration* (New York: Routledge, 1990).

91. Paula Hamilton, "The Knife Edge: Debates about Memory and History," in Kate Darian-Smith and Paula Hamilton, eds., *Memory and History in Twentieth-Century Australia* (Melbourne: Oxford University Press, 1994), pp. 9–32.

92. Mary Margaret Steedly, *Hanging without a Rope: Narrative Experience in Colonial and Postcolonial Karoland* (Princeton, N.J.: Princeton University Press, 1993), p. 22.

93. Quotation is Jean Duruz, "Suburban Houses Revisited," in Darian-Smith and Hamilton, *Memory and History*, p. 176.

94. For a persuasive argument along these lines see Eleni Coundoriotis, *Claiming History: Colonialism, Ethnography and the Novel* (New York: Columbia University Press, 1999).

95. Here I borrow from Echevarría, *Myth and Archive*, p. 26.

96. See Dominick LaCapra: "The dream of a 'total history' corroborating the historian's own desire for mastery of a documentary repertoire . . . has of course been a lodestar of historiography." Cited in Susan Stanford Friedman, *Mappings* (Princeton, N.J.: Princeton University Press, 1998), p. 199.

97. Rajeswari Sunder Rajan, "The Feminist Plot and the Nationalist Allegory: Home and World in Two Indian Women's Novels in English," *Modern Fiction Studies* 39, 1 (1993): 76.

98. I am drawing here on Victoria Rosner's incisive reading of Doris Lessing's work; see Rosner, "Home Fires: Doris Lessing, Colonial Architecture, and the Reproduction of Mothering," *Tulsa Studies in Women's Literature* 18, 1 (spring 1999): 79. For a different discussion of this same question see Cecily Devereux, "A Process of Being Re-Anglicized: 'Colonial' Houses and 'Post-colonial' Fiction," on-line; available at: http://www.arts.uwo.ca/~andrewf/anzsc/anzsc12/devereaux12.htm.

99. Rosemary Marangoly George, *The Politics of Home: Postcolonial Relocations and Twentieth Century Fiction* (Cambridge: Cambridge University Press, 1996), p. 6.

100. Quotation in Krishnan Kumar, "Home: The Promise and Predicament of Private Life at the end of the Twentieth Century," in Jeff Weintraub and Krishnan Kumar, eds., *Public and Private in Thought and Practice: Perspectives on a Grand Dichotomy* (Chicago: University of Chicago Press, 1997), p. 204.

Chapter 2

1. Meera Syal, *Anita and Me* (London: Flamingo, 1996), p. 35. Italics added. For approximations in another familial context see Susan Maushart, *Sort of a*

Place Like Home: Remembering the Moore River Native Settlement (n.p.: Freemantle Arts Center Press, 1993).

2. Hemangini's father was Nilmoney Motilal. She is described as coming from "a well-to-do and highly orthodox Brahmin family of Calcutta." See Sadhona Bonnerjee and Janaki Majumdar, *W. C. Bonnerjee and Hemangini* (Calcutta: New Sakti Press, 1975), p. 7.

3. She died in England; she had returned there after her husband's death in 1947. Sally Singh, personal communication, November 21, 1996.

4. This would seem especially apt, given what Sheldon Pollock has argued about the importance of literary historical practices for nationalism and cosmopolitanism in India and elsewhere. See his "Literary History, Indian History, World History," *Social Scientist* 23, 1-12 (October-December 1995): 112-42.

5. Tanika Sarkar, "A Book of her Own. A Life of Her Own: Autobiography of a Nineteenth-Century Woman," *History Workshop Journal* 36 (1993): 35-65; Carolyn Steedman, *Landscape for a Good Woman: A Story of Two Lives* (New Brunswick, N.J.: Rutgers University Press, 1987); and Steedman, "Inside, Outside, Other: Accounts of National Identity in the Nineteenth Century," *History of the Human Sciences* 8, 4 (1995): 59-76.

6. Kwame Anthony Appiah, *In My Father's House: Africa in the Philosophy of Culture* (New York: Oxford University Press, 1992). For examples of Indian men's autobiographies that foreground the village, see Paramananda Dutt, ed., *Memoirs of Motilal Ghose* (Calcutta: Amrita Bazar Patrika Office, 1935), and Prafula Mohanti, *My Village, My Life: Portrait of an Indian Village* (New York: Praeger, 1973). An interesting exception is the chapter "My Mother's Village" in Nirad C. Chaudhuri, *The Autobiography of an Unknown Indian* (Bombay: Jaico, 1971). For an extended discussion see Sudesh Mishra, "The Two Chaudhuris: Historical Witness and Pseudo-Historian," *Journal of Commonwealth Literature* 23 (1988): 7-15.

7. For the Bengali *bhadralok* family romance see Dipesh Chakrabarty, *Provincializing Europe: Postcolonial Thought and Historical Difference* (Princeton, N.J.: Princeton University Press, 2000), chap. 8.

8. See Paul Gilroy in Vikki Bell, "Historical Memory, Global Movement and Violence: Paul Gilroy and Arjun Appadurai in Conversation," *Theory, Culture and Society* 16, 2 (1999): 25; Arjun Appadurai, ed., *The Social Life of Things: Commodities in Cultural Perspective* (Cambridge: Cambridge University Press, 1986); and Himani Bannerji, Shahrzad Mojab, and Judith Whitehead, eds., *Of Property and Propriety: The Role of Gender and Class in Imperialism and Nationalism* (Toronto: University of Toronto Press, 2001).

9. Partha Chatterjee, "The Nationalist Resolution of the Woman Question," in Kumkum Sangari and Sudesh Vaid, eds., *Recasting Women: Essays in Colonial History* (Delhi: Kali for Women, 1989), pp. 233-53; and Chakrabarty, *Provincializing Europe*.

10. See Rosemary Marangoly George, "Recycling: Long Routes to and from Domestic Fixes," in her edited collection, *Burning Down the House: Recycling Domesticity* (Boulder, Colo.: Westview Press, 1998), p. 3.

11. Chakrabarty, *Provincializing Europe*, p. 226.

12. See Tanika Sarkar, "The Hindu Wife and the Hindu Nation: Domesticity and Nationalism in Nineteenth-Century Bengal," *Studies in History* 8, 2 (1992): 213-35; also her "Rhetoric against Age of Consent: Resisting Colonial

Reason in the Death of a Child-Wife," *Economic and Political Weekly* 28, 36 (September 4, 1993): 1869–78; Padma Anagol-McGinn, "The Age of Consent Act (1891) Reconsidered: Women's Perspectives and Participation in the Child-Marriage Controversy in India," *South Asia Research* 12, 2 (1992): 100–118; Meera Kosambi, "The Meeting of the Twain: The Cultural Confrontation of Three Women in Nineteenth-Century Maharashtra," *Indian Journal of Gender Studies* 1, 1 (1994): 1–22; Himani Bannerji, "Fashioning a Self: Education Proposals for and by Women in Popular Magazines in Colonial Bengal," *Economic and Political Weekly* (October 26, 1991): 50–62; Antoinette Burton, "From 'Child-Bride' to 'Hindoo Lady': Rukhmabai and the Debate about Sexual Respectability in Imperial Britain," *American Historical Review* 104, 4 (October 1998): 1119–46; Rosalind O'Hanlon, ed., *A Comparison between Men and Women: Tarabai Shinde and the Critique of Gender Relations in Colonial India* (Madras: Oxford University Press, 1994); and Meera Kosambi, ed., *Pandita Ramabai through Her Own Words—Selected Works* (Delhi: Oxford University Press, 2000).

13. Tanika Sarkar, *Words to Win: The Making of Amar Jiban: A Modern Autobiography* (New Delhi: Kali for Women, 1999), pp. 30, 27–28.

14. Ibid., p. 28.

15. Ibid., p. 3.

16. Malavika Karlekar, *Voices from Within: Early Personal Narratives of Bengali Women* (Delhi: Oxford University Press, 1993).

17. For a discussion of this with respect to Indian travelers in the west, see Inderpal Grewal, *Home and Harem: Nation, Gender, Empire and Cultures of Travel* (Durham, N.C.: Duke University Press, 1996), and Antoinette Burton, *At the Heart of the Empire: Indians and the Colonial Encounter in Late-Victorian Britain* (Berkeley: University of California Press, 1998).

18. Srabashi Ghosh, "Changes in Bengali Social Life as Recorded in Autobiographies by Women," *Economic and Political Weekly* 21, 43 (October 25, 1986): 93.

19. Nicholas B. Dirks, "*The Home and the World*: The Invention of Modernity in Colonial India," in Robert A. Rosenstone, ed., *Revisioning History: Film and the Construction of a New Past* (Princeton, N.J.: Princeton University Press, 1995) p. 55.

20. Janaki Penelope Agnes Majumdar, "Family History" (1935), typescript, p. 1. The original, handwritten version is in the possession of Janaki Majumdar's grandson, Amar Singh, and I am grateful to him for allowing me to consult it. All citations hereafter refer to the typescript (TS) as FH. See also A. Burton, ed., *Janaki Majumdar's "Family History"* (Delhi: Oxford University Press, forthcoming).

21. FH, p. 8.

22. See Sarkar, *Words to Win*.

23. Anandibai Joshee (1865–87) also recalled her mother as a disciplinarian; see Meera Kosambi, "Anandibai Joshi: Retrieving a Fragmented Feminist Image," *Economic and Political Weekly* 31, 49 (December 7, 1996): 3190. For a discussion of mothers in Indian men's autobiographies see Judith Walsh, *Growing Up in British India: Indian Autobiographers on Childhood and Education under the Raj* (New York: Holmes and Meier, 1983).

24. FH, p. 32.

25. Bonnerjee and Majumdar, *W. C. Bonnerjee and Hemangini*, p. 13.

26. FH, p. 36.

27. Ibid.

28. The story of W. C. Bonnerjee's time in Britain is more complex, as his letters home testify. See John McLane, "The Early Congress, Hindu Populism, and the Wider Society," in Richard Sisson and Stanley Wolpert, eds., *Congress and Indian Nationalism: The Pre-Independence Phase* (Berkeley: University of California Press, 1988); and Manickal Mukherjee, *W. C. Bonnerjee: Snapshots from His Life and Letters* (Calcutta: Deshbandhu Book Depot, 1949).

29. FH, p. 39.

30. There is evidence that her mother continued to visit the household of her family of origin at Bowbazar: a site commonly understood as "bahu," or bride's bazaar, while Bonnerjee was in Britain—a regular holiday outing that she evidently anticipated with great pleasure; see FH, p. 33, and P. Thankappan Nair, "The Growth and Development of Old Calcutta," in Sukanta Chaudhuri, ed., *Calcutta: The Living City*, vol. 1, *The Past* (Calcutta: Oxford University Press, 1990), p. 17. Judy Yung notes that nineteenth-century Chinese women whose husbands went to America were often separated for a decade, though the cultural contexts in which the separation was played out differed. See *Unbound Feet: A Social History of Chinese Women in San Francisco* (Berkeley: University of California Press, 1995).

31. FH, pp. 34–35.

32. FH, p. 40.

33. Doorga Mohan Doss, "'Europe-Returned' Hindoos," *Statesman*, February 22, 1878; quoted in N. Krishnaswamy and Archana S. Burde, *Linguistic Colonialism and the Expanding English Empire: The Politics of Indians' English* (Oxford: Oxford University Press, 1998), pp. 102–3.

34. After 1889 Entally became an "added area ward" under Calcutta Corporation; before that it had been a "suburb." See Nair, "The Growth and Development of Old Calcutta," p. 13. In the 1880s it would have been referred to locally as "Intally," as in Ramanath Das's grid map of 1884. See Keya Dasgupta, "A City away from Home: The Mapping of Calcutta," in Partha Chatterjee, ed., *Texts of Power: Emerging Disciplines in Colonial Bengal* (Minneapolis: University of Minnesota Press, 1995), p. 156.

35. FH, p. 40.

36. FH, p. 41. For an account of a much differently ordered Bengali household around the same period see Shudha Mazumdar, *Memoirs of an Indian Woman*, edited with an introduction by Geraldine Forbes (New York: Sharpe, 1989), chap. 1.

37. Dipesh Chakrabarty, "The Difference-Deferral of (A) Colonial Modernity: Public Debates on Domesticity in British Bengal," *History Workshop Journal* 36 (1993): 1–33.

38. Himani Bannerji, "Attired in Virtue: The Discourse on Shame (*Lajja*) and Clothing of the *Bhadramahila* in Colonial Bengal," in Bharati Ray, ed., *From the Seams of History* (Delhi: Oxford University Press, 1995), pp. 71–73.

39. FH, p. 42. See also Bannerji, "Attired in Virtue," and Emma Tarlo, *Clothing Matters: Dress and Identity in India* (Chicago: University of Chicago Press, 1996), especially chap. 2.

40. Nair, "The Growth and Development of Old Calcutta," p. 18.

41. FH, pp. 42–43.

42. FH, p. 33.

43. FH, p. 42.

44. FH, p. 44.

45. This was of course a microcosm of at least some Victorian English attitudes toward Indians. Bengalis were the objects of derision and scorn in particular ways: "A low-lying people in a low-lying land . . . with the intellect of a Greek and the grit of a rabbit" was "a favorite British sneer." See John H. Roselli, "The Self-Image of Effeteness: Physical Education and Nationalism in Nineteenth-Century Bengal," *Past and Present* 86 (February 1980): 121.

46. FH, p. 46.

47. FH, p. 45.

48. Ibid.

49. This is the same group to which Edmond Gosse and his family belonged. In fact, Gosse records meeting an "Asiatic" lady at one of the meetings (she was married to an Irishman so was probably not Hemangini). See his *Father and Son* (New York: Norton, 1963), pp. 11 and 44.

50. FH, p. 40. There are varying views in "Family History" as to when Hemangini first became exposed to Christianity in a formal sense. Janaki's sister Nellie believed that it was W. C. Bonnerjee who encouraged her mother to embrace Christianity in the first place—according to her, "he thought it would be easier for her when she had to live in England" if she did (FH, 40). Janaki clearly associated her father's own heterodoxy with his first trip to Britain, when "he was glad to break away completely from Hinduism . . . [which] had never had any appeal for him, and he was always very much against what he used to call 'priestcraft,' by which priests of all religions are want [*sic*] to prey upon the ignorance and superstition of the masses." Bonnerjee was evidently also impressed by the lectures of Charles Bradlaugh and Annie Besant, who were frequent and controversial critics of Christian orthodoxy in the 1860s and 1870s—a circumstance that makes it somewhat hard to believe that he "requested" Hemangini to convert, as Nellie later claimed (FH, 40).

51. FH, p. 34.

52. FH, p. 51.

53. Ibid.

54. Ibid.

55. FH, p. 82.

56. FH, p. 53.

57. FH, p. 87.

58. Swapna Mitra Banerjee, "Middle-Class Women and Domestics in Colonial Calcutta, 1900–1947" (Ph. D. diss., Temple University, 1998).

59. Moira Donald, "Tranquil Havens? Critiquing the Idea of Home as the Middle-Class Sanctuary," in Inga Bryden and Janet Floyd, eds., *Domestic Space: Reading the Nineteenth-Century Interior* (Manchester, England: Manchester University Press, 1999), pp. 103–20.

60. Toni Morrison, *Playing in the Dark: Whiteness and the Literary Imagination* (New York: Vintage, 1993).

61. FH, p. 53.

62. Amos Rapoport, "Housing as Culture," in Lisa Taylor, ed., *Housing: Symbol, Structure, Site* (New York: Cooper-Union Museum with the Smithsonian, 1990), p. 15.

63. FH, p. 56.

64. FH, p. 57.

65. FH, pp. 56–57.

66. FH, p. 57.

67. FH, p. 34.

68. FH, p. 54.

69. FH, p. 57.

70. Ibid.

71. Ibid.

72. Annmarie Adams, *Architecture in the Family Way: Doctors, Houses, and Women, 1870–1900* (Montreal: McGill–Queen's University Press, 1996), p. 3; see also Kerreen Reiger, *The Disenchantment of Home: Modernizing the Australian Family Home, 1880–1940* (Melbourne: Oxford University Press, 1985).

73. Leora Auslander, "The Gendering of Consumer Practices in Nineteenth-Century France," in Victoria de Grazia, ed., *The Sex of Things: Gender and Consumption in Historical Perspective* (Berkeley: University of California Press, 1996), p. 95.

74. Donald, "Tranquil Havens?" p. 106.

75. This remained true long after the Majumdars had left Calcutta for Darjeeling in the wake of World War I. Janaki's grandson's wife, Sally Singh, believes that "the family's identity was very tied to the house in Darjeeling, Point Clear. Some of its best furniture came from the house in Calcutta, then was shipped to London. The reconstruction of the family again took place through the memories of that house. I think it was very necessary for them to have this 'created' base as almost all the descendants ended up in England, Canada and the States where they were unknowns. No one recognized them as descendants of W. C. Bonnerjee, they were just 'Indians.'" Personal communication, November 21, 1996.

76. FH, p. 58.

77. FH, p. 60.

78. FH, p. 61.

79. FH, p. 62.

80. FH, p. 63. New houses were not required to have a privy or water-closet in England until the Public Health Act of 1875. See Sally Mitchell, *Daily Life in Victorian England* (Westport, Conn.: Greenwood Press, 1996), p. 117.

81. See Hermann Muthesius, *The English House* (New York: Rizzoli, 1979), p. 162; and Ralph Dutton, *The English Interior, 1500 to 1900* (London: Batsford, 1954).

82. Homi Bhabha, "Of Mimicry and Man: The Ambivalence of Colonial Discourse," in *The Location of Culture* (New York: Routledge, 1994), p. 89.

83. Ghassan Hage, "The Spatial Imaginary of National Practices: Dwelling-Domesticating/Being-Exterminating," *Environment and Planning D: Society and Space* 14 (1996): 466.

84. Meredith Borthwick, *The Changing Role of Women in Bengal, 1849–1905* (Princeton, N.J.: Princeton University Press, 1984).

85. FH, p. 64.

86. See Ann Stoler and Karen Strassler, "Castings for the Colonial: Memory Work in 'New Order' Java," *Comparative Studies in Society and History* (2000): 11.

87. Thanks to Angela Woollacott for this formulation.

88. FH, p. 66. As John Coffey has detailed, Moody and Sankey's mission to Britain was in the 1870s, the decade of Hemangini's conversion, which explains

the centrality of their hymn book to her conversion experience. See his "Democracy and Popular Religion: Moody and Sankey's Mission to Britain, 1873-75," in Eugenio Biagini, ed., *Citizenship and Community: Liberals, Radicals and Collective Identities in the British Isles, 1865-1931* (Cambridge: Cambridge University Press).

89. FH, p. 72.

90. I am indebted to Laura Mayhall for this point.

91. FH, p. 64.

92. FH, p. 65.

93. FH, p. 76.

94. Ibid.

95. FH, p. 75.

96. FH, p. 104.

97. FH, p. 105.

98. FH, p. 106.

99. Gertie was Gertrude Blair, a white Englishwoman. Nellie, Janaki's older sister, married Gertie's brother, George Blair. If these interracial marriages were upsetting to the Bonnerjees, Janaki does not record it, though she does make reference to Indian contemporaries of her father's whose children's relationships with English people caused family dissension. See FH, p. 21, and Burton, *At the Heart of the Empire*, chap. 2.

100. FH, p. 107.

101. FH, p. 108.

102. FH, pp. 110-11.

103. Maxine Hong Kingston, *The Woman Warrior* (New York: Knopf, 1976), p. 8.

104. FH, p. 91.

105. FH, pp. 92-93.

106. Nupur Chaudhuri suggests that the Santa Devi and Sita Devi, two Bengali novelists contemporary with Janaki Majumdar, wrote female characters who had clearly been exposed to English classics like those of Dickens by the 1920s. See her "Nationalism and Feminism in the Writings of Santa Devi and Sita Devi," in Bishnupriya Ghosh and Brinda Bose, eds., *Interventions: Feminist Dialogues on Third World Women's Literature and Film* (New York: Garland, 1997), p. 35.

107. FH, p. 112. For more on the National Indian Association see Burton, *At the Heart*, chap. 2.

108. FH, p. 113.

109. FH, p. 113.

110. FH, p. 113. As Dipesh Chakrabarty notes, a number of Marwari merchants made their fortunes in the Calcutta jute mills in the first quarter of the twentieth century. See his *Rethinking Working-Class History* (Princeton University Press, 1989), pp. 52-53, and Amya Kumar Bagchi, "Wealth and Work in Calcutta," in Chaudhuri, *Calcutta: The Living City*, p. 216.

111. Thanks to Mahua Sarkar for this point. Although no such "obituary" was written for No. 8 Bedford Park, later Janaki was to note that it had become an "Old People's Home . . . accommodating fourteen women and nine men, and has a long waiting list. It looks extremely nice and well cared for, though the neighbourhood has changed almost beyond recognition." Janaki Majumdar, *Pramila: A Memoir* (n.p.: privately printed, c. 1974), p. 7. For another example of

the relationship between memory, desire, and the interiors of home, see Suzannah Lessard, *The Architect of Desire: Beauty and Danger in the Stanford White Family* (New York: Dial Press, 1996).

112. The memoir has not been published until now; see Burton, *Janaki Majumdar's "Family History."*

113. I am exceedingly grateful to Elise Weinbaum and the "Modern Girl" group at the University of Washington, Seattle, for pressing me on this question.

114. Janaki collaborated with Sadhona Bonnerjee in a pamphlet (see note 2 earlier) that appears to draw heavily on her "Family History," especially for the section on Hemangini. She also wrote a small essay on her sister, *Pramila*, which was privately printed; copies are held by the family.

115. FH, p. 54.

116. Judith Brown, "The Mahatma in Old Age: Gandhi's Role in Indian Political Life, 1935–1942," in Sisson and Wolpert, *Congress and Indian Nationalism: The Pre-Independence Phase*, p. 188.

117. FH, 27. This comment emerges in the context of a story about one of P. M.'s nephews, who was drawn in by the Swaraj agitation in 1921 and wanted to give up preparing for his Intermediate Arts Examination. P. M. dissuaded him from this; Janaki wrote: "He has never regretted it, when he sees how others of his contemporaries who 'came out' in the first flush of eager enthusiasm now swell the ranks of the unemployed. Mahatma Gandhi's ideas were sound, but unfortunately, the bulk of mankind being what it is, at that time little could be done by non-co-operating students, though the spinning and Khadar campaign had a lasting effect on Manchester trade."

118. Bharati Ray, "Calcutta Women in the Swadeshi Movement (1903–1910): The Nature and Implications of Participation," in Pradip Sinha, ed., *The Urban Experience: Calcutta* (Calcutta: Riddhi, 1987); Madhu Kishwar, "Gandhi on Women," *Race and Class* 28, 1 (1986): 43–61; Sujata Patel, "Construction and Reconstruction of Women in Gandhi," *Economic and Political Weekly* (February 20, 1988): 377–87; Geraldine Forbes, "The Politics of Respectability: Indian Women and the INC," in D. A. Low, ed., *The INC: Centenary Hindsights* (Delhi: Oxford University Press, 1988), and *The New Cambridge History of India*, vol. 4, pt. 2, *Women in Modern India* (Cambridge: Cambridge University Press, 1996); and Radha Kumar, *The History of Doing: An Illustrated Account of Movements for Women's Rights and Feminism in India, 1800–1990* (London: Verso, 1994).

119. Sudeshna Banerjee, "Spirituality and Nationalist Domesticity: Rereading the Relationship," *Calcutta Historical Journal* 19–20 (1997–98): especially 180–97. I am grateful to Tony Ballantyne for this reference.

120. Ibid., p. 197.

121. Ibid., p. 180. *Stridharma*, the publication of the Women's Indian Association, was a primary site for this. See Mary Hancock, "Gendering the Modern: Women and Home Science in British India," in Antoinette Burton, ed., *Gender, Sexuality and Colonial Modernities* (London: Routledge, 1999); Shahida Lateef, *Muslim Women in India: Political and Private Realities* (New Delhi: Kali for Women, 1990), p. 84; Mrinalini Sinha, "The Lineage of the 'Indian' Modern: Rhetoric, Agency, and the Sarda Act in Late Colonial India," in Burton, *Gender, Sexuality and Colonial Modernities*, pp. 207–21; Sinha, "Suffragism and Internationalism: The Enfranchisement of British and Indian Women under an Imperial State," *Indian Economic and Social History Review* 36 (October–December 1999): 461–84;

reprinted in Ian Fletcher, Philippa Levine, and Laura Mayhall, eds., *Women's Suffrage in the British Empire: Citizenship, Race, and Nation* (London: Routledge, 2000), pp. 224–39; and Sinha, "Refashioning Mother India: Feminism and Nationalism in Late-Colonial India," *Feminist Studies* 28, 3 (fall 2000): 623–44.

122. Kamala Visweswaran, "Small Speeches, Subaltern Gender: Nationalist Ideology and Its Historiography," in Shahid Amin and Dipesh Chakrabarty, eds., *Subaltern Studies 9* (Delhi: Oxford University Press, 1996), pp. 83–125.

123. See also Susan Koshy's analysis of Suleri's memoir, "Mother-Country and Fatherland: Re-membering the Nation in Sara Suleri's *Meatless Days*," in Ghosh and Bose, *Interventions*, pp. 45–61.

124. Dirks, "*The Home and the World*," p. 56.

125. Rosemary Marangoly George, *The Politics of Home: Postcolonial Relocations and Twentieth-Century Fiction* (Cambridge: Cambridge University Press, 1996), p. 137.

126. Mrinalini Sinha, "Gender in the Critiques of Colonialism and Nationalism: Locating the 'Indian Woman,'" in Joan Scott, ed., *Feminism and History* (New York: Oxford University Press, 1996), p. 482.

127. Kosambi, "Anandibai Joshi," p. 3196.

128. Frederic Jameson, "Third-World Literature in the Era of Multinational Capitalism," *Social Text* 15 (fall 1986): 65–88; see also Aijaz Ahmad, *In Theory: Nations, Classes, Literatures* (London: Verso, 1992).

129. Many thanks to Laura Mayhall for encouraging me to reflect on this point.

130. Susie Tharu and K. Lalita, eds., *Women Writing in India 600 B.C. to the Present*, vol. 1, *600 B.C. to the Early Twentieth Century* (New York: Feminist Press, 1991).

131. Sarkar, *Words to Win*, p. 13.

132. I am drawing on the version translated by Kusumavati Deshpande, *Ranade: His Wife's Reminiscences*, from Ramabai Ranade's Marathi original, *Amchya Ayuskahtil Kahi Athvanni* (Delhi: Ministry of Information and Broadcasting, 1963).

133. See Burton, *Janaki Majumdar's "Family History."* Although in this chapter I have generally avoided drawing parallels between "Family History" and other texts produced by Western women in this period, it is helpful in this context, I think, to consider Janaki Majumdar's work as an example of what Alison Light calls "conservative modernity." See her *Forever England: Femininity, Literature and Conservatism between the Wars* (London: Routledge, 1991).

134. For domestic genealogies and colonialism see Anne McClintock, "Family Feuds: Gender, Nationalism and the Family," *Feminist Review* 44 (1993): 61–80.

135. FH, p. 1.

136. George, *The Politics of Home*, p. 6.

Chapter 3

1. *Times of London*, October 29, 1932.

2. The first epigraph is from a quotation in Susie Tharu and K. Lalita, eds.,

Women Writing in India, 600 B.C. to the Present, vol. 1, *600 B.C. to the Early Twentieth Century* (New York: Feminist Press, 1991), p. 393. Hyder was a writer and one of the originators of the idea of the All-India Muslim Ladies' Conference. Having designed and popularized the *burqa,* she "took the bold step of discarding purdah in 1923 when she joined the freedom struggle" (391). Steve Poulos calls her "the most important women writer in Urdu prior to Ismat Chugtai." Poulos, "Feminine Sense and Sensibility: A Comparative Study of Six Modern Women Short Fiction Writers in Hindi and Urdu: Rashid Jahan, Ismat Chughtai, Qurratulain Hyder, Mannu Bhandari, Usha Priyamvada, Vijay Chauhan" (Ph.D. diss., University of Chicago, 1975), p. 11.

3. Shahida Lateef, *Muslim Women in India: Politics and Private Realities* (New Delhi: Kali for Women, 1990), pp. 74–94.

4. Lata Mani, *Contentious Traditions: The Debate on Sati in Colonial India* (Berkeley: University of California Press, 1998).

5. Cornelia Sorabji, "Concerning Purdahnashins," September 1917, typescript, MSS EUR F165/199, Oriental and India Office Library, London, p. 1. All call numbers cited in this chapter hereafter are of this library.

6. Reviews of *Love and Life beyond the Purdah,* by Cornelia Sorabji, *Yorkshire Post,* February 5, 1902; *Saturday Review,* December 12, 1901, MSS EUR F165/197.

7. Review of *India Calling* by Cornelia Sorabji, *British Weekly,* February 28, 1935, MSS EUR F165/197.

8. For an account of her early antinationalism (i.e., in the 1880s and 1890s) see Antoinette Burton, *At the Heart of the Empire: Indians and the Colonial Encounter in Late-Victorian Britain* (Berkeley: University of California Press, 1998), chap. 3.

9. Cornelia Sorabji, "Mahatma Gandhi," *Nineteenth Century and After* 100 (September 1926): 368–79, and "The Gandhi Apocrypha," *Nineteenth Century and After* 110 (November 1931): 594–601. For an example of an earlier incarnation of Sorabji's antinationalism, see her "Stray Thoughts of an Indian Girl," *Nineteenth Century* (October 1891).

10. See Mrinalini Sinha, ed., *Mother India* (Delhi: Kali for Women, 1998; Ann Arbor: University of Michigan Press, 2000), especially her introduction, pp. 1–62; and Catherine Candy, "The Inscrutable Irish-Indian Feminist Management of Anglo-American Hegemony," *Journal of Colonialism and Colonial History* 2, 1 (Spring 2001); available at: www.jhu.edu/journals/jcch.

11. MSS EUR F 165/183.

12. MSS EUR F 165/187; Samuel Hoare to Cornelia Sorabji, August 12, 1933; Sorabji to Salisbury, September 21, 1933; Sorabji to Lady Elena Richmond, February 26, 1934, MSS EUR F165/46. At times Sorabji's very public views on nationalism and the political situation in India got her official reprimands; see A. Marr to Sorabji, July 1914, MSS EUR F165/127.

13. See Cornelia Sorabji to Mr. Morrison, January 21, 1943, IOL L/P&J/12/455. Thanks to Rozina Visram for this reference. For a critical analysis of this characterization and the ideological work it has done, see Sonita Sarker, "Unruly Subjects: Cornelia Sorabji and Ravinder Randhawa," in Sonita Sarker and Esha Niyogi De, eds., *Trans-Status Subjects: Gender in the Globalization of South and Southeast Asia* (Durham, N.C.: Duke University Press, forthcoming).

14. See Burton, *At the Heart,* chap. 3.

15. Cornelia Sorabji, *Therefore: An Impression of Sorabji Kharsedji Langrana*

and His Wife Franscina (Oxford: Oxford University Press, 1934); Susie Sorabji: Christian-Parsee Educationalist of Western India: A Memoir by Her Sister (London: Oxford University Press, 1932).

16. See Burton, At the Heart, p. 116–17.

17. Sorabji, "Concerning Purdahnashins," pt. 2, p. 21.

18. Burton, At the Heart, p. 133.

19. Recounted by Sorabji in "Note A," appendix J, June 21, 1911, MS EUR F165/122. "I was appointed in 1904 to a post which I myself was to create in relation to the Court of Wards zenana. . . . When the Government of Bengal asked me to initiate the scheme, and offered me a retainer of Rs.200 with fixed fees for special work on visits to wards, I accepted." The House of Commons question was put by Arthur Elliot; see note C, MSS EUR F165/22.

20. Mahua Sarkar, "Muslim Women and the Politics of (In)visibility in Late Colonial Bengal," Journal of Historical Sociology 14, 2 (June 2001): 226–50.

21. This was a title that Rozina Visram has argued captured the lowly status of the post; it was also a title that varied in Sorabji's usage to include "Legal Advisor" or "Lady Advisor," according to context and audience. See Rozina Visram, Ayahs, Lascars and Princes: The Story of Indians in Britain, 1700-1947 (London: Pluto, 1986), p. 189.

22. As an interesting counterpoint, Maggie Papakura (1882–1930) was a Maori woman who earned a degree at Oxford that resulted in the posthumous publication of the first account of Maori life by a Maori woman scholar in 1938. See Makereti, The Old-Time Maori (Auckland: New Women's Press, 1986). I am grateful to Tony Ballantyne for making this text available to me.

23. Bernard S. Cohn, Colonialism and Its Forms of Knowledge (Princeton, N.J.: Princeton University Press, 1996); Nicholas B. Dirks, "Colonial Histories and Native Informants: Biography of an Archive," in Carol Breckenridge and Peter van der Veer, eds., Orientalism and the Postcolonial Predicament: Perspectives on South Asia (Philadelphia: University of Pennsylvania Press, 1993): pp. 279–313; C. A. Bayly, Empire and Information: Intelligence Gathering and Social Communication in India, 1780-1870 (Cambridge: Cambridge University Press, 1999); Martin Moir, "Kaghazi Raj: Notes in the Documentary Basis of Company Rule, 1773-1858," Indo-British Review 21, 2 (1993): 185–92.

24. Richard Suarez-Smith, "Rule-by-Record and Rule-by-Report: Complementary Aspects of the British Imperial Rule of Law," in Veena Das, ed., The World and the Word: Fantasy, Symbol and Record (Delhi: Sage, 1986), p. 153; see also Rule by Records: Land Registration and Village Custom in Early British Punjab (Delhi: Oxford University Press, 1996).

25. Suarez-Smith, "Rule-by-Record," p. 154.

26. Arjun Appadurai, "Number in the Colonial Imagination," in van der Veer and Breckenridge, Orientalism and the Postcolonial Predicament, pp. 314–40.

27. Janaki Nair, "Uncovering the Zenana: Visions of Indian Womanhood in Englishwomen's Writings, 1813–1940," Journal of Women's History 2 (spring 1990): 8–34. For the back-history of the investment of the colonial state in the sphere of the domestic see Radhika Singh, A Despotism of Law: Crime and Justice in Early Colonial India (Delhi: Oxford University Press, 1998).

28. Cornelia Sorabji, India Calling: The Memories of Cornelia Sorabji (London: Nisbet, 1934), p. 299. See also Chandani Lokugé, ed., India Calling: The Memories of Cornelia Sorabji, India's First Woman Barrister (Delhi: Oxford University Press, 2001).

Here I am echoing James Scott, *Seeing Like a State: How Certain Schemes to Improve the Human Condition Have Failed* (New Haven, Conn.: Yale University Press, 1998).

29. For an instructive account of how official reports reveal a variety of narrated subjectivities see Angela Woollacott, "The Fragmented Subject: Feminist History, Official Records and Self-Representation," *Women's Studies International Forum* 21, 4 (1998): 329–39.

30. Board of Revenue Bengal: Report of Lady Advisor to the Court of Wards Bengal for 1919–20, p. 125, MSS F165/183.

31. Ibid.

32. For Das see MSS EUR F165/140; for the lantern shows see Board of Revenue Bengal, Report of Lady Advisor to the Court of Wards Bengal for 1914–1915, MSS EUR F165/141.

33. Sorabji, "Concerning Purdahnashins," part 1.

34. See Clifford, *Seeing Like a State;* and Sorabji, "Prospice: The New India," *Nineteenth Century and After* 109 (February 1931): 176.

35. Board of Revenue Bengal, Report of Lady Advisor to the Court of Wards Bengal for 1919–20, p. 4.

36. Cornelia Sorabji, "Zenana Dwellers: The Selfless Women of Hinduism, Keepers of the God-Rules," *Asia* (March 1924): 173.

37. Board of Revenue Bengal, Report of Lady Advisor to the Court of Wards Bengal for 1919–20, p. 28.

38. Proof for "The Position of Women in India" (n.d.), MSS EUR F165/58.

39. Note 1 (n.d.); note 2 (1911).

40. Ibid.

41. See Burton, *At the Heart,* chap. 3.

42. Note 1 (n.d.); note 2 (1911).

43. Ibid.

44. See Sorabji, Diaries, 1927–29 and /127, MSS EUR F165/89 and F165/90.

45. Miscellaneous correspondence, IOL L/I/1/1520, file no. 8. I am indebted to Rozina Visram for providing me with the reference number for this file.

46. Board of Revenue Bengal, Report of Lady Advisor to the Court of Wards Bengal for 1919–20, p. 22.

47. Here I borrow from his *Hybrid Cultures: Strategies for Entering and Leaving Modernity* (Minneapolis: University of Minnesota Press, 1995), p. 125.

48. See James Clifford, "On Ethnographic Allegory," in James Clifford and George E. Marcus, eds., *Writing Culture: The Poetics and Politics of Ethnography* (Berkeley: University of California Press, 1986), pp. 98–121.

49. Maharani of Banailli to Cornelia Sorabji, May 21, 1927, MSS EUR F165/145.

50. Ibid.

51. Maharani of Banailli to Cornelia Sorabji, July 15, 1927, MSS EUR F165/145.

52. See Susan Pederson, "National Bodies, Unspeakable Acts: The Sexual Politics of Colonial Policy-Making," *Journal of Modern History* 63 (December 1991): 647–80; Angela Woollacott, "Inventing Commonwealth and Pan-Pacific Feminisms: Australian Women's International Activism," *Gender and History* 10, 3

(1998): 425–48; Fiona Paisley, *Loving Protection? Australian Feminism and Aboriginal Women's Rights 1919–1939* (Melbourne: Melbourne University Press, 2000); Nayan Shah, *Contagious Divides: Epidemics and Race in San Francisco's Chinatown* (Berkeley: University of California Press, 2001), especially chaps. 3 and 4; and Barbara Ramusack, "Embattled Advocates: The Debate over Birth Control in India, 1920–1940," *Journal of Women's History* 1, 2 (fall 1989): 34–64.

53. I am grateful to Barbara Ramusack for raising this question.

54. See Dipesh Chakrabarty, *Provincializing Europe: Postcolonial Thought and Historical Difference* (Princeton, N.J.: Princeton University Press, 2000), p. 216.

55. Board of Revenue Bengal: Report of Lady Advisor to the Court of Wards Bengal for 1914–1915, p. 2.

56. Board of Revenue Bengal: Report of Lady Advisor to the Court of Wards Bengal for 1919–20, p. 5.

57. Ibid.

58. Letter to Lady Elena Richmond, February 5, 1931, MSS EUR F165/46.

59. August 5, 1934, MSS EUR F165/96.

60. "Note A," appendix J, June 21, 1911, MSS EUR F165/122.

61. Though the notion of an imperial historicity is central to Chakrabarty's argument in *Provincializing Europe*, the extent to which that is constitutively gendered—at the site of history itself rather than simply in the domestic—is not fully explored.

62. Sorabji, *India Calling*, p. 99.

63. Ibid., p. 67.

64. Thanks to Barbara Ramusack for this information.

65. Ibid., p. 70.

66. See Rita Felski, *The Gender of Modernity* (Cambridge, Mass.: Harvard University Press, 1995), pp. 1–18, and Griselda Pollock, *Vision and Difference: Femininity, Feminism and the Histories of Art* (London: Routledge, 1988). Thanks to Angela Woollacott for directing my attention to these references. See also Andreas Hussyen, *After the Great Divide: Modernism, Mass Culture, Postmodernism* (Bloomington: Indiana University Press, 1986).

67. Felski, *The Gender of Modernity*, p. 14.

68. See *At the Heart*, chapter 3.

69. See Pradip Kumar Datta, *Carving Blocks: Communal Ideology in Early Twentieth-Century Bengal* (Delhi: Oxford University Press, 1999).

70. See John Urry, "The Tourist Gaze 'Revisited,'" *American Behavioral Scientist* 36, 2 (November 12, 1993). 171 86, especially 179

71. Ibid., p. 177.

72. Tim Edensor (quoting C. Rojek), *Tourists at the Taj: Performance and Meaning as a Symbolic Site* (London: Routledge, 1998), p. 16.

73. Sorabji, *India Calling*, part 5.

74. Ibid., p. 230.

75. Board of Revenue Bengal: Report of Lady Advisor to the Court of Wards Bengal for 1915–16; "Supply of Motor to L.A.'s Office," MSS EUR F165/96.

76. See for example Board of Revenue Bengal, Report of Lady Advisor to the Court of Wards Bengal for 1915–16.

77. See Chakrabarty, "The Idea of Provincializing Europe," introduction to *Provincializing Europe*.

78. Review of *India Calling*, by Cornelia Sorabji, *Dublin Evening Herald*, January 18, 1935, MSS EUR F165/197.

79. Kamala Visweswaran, "Small Speeches, Subaltern Gender: Nationalist Ideology and Its Historiography," in Shahid Amin and Dipesh Chakrabarty, eds., *Subaltern Studies 9* (Delhi: Oxford University Press, 1996), pp. 83–125; Kalpana Dutt (Joshi), *Chittagong Armoury Raiders Reminiscences* (New Delhi: People's Publishing House, 1979).

80. MSS EUR F 165/197; and also her essay, "Gandhi Interrogated," *Atlantic Monthly* (April 1932).

81. "The Lineage of the 'Indian' Modern: Rhetoric, Agency, and the Sarda Act in Late Colonial India," in Antoinette Burton, ed., *Gender, Sexuality and Colonial Modernities* (London: Routledge, 1999), pp. 207–21; "Refashioning Mother India: Feminism and Nationalism in Late-Colonial India," *Feminist Studies* 28, 3 (fall 2000): 623–44; and "Suffragism and Internationalism: The Enfranchisement of British and Indian Women Under an Imperial State," *Indian Economic and Social History Review* 36 (October–December 1999): 461–84; reprinted in Ian Fletcher, Philippa Levine and Laura Mayhall, eds., *Women's Suffrage in the British Empire: Citizenship, Race, and Nation* (Routledge: London, 2000), pp. 224–39.

82. Cornelia Sorabji, "Indian Women of 'The Outside': The Emancipated Who, with no Book of Rules, Have Attained New Spheres of Freedom," *Asia* (April 1924).

83. Ibid.

84. Cornelia Sorabji, *Between the Twilights* (London: Harper, 1908), p. 6.

85. Cornelia Sorabji, "A Bengali Woman Revolutionary," *Nineteenth Century and After* 112 (November, 1933): 604.

86. It was, in her estimation, a nationalism "which sought little more than the revival of home-industries and the Indianising of the Services so as to secure posts and 'key' positions to Indians, and particular to Bengali-Hindus." Ibid., p. 604.

87. Ibid., p. 605.

88. Parama Roy, *Indian Traffic: Identities in Question in Colonial and Postcolonial India* (Berkeley: University of California Press, 1998), pp. 41–70; Michael Silvestri, "The Thrill of 'Simply Dressing Up': The Indian Police, Disguise, and Intelligence Work in Colonial India," *Journal of Colonialism and Colonial History* 2, 2 (2001).

89. Ibid., p. 606.

90. I am grateful to Angela Woollacott for this observation.

91. Lateef, *Muslim Women in India*, p. 81.

92. Sorabji, "A Bengali Woman Revolutionary," p. 606.

93. Tirtha Mandal, *Women Revolutionaries of Bengal, 1905–1939* (Calcutta: Minerva, 1991), p. 3; and Geraldine Forbes, "Goddesses or Rebels? The Women Revolutionaries of Bengal," *Oracle* 11, 2 (April 1980): 1–15.

94. Sorabji, "A Bengali Woman Revolutionary," p. 607.

95. Ibid., p. 608.

96. Christopher Pinney, *Camera Indica: The Social Life of Indian Photographs* (Chicago: University of Chicago Press, 1998), p. 45; see also Béatriz Colomina, "Excerpts from 'The Split Wall': Domestic Voyeurism," in Jane Rendell, Barbara Penner, and Iain Borden, *Gender, Space, Architecture* (London: Routledge, 2000), pp. 314–20.

97. Sorabji, "A Bengali Woman Revolutionary," p. 610.

98. Sorabji, "Concerning Purdahnashins," p. 11.

99. *Bengal League of Social Service for Women: Handbook* (Calcutta, 1929), MSS EUR F165/163. Not incidentally, perhaps, Srimati Chandrabati Koer donated Rs. 500 to this group, p. 6. For a discussion of Muslim women and feminism in twentieth-century India see Azra Asghar Ali, *The Emergence of Feminism among Indian Muslim Women* (London: Oxford University Press, 2000).

100. Sorabji to Lady Elena Richmond, February 9, 1933, MSS EUR F165/46. For an account of the history of Bengali Hindu women's representations of Muslims, especially with respect to the zenana, see Sarkar, "Muslim Women and the Politics of (In)visibility," pp. 226–50. For more on Begum Shah Nawaz see Ali, *The Emergence of Feminism.*

101. Sally Alexander, *Becoming a Woman, and Other Essays in Nineteenth and Twentieth Century Feminist History* (New York: New York University Press, 1995), p. 234.

102. See Forbes, "Goddesses or Rebels?" and Purnima Bose, "Engendering the Armed Struggle: Women, Writing, and the Bengali Terrorist Movement," in Thomas Foster, Carol Siegel, and Ellen E. Berry, eds., *Bodies of Writing, Bodies in Performance* (New York: New York University Press, 1996), pp. 145–83.

103. Cornelia Sorabji, "Indian Women of 'The Outside,'" p. 307.

104. Ibid., pp. 329, 331.

105. Cornelia Sorabji, "The Women of India: Behind the Purdah," London *Times*, February 18, 1930.

106. Sorabji, "A Bengali Woman Revolutionary," pp. 610–11.

107. Ibid., p. 609.

108. Sorabji, "Indian Women of 'The Outside,'" p. 304.

109. Isabel Hartog, "The Awakening of Indian Womanhood," *Contemporary Review* 136 (November 1929): 607. Margaret Cousins's 1922 book was similarly titled; see her *The Awakening of Asian Womanhood* (Madras: Ganesh, 1922).

110. See Antoinette Burton, *Burdens of History: British Feminists, Indian Women and Imperial Culture, 1865–1915* (Chapel Hill: University of North Carolina Press, 1994); for the Begum see Siobhan Hurley, "Out of India: The Journeys of the Begum of Bhopal, 1901–1930," *Women's Studies International Forum* 21, 3 (1998): 263–76.

111. Thanks to Barbara Ramusack for insisting on this point.

112. See Madhu Kishwar, "Gandhi on Women," *Race and Class* 28, 1 (1986): 43–61, and Sujata Patel, "Construction and Reconstruction of Women in Gandhi, *Economic and Political Weekly* (February 20, 1988): 377–87. For a different take see Richard G. Fox, "Gandhi and Feminized Nationalism in India," in Brackette Williams, ed., *Women Out of Place: The Gender of Agency and the Race of Nationality* (New York: Routledge, 1996), pp. 37–49.

113. Cornelia Sorabji, *India Recalled* (London: Nisbet, 1936), pp. vii, viii, x.

114. Ibid., p. viii.

115. For her failing sight, including hemorrhaging in the eyes, see Sorabji to Lady Helena Richmond, February 1, 1932, MSS EUR F165/46. According to her, whenever she visited remote Indian villages, "we hear only of the films Gandhi figures in and his Talkies." Sorabji to Lady Elena Richmond, June 5, 1931, MSS EUR F165/46. See also Anna Grimshaw, "The Eye in the Door: Anthropology, Film, and the Exploration of Interior Space," in Marcus Banks and

Howard Murphy, eds., *Rethinking Visual Anthropology* (New Haven, Conn.: Yale University Press, 1997), pp. 36–52.

116. Review of *India Recalled* by Cornelia Sorabji, MSS EUR F 165/197.

117. Sorabji, *India Recalled*, p. x.

118. Ibid., p. xiii.

119. The fact that Sorabji was going gradually blind in this period may help to explain why the promise of film and the camera appealed to her.

120. Sorabji, *India Recalled*, p. 19.

121. Ibid., p. 20.

122. See Ava Baron and Susan E. Klepp, "'If I Didn't Have My Sewing Machine . . .' Women and Sewing Machine Technology," in Joan M. Jensen and Sue Davidson, eds., *A Needle, a Bobbin, a Strike: Women Needleworkers in America* (Philadelphia: Temple University Press, 1984), p. 37.

123. Sorabji, *India Recalled*, p. 18.

124. Ibid., pp. 257 and 280.

125. Felski, *The Gender of Modernity*, p. 2.

126. I borrow this term from Geeta Kapur's analysis of Amrita Sher-Gil. See her "Body as Gesture: Indian Women Artists at Work," in Vidya Dehejia, ed., *Representing the Body: Gender Issues in Indian Art* (New Delhi: Kali for Women, 1997), p. 170.

127. Sorabji to Lady Elena Richmond, August 6, 1936, MSS EUR F 165/49.

128. Sorabji to Lady Elena Richmond, August 25, 1936, and September 10, 1936, MSS EUR F165/49.

129. For *India Calling* see Sorabji to Lady Elena Richmond, May 1, 1934, and June 8, 1934, MSS EUR Fa65/96; for *India Recalled* see Sorabji to Lady Elena Richmond, May 5, 1936, MSS EUR F165/49.

130. Sorabji to Lady Elena Richmond, n.d. [but appears to be early 1936], MSS EUR F165/49.

131. Sorabji to Lady Elena Richmond, February 9, 1933, MSS EUR F165/46.

132. Sorabji to Lady Elena Richmond, September 11, 1936, MSS EUR F165/49.

133. Sorabji to Lady Elena Richmond, August 15, 1936, MSS EUR F165/49.

134. See Alice Gambrell, *Women Intellectuals, Modernism, and Difference: Transatlantic Culture, 1919–1945* (Cambridge: Cambridge University Press, 1997), chap. 1.

135. Abdul JanMohammed, "Worldliness-without-World, Homelessness-as-Home: Toward a Definition of the Specular Border Intellectual," in Michael Sprinker, ed., *Edward Said: A Critical Reader* (Cambridge, Mass.: Blackwell, 1992), pp. 96–120. See also Gita Rajan, "(Con) Figuring Identity: Cultural Space of the Indo-British Border Intellectual," in Gisela Brinker-Gabler and Sidonie Smith, eds., *Writing New Identities: Gender, Nation, and Immigration in Contemporary Europe* (Minneapolis: University of Minnesota Press, 1997), pp. 78–99.

136. Kapur, "Body and Gesture," p. 172. The fact that Sher-Gil's parentage was mixed—her father was Punjabi and her mother a Hungarian—makes her an especially interesting modernist hybrid, not unlike Sorabji in her angular relationship to "Indianness." In addition, her orientation as an art student was to Paris, not Britain. See K. G. Subramanyam, "Amrita Sher-Gil and the East-West

Dilemma," in Vivan Sundaram et al., *Amrita Sher-Gil* (Bombay: Tata Press, 1972), pp. 63–72.

137. Kapur, "Body and Gesture," pp. 168, 173. Like a variety of imperialist sympathizers, Sorabji was attracted to Hindu women's culture "as it was 'traditionally'"—that is, when she first encountered it. See Renato Rosaldo, "Imperialist Nostalgia," *Representations* 26 (spring 1989): 107.

138. This connection is prompted by Charles W. Hayford's essay, "The Storm over the Peasant: Orientalism and Rhetoric in Constructing China," in Jeffrey Cox and Sheldon Stromquist, eds., *Contesting the Master Narrative: Essays in Social History* (Iowa City: University of Iowa Press, 1998), especially pp. 164–66, which focus on Buck.

139. See Cynthia Nelson, "Biography and Women's History: On Interpreting Doria Shafik," in Nikki Keddie and Beth Baron, eds., *Women in Middle Eastern History: Shifting Boundaries in Sex and Gender* (New Haven, Conn.: Yale University Press, 1991), pp. 31–33, and my own *Burdens of History: British Feminists, Indian Women and Imperial Culture, 1865–1915* (Chapel Hill: University of North Carolina Press, 1994).

140. Williams's schema is recounted in Nestor Garcia Canclini, *Hybrid Cultures* (Minneapolis: University of Minnesota Press), p. 138.

141. See Gyan Prakash, "Science between the Lines," in Shahid Amin and Dipesh Chakrabarty, eds., *Subaltern Studies 9: Writings on South Asian History and Society* (Delhi: Oxford University Press, 1996), p. 59.

142. James Young, *The Texture of Memory: Holocaust Memorials and Meaning* (New Haven, Conn.: Yale University Press, 1993), pp. vii–xi.

143. David Lloyd, *Ireland after History* (Notre Dame, Ind.: Field Day, 1999), p. 2.

144. Arjun Appadurai, *Modernity at Large: Cultural Dimensions of Globalization* (Minneapolis: University of Minnesota Press, 1996), p. 2; see also Jasodhara Bagchi, "Europe and the Question of Modernity," *Social Scientist* 24, 7–8 (August 1996): 10.

145. Arjun Appadurai, "The Past as a Scarce Resource," *Man* 16 (1981): 204 and 217.

146. I am indebted to Tony Ballantyne for this provocative suggestion.

147. I am borrowing here from Susan Stewart, *On Longing: Narratives of the Miniature, the Gigantic, the Souvenir, the Collection* (Baltimore: Johns Hopkins University Press, 1984).

Chapter 4

1. Ritu Menon and Kamla Bhasin, *Borders and Boundaries: Women in India's Partition* (New Brunswick, N.J.: Rutgers University Press, 1998), and Urvashi Butalia, *The Other Side of Silence: Voices from the Partition of India* (Delhi: Oxford University Press, 1998).

2. Amrit Srinivasan, "The Survivor in the Study of Violence," in Veena Das, ed., *Mirrors of Violence: Communities, Riots and Survivors in South Asia* (Delhi: Oxford University Press, 1990), p. 307.

3. Quotation is from Butalia, *Other Side of Silence*, p. 6.

4. For an account of the general disinterest, until recently, in popular con-

structions of partition and its meanings see Gyanendra Pandey, "The Prose of Otherness," in David Arnold and David Hardiman, eds., *Subaltern Studies 8: Essays in Honor of Ranajit Guha* (New Delhi: Oxford University Press, 1994), pp. 188–221; see also Pandey's recent book, *Remembering Partition* (Cambridge: Cambridge University Press, 2001).

5. Intizar Husain (b. 1925), "The Stairway," in Saros Cowasjee and K. S. Duggal, eds., *Orphans of the Storm: Stories on the Partition of India* (New Delhi: UBS, 1995), p. 128; see also Ian Bedford, "Intizar Husain's 'An Unwritten Epic' and the 'Matter of Pakistan,'" *Journal of Commonwealth Literature* 28 (1993): 16–32.

6. Kartar Singh Duggal (b. 1917), "A New Home," in Cowasjee and Duggal, *Orphans*, pp. 104–8.

7. Jyotirmoyee Devi (b. 1894), *The River Churning: A Partition Novel* (New Delhi: Kali for Women, 1995; written in 1947 under the title *Epar Ganga Opar Ganga*, or "The Woman Chapter in History"), pp. xxvii, 4.

8. Saadat Hasan Manto (1912–55), "Toba Tek Singh," in Cowasjee and Duggal, *Orphans*, pp. 145–57.

9. Butalia, *The Other Side of Silence*, p. 24.

10. Ibid., p. 28.

11. Ibid., p. 38.

12. See Mary J. Carruthers, *The Book of Memory: A Study of Memory in Medieval Culture* (Cambridge: Cambridge University Press, 1990), and Jonathan Spence, *The Memory Palace of Matteo Ricci* (New York: Penguin, 1985).

13. See Menon and Bhasin, *Borders and Boundaries*, pp. 8–21.

14. See Homi Bhabha, "The World in the Home," in Anne McClintock, Aamir Mufti, and Ella Shoat, eds., *Dangerous Liaisons: Gender, Nation and Postcolonial Perspectives* (Minneapolis: University of Minnesota Press, 1997), p. 448.

15. Ibid., p. 454.

16. Mushirul Hasan and M. Assaduddin, eds., *Image and Representation: Stories of Muslim Lives in India* (New Delhi: Oxford University Press, 2000), p. 4. Here they are drawing expressly on Terry Eagleton's *Criticism and Ideology* (London: Prometheus Books, 1976). Other scholars are more skeptical about this proposition; see Ian Talbot, *Freedom's Cry: The Popular Dimension in the Pakistan Movement and Partition Experience in Northwest India* (Karachi: Oxford University Press, 1996) especially chap. 3.

17. Mushirul Hasan, *Legacy of a Divided Nation: India's Muslims Since Independence* (Boulder, Colo.: Westview Press, 1997), p. 62.

18. This is the very justification that the publishers of Mumtaz Shah Nawaz's *The Heart Divided* use to introduce this little-known novel to the public. The novel was written in 1948, originally published by Mumtaz Publications, Lahore, in 1957, and reissued by ASR Publications (Lahore) in 1990.

19. Ayesha Jalal, "Secularists, Subalterns and the Stigma of 'Communalism': Partition Historiography Revisited," *Indian Economic and Social History Review* 33, 1 (January–March 1996): 93–104.

20. Here I draw on Eleni Coundoriotis, *Claiming History: Colonialism, Ethnography and the Novel* (New York: Columbia University Press, 1999), p. 20; Leo Ou-fan Lee, *Shanghai Modern: The Flowering of a New Urban Culture in China, 1930–1945* (Cambridge, Mass.: Harvard University Press, 1999), p. 301; and Barbara Melosh, "Historical Memory in Fiction: The Civil Rights Movement in Three Novels," *Radical History Review* 40 (1988): 64–76.

21. Attia Hosain, *Sunlight on a Broken Column* (New Delhi: Penguin, 1988; original 1961), p. 46.

22. Ranajit Guha, "The Migrant's Time," *Postcolonial Studies* 1, 2 (1998): 155–60.

23. Nirmala Bannerjee, "Whatever Happened to the Dreams of Modernity? The Nehruvian Era and Women's Position," *Economic and Political Weekly* (April 25, 1998): WS 2–7.

24. See Claudia Tate, *Domestic Allegories of Political Desire: The Black Heroine's Text at the Turn of the Century* (New York: Oxford University Press, 1992). As Ranabir Samaddar reminds us, partition cannot and should not be deracinated from the decolonizing context in which it occurred, and in which it must be historicized. See his "The History that Partition Creates," in his edited collection, *Reflections on Partition in the East* (New Delhi: Vikas, 1997), p. 1.

25. Jean Pickering, "Remembering D-Day," in Jean Pickering and Suzanne Kehde, eds., *Narratives of Nostalgia: Gender and Nationalism* (New York: Macmillan, 1997), p. 183.

26. See Rosie Llewellyn-Jones, "Lucknow, City of Dreams," in Violette Graff, ed., *Lucknow: Memories of a City* (Delhi: Oxford University Press, 1997), p. 60.

27. Violette Graff, introduction to *Lucknow*, p. 3.

28. Hosain, *Sunlight*, p. 14.

29. E-mail correspondence, Shama Habibullah, 2000. In her 1971 autobiography, Jahan Ara Shanawaz (b. 1896, hence seventeen years older than Hosain) remembered that her father "used to get a new novel every month from Thacker Spink and Co., of London, as a standing order had been placed with them to send him the best novel of the month. Often, after reading a good story, he would relate it to us in Urdu. Once, when he told us the story of one of Rider Haggard's new novels called *Swallow*, I asked Father to give me the book. At that time, I could read very little English, but the desire to study the book made me work hard and I began to understand English well within a short time." *Father and Daughter: A Political Autobiography* (Lahore: Nigarishat, 1971), p. 15.

30. Though not all the women in Minault's book are purdahnashin. See Gail Minault, *Secluded Scholars: Women's Education and Muslim Social Reform in Colonial India* (Delhi: Oxford University Press, 1998), as well as her "Other Voices, Other Rooms: The View from the Zenana," in Nita Kumar, ed., *Women as Subjects: South Asian Histories* (Charlottesville: University of Virginia Press, 1994), p. 108.

31. Anita Desai, introduction to Attia Hosain, *Phoenix Fled and Other Stories* (New Delhi: Penguin, 1989), p. xlii.

32. Ibid. She majored in English literature, economics, and politics. See Laura Bondi, "An Image of India by an Indian Woman: Attia Hosain's Life and Fiction" (M.A. thesis, Universita Degli Stufio Venezia, 1993), provided courtesy of the author, p. 8.

33. Marjorie A. Dimmitt, *Isabella Thoburn College: A Record from Its Beginnings to Its Diamond Jubilee, 1961*, p. 102; see also Maina Chawla Singh, *Gender, Religion and "Heathen" Lands: American Missionary Women in South Asia (1860s–1940s)* (New York: Garland, 2000), chap. 7 (on the history of Thoburn College).

34. Patrick Colm Hogan attributes a purer Marxism to her work than I do; see his *Colonialism and Cultural Identity: Crises of Tradition in the Anglophone Literatures of India, Africa and the Caribbean* (Albany: SUNY Press, 2000), pp. 263 and

265, and especially what he calls her "universal categories of economic structure," p. 272.

35. Francis Robinson, "The Re-emergence of Lucknow as a Major Political Centre, 1899–early 1920s," in Graff, *Lucknow*, p. 197.

36. Ibid.; see also Peter Reeves, "Lucknow Politics, 1920–1947," in Graff, *Lucknow*, pp. 213–26; and Sanjay Joshi, *Fractured Modernity: Making of a Middle Class in Colonial North India* (New Delhi: Oxford University Press, 2001).

37. Robinson, "The Re-emergence of Lucknow," pp. 203–8. This was also the period in which debates about, and the founding of, a Muslim University at Aligarh were taking place; see Gail Minault and David Lelyveld, "The Campaign for a Muslim University," *Modern Asian Studies* 8, 2 (1974): 145–89.

38. Robinson, "The Re-emergence of Lucknow," p. 199.

39. Bondi, "An Image of India," p. 10.

40. Quotation is Rumina Seth, *Myths of the Nation: National Identity and Literary Representation* (Oxford: Clarendon Press, 1999), p. 1.

41. Shabana Mahmud, "*Angare* and the Founding of the Progressive Writers' Association," *Modern Asian Studies* 30, 2 (1996): 448–49; and Steven Poulos, "Feminine Sense and Sensibility: A Comparative Study of Six Modern Women Short Fiction Writers in Hindi and Urdu: Rashid Jahan, Ismat Chughtai, Qurratulain Hyder, Mannu Bhandari, Usha Priyamvada, Vijay Chauhan" (Ph.D. diss., University of Chicago, 1975), pp. 16–19.

42. Mahmud, "*Angare*," pp. 448–49.

43. Ibid., p. 450.

44. The short stories of Premchand (1880–1936) were the subject of a government ban in 1909 in the antisedition, pro-swadeshi climate following the partition of Bengal in 1905; see David Rubin, ed., *Widows, Wives and Other Heroines: Twelve Stories by Premchand* (Delhi: Oxford University Press, 1998), p. xi.

45. Mahmud, "*Angare*," pp. 450–52.

46. For Chugtai (1915–91) see Sukrita Paul Kumar and Sadique, eds., *Ismat: Her Life and Times* (New Delhi: Katha, 2000). A short story writer, she was most famous as the author of "The Quilt," first published in 1944, as "Lihaaf," to great notoriety—see *The Quilt and Other Stories* (New Delhi: Kali for Women, 1990); she was also a novelist—see for example *The Crooked Line* (New Delhi: Kali for Women, 1995), first published as *Terhi Lakeer* in 1945. Poulos, "Feminine Sense and Sensibility," was one of the earliest to treat women writers of this generation as a collectivity.

47. E-mail correspondence with Attia's daughter, Shama Habibullah, July 27, 1999. According to Habibullah, her mother was not herself a member of the PWA "but was influenced by, and supported, their ideas. The connection came through her contacts in Lucknow, particularly because her friend 'Bunny' Zaheer introduced her to Mulk Raj Anand. . . . [S]he was encouraged to write by Mulk, but most strongly by Sarojini Naidu." For a variety of accounts of the PWA, its origins, and its international connections see Carlo Coppola, ed., pamphlet titled "Marxist Influences in South Asian Literatures" (East Lansing, Mich., 1974).

48. Bondi, "An Image," p. 9; see also BBC Written Archives Centre (Caversham Park, Reading), scripts microfilm collection: "Passport to Friendship," recorded January 26, 1965.

49. Jehan (1905–52) was a medical doctor, short story writer, and author of

one-act plays, as well as one of the chief organizers of the PWA. See Ralph Russell, ed., *Hidden in the Lute: An Anthology of Two Centuries of Urdu Literature* (Delhi: Viking, 1995). For a reprint of her story "The Veil," see pp. 34–46.

50. He was the eldest son of Shaikh Mohammed Habibullah, vice chancellor of Lucknow University and *taluqdar* of Saidananpur. His mother Inam was the sister of Attia's mother Nisar. Courtesy of Shama Habibullah, e-mail correspondence, October 27, 1999.

51. See Desai, introduction to *Phoenix Fled*, p. xii.

52. Bondi, "An Image of India," p. 8.

53. Ibid.

54. Ibid., pp. 11–12.

55. He had been the textile commissioner during the war and then the supply commissioner, responsible for civilian supplies in south and southeast Asia. Between 1945 and Independence he was in charge of working out trade requirements and the redistribution of trade assets—all this according to his daughter, Shama Habibullah, e-mail correspondence, October 8, 1999. For Bharucha's interview see *Biblio* (July–August 1998): 21.

56. Rashid Jehan was also involved in All India Radio in Lucknow, for which she wrote and produced plays. Poulos, "Feminine Sense and Sensibility," pp. 20–21.

57. BBC Written Archives Centre (Caversham Park, Reading), scripts microfilm collection.

58. BBC Written Archives Centre, scripts microfilm collection: "Passport to Friendship," recorded January 28, 1965.

59. BBC Written Archives Centre, Attia Hosain to Owen Leeming, July 12, 1961.

60. BBC Written Archives Centre, Terence Cooper [for London Calling Asia] to Attia Hosain, December 29, 1954.

61. BBC Written Archives Centre, scripts microfilm collection: "Exhibition of Indian Art" for Weekend Review, May 28, 1956 ["All Scripts Destroyed"]; and Attia Hosain to K. M. Brown, September 7, 1956.

62. BBC Written Archives Centre, Richard Daly to the BBC, March 30, 1956.

63. BBC Written Archives Centre, B. C. Horton to Attia Hosain, April 5, 1956. According to the transcript it was in fact repeated; it aired first on Friday, March 30, 1956, and was rebroadcast on Friday, April 13, 1956. Later, in the context of a letter about another script, Horton wrote, "I only hope that writing down all the difficulties [of the script] has not discouraged you from continuing your novel!" Horton to Hosain, May 1, 1956.

64. Attia told Laura Bondi in 1997 that she wrote the novel in three places: India, Pakistan, and Britain; "An Image," p. 7. In an interview with Anuradha Needham, Hosain named these three places as Buckinghamshire (Britain), Rahim Yaar Khan (Pakistan), and Katmandu (Nepal). Interview notes, courtesy of Anuradha Needham.

65. BBC Written Archives Centre, scripts microfilm collection: "A Conversation on Homesickness," recorded March 6, 1956.

66. Ibid., p. 1.

67. Ibid., pp. 3–4.

68. Ibid., p. 7.

69. Ibid., p. 5.

70. Thanks to David Prochaska for helping me to appreciate this point.

71. See chapter 2.

72. Mulk Raj Anand, "Attia Hosain: A Profile," in Attia Hosain, *Sunlight on a Broken Column* (Delhi: Gulab Vazirani for Arnold-Heinemann, 1979), p. xi.

73. BBC Written Archives Centre, scripts microfilm collection: "A Conversation on Homesickness," p. 6.

74. Quoted in Sandra Ponzanesi, "Paradoxes of Postcolonial Culture: Feminism and Diaspora in South Asian and Afro-Italian Women's Narratives" (M.A. thesis, University of Utrecht, 1999), p. 71; manuscript provided courtesy of the author. See also Meena Alexander on Sarojini Naidu and "the inner shelters of domesticity" in her essay "Outcaste Power: Ritual Displacement and Virile Maternity in Indian Women Writers," *Journal of Commonwealth Literature* 24 (1989): 16.

75. Hosain quoted in Desai, introduction to *Phoenix Fled*, p. xiii. Italics in original.

76. Meenakshi Mukherjee, *Realism and Reality: The Novel and Indian Society* (New Delhi: Oxford University Press, 1985), and *The Perishable Empire: Essays on Indian Writing in English* (New Delhi: Oxford University Press, 2000); Jasbir Jain, *Feminizing Political Discourse: Women and the Novel in India, 1857–1905* (Jaipur: Rawat, 1997).

77. Firdous Azim, *The Colonial Rise of the Novel* (London: Routledge, 1992), and Suvir Kaul, *Poems of Nation, Anthems of Empire: English Verse in the Long Eighteenth Century* (Charlottesville: University Press of Virginia, 2000), p. 11.

78. Anand, "Profile," p. x.

79. Bondi, "An Image," p. 10, 7, and Nilufer E. Bharucha, "I Am a Universalist-Humanist" (interview with Attia Hosain), *Biblio* (July–August 1998): 20. I am grateful to Ania Loomba for bringing this to my attention and to Deborah Hughes for hunting it down for me. The interrelationship of the novel to the autobiography is echoed in the corpus of Hosain's contemporary Ismat Chugtai, whose autobiography "reads like detailed notes for *The Crooked Line.*" Tahira Naqvi, introduction to *The Crooked Line* (Kali, 1995), p. xiv.

80. Bharucha, "I Am a Universalist-Humanist," p. 20.

81. According to Murdoch, "A novel must be a house for free people to live in." Quoted in Bhabha, "The World in the Home," p. 446.

82. For an elaboration of this idea see Gaston Bachelard, *The Poetics of Space* (1964; Boston: Beacon Press, 1994), especially chaps. 1 and 2.

83. Hosain, *Sunlight* (1961), p. 16.

84. Ibid.

85. Ibid., p. 98.

86. Ibid., p. 165.

87. Anand, "Profile," p. i. For an entirely different kind of profile, see Mulk Raj Anand, "E. M. Forster: A Personal Recollection," *Journal of Commonwealth Literature* 18 (1983): 80–83, and *Conversations in Bloomsbury* (London: Wildwood House, 1981). He also wrote the afterword to Ranjana Harish, ed., *Indian Women's Autobiographies* (New Delhi: Arnold, 1993), pp. 213–16.

88. Ibid., pp. vii and xiv.

89. He was also involved in India League in Britain; see his "In Conversation with H. G. Wells," *Journal of Commonwealth Literature* 18 (1983): 84–90.

90. Attia Hosain, "Seclusion of Women," in Shyam Kumari Nehru, ed., *Our Cause: A Symposium by Indian Women* (Allahabad: Kitabistan, n.d. [1952?]), p. 206. I am grateful to David Doughan for initially drawing my attention to this text and to Gail Minault for reminding me of it many years later.

91. See Shahida Lateef, *Muslim Women in India: Political and Private Realities* (New Delhi: Kali for Women, 1990), p. 81.

92. *Sunlight* (1961), p. 119.

93. Ibid., pp. 120–21.

94. See Lawrence J. Taylor, "Re-entering the West Room: On the Power of Domestic Spaces," in Donna Birdwell-Pheasant and Denise Lawrence-Zúñiga, eds., *House Life: Space, Place and Family in Europe* (New York: Berg, 1999), p. 224.

95. Guha, "The Migrant's Time"; see also Julia Kristeva, "Women's Time," in Toril Moi, ed., *The Kristeva Reader* (New York: Columbia University Press, 1986), pp. 187–213.

96. See Susie Tharu, "The Impossible Subject: Caste and Desire in the Scene of the Family," in Rajeswari Sunder Rajan, ed., *Signposts: Gender Issues in Post-Independence India* (New Delhi: Kali for Women, 1999), pp. 187–203.

97. Ann Stoler and Karen Strassler, "Castings for the Colonial: Memory Work in 'New Order' Java," *Comparative Studies in Society and History* (2000): 11.

98. For a discussion of the postcolonial bildungsroman in the Caribbean see Maria H. Lima, "Decolonizing Genre: Caribbean Women Writers and the Bildungsroman" (Ph.D. diss., University of Maryland, College Park, 1993).

99. Desai, introduction to *Phoenix Fled*, p. xx.

100. Bondi, "An Image," p. 12.

101. Mary Louise Pratt, "The Short Story: The Long and the Short of It," in Charles May, ed., *The New Short Story Theories* (Athens: Ohio University Press, 1994), pp. 91–113.

102. Bondi, "An Image," p. 13.

103. Ibid., p. 189.

104. Many years later, recalling how specific servants prompted specific stories, Hosain told Nilufer Bharucha a revealing anecdote. "'The Street of the Moon' is based on several people I knew. In my father-in-law's house there was an old cook like Kalloo, who had a much younger wife. I knew a woman like his young wife. She didn't know that she was a model for my character. Whenever I met her I laughed to myself that she didn't know how she ended up in my story— in the prostitutes' quarter!" Bharucha, "I Am a Universalist-Humanist," p. 20.

105. Hosain, *Sunlight* (1961), p. 83.

106. Ibid., p. 29.

107. Ibid., p. 140.

108. Ibid., p. 104.

109. Ibid., p. 105.

110. Ibid.

111. Ibid., p. 161.

112. Ibid., p. 134.

113. Ibid., p. 138.

114. See Mary Beth Tierney-Tello, *Allegories of Transgression and Transformation: Experimental Fiction by Women Writing under Dictatorship* (Albany: SUNY Press, 1996), p. 13.

115. Hosain, *Sunlight* (1961), p. 168.

116. Ibid., p. 147.

117. Ibid., p. 289.

118. Ibid., p. 230.

119. Ibid., pp. 222–23.

120. Ibid., p. 267.

121. Susan Stewart, *On Longing: Narratives of the Miniature, the Gigantic, the Souvenir, the Collection* (Baltimore: Johns Hopkins University Press, 1984).

122. Hosain, *Sunlight* (1961), p. 270.

123. Ibid., p. 267.

124. Ibid.

125. Ibid., p. 286.

126. Ibid., p. 272.

127. Ibid., p. 273.

128. Here, what Patrick Colm Hogan calls Aunt Abida's "class-based traditionalism" might be applied to Saira as well. See Hogan, *Colonialism and Cultural Identity*, p. 287.

129. Hosain, *Sunlight*, p. 284.

130. Ibid., p. 289.

131. Salman Rushdie, "Letter from India: A Dream of Glorious Return," *New Yorker*, June 19 and 26, 2000, pp. 95–112.

132. See Eric Santner, *Stranded Objects: Mourning, Memory and Film in Postwar Germany* (Ithaca, N.Y.: Cornell University Press, 1991).

133. Hosain, *Sunlight* (1961), p. 279.

134. Ibid., p. 313.

135. Ibid., p. 304.

136. Theodor Adorno, "Refuge for the Homeless," in *Minima Moralis: Reflections from Damaged Life* (Surrey, England: Gresham Press, 1974), p. 38. For a contemporary, postcolonial echo of this dilemma see Dipesh Chakrabarty, "*Adda*, Calcutta: Dwelling in Modernity," *Public Culture* 11, 1 (1999): 109.

137. Adorno, "Refuge," p. 39.

138. Vinay Lal, "Genocide, Barbaric Others, and the Violence of Categories: A Response to Omar Bartov," *American Historical Review* 103, 4 (October 1998): 1187–90. Radha Kumar is interested in making similar connections in her book *Divide and Fall? Bosnia in the Annals of Partition* (London: Verso, 1997). While it is not very common in fiction, references to partition as a holocaust do arise, at least in translation; see for example Rajinder Singh Bedi, "Lajwanti," in Cowasjee and Duggal, *Orphans*, p. 67.

139. Graff, introduction to *Lucknow*, p. 1.

140. This is Desai writing about *Phoenix Fled* in her introduction to it, p. xxi.

141. Bondi, "An Image," pp. 3 and 12.

142. Bharucha, "I Am a Universalist-Humanist," pp. 20–21.

143. Alice Walker, "Reassurance," in *Revolutionary Petunias and Other Poems* (New York: Harcourt Brace Jovanovich, 1973), p. 33.

Epilogue

1. Francis Fukuyama, *The End of History and the Last Man* (New York: Avon Books, 1993).

2. Tony Judt, "The End of History," *New Republic,* May 14, 2001, pp. 36–41.

3. The quotation is from Robin Winks, ed., *The Oxford History of the British Empire,* vol. 5, *Historiography* (Oxford: Oxford University Press, 1999), p. 659. For a more temperate assessment of the state of the archive in the South Asian context see Tony Ballantyne, "Archive, Discipline, State: Power and Knowledge in South Asian Historiography," *New Zealand Journal of Asian Studies* 3, 1 (June 2001): 87–105.

4. See Joyce Appleby, Lynn Hunt, and Margaret Jacob, *Telling the Truth about History* (New York: Norton, 1994), and Lynn Hunt, "Where Have All the Theories Gone?" *Perspectives* 40, 3 (March 2002): 5–7.

5. See Susan Geiger, "Life Histories of Women in Nationalist Struggle in Tanzania: Lessons Learned" (Dar es Salaam: Tanzania Gender Networking Program, 1996), p. 4, and *TANU Women: Gender and Culture in the Making of Tanganyikan Nationalism, 1955–1965* (Portsmouth, N.H.: Heinemann, 1997).

6. Charles Villa-Vicencio, "On the Limitations of Academic History: The Quest for Truth Demands Both More and Less," in Wilmot James and Linda Van de Vijver, eds., *After the TRC: Reflections on Truth and Reconciliation in South Africa* (Cape Town: David Philip, 2000; Athens, Ohio: Ohio University Press, 2001), pp. 21–31.

7. Jacques Derrida, *Archive Fever* (Chicago: University of Chicago Press, 1995).

8. Paul J. Voss and Marta L. Werner, "Toward a Poetics of the Archive," *Studies in the Literary Imagination* (special issue: "The Poetics of the Archive"), 32, 1 (spring 1999): i.

9. How grateful I am to Herman Bennett and Madhavi Kale for reminding me, separately and together, of this crucial point. As Sheldon Pollock has remarked, history "hardly seems meaningful any longer in a world where last week's news seems to be history enough." "Cosmopolitan and Vernacular in History," *Public Culture* 12, 3 (2000): 597.

10. For discussions of this in the context of British and British imperial history see Madhavi Kale, *Fragments of Empire: Capital, Slavery, and Indian Indentured Labor Migration in the British Caribbean* (Philadelphia: University of Pennsylvania Press, 1999); Antoinette Burton, "Who Needs the Nation? Interrogating 'British' History," *Journal of Historical Sociology* 10, 3 (1997): 227–48; and Burton, "Thinking beyond the Boundaries: Empire, Feminism and the Domains of History," *Social History* 26, 1 (2001): 60–71.

11. This is in part what Roger Chartier refers to when he references "the edge of the cliff" made visible by thinkers like Michael Foucault and Michel de Certeau. See Roger Chartier, *On the Edge of the Cliff: History, Language, and Practices* (Baltimore: Johns Hopkins University Press, 1997), and the forum "Critical Pragmatism, Language, and Cultural History: On Roger Chartier's *On the Edge of the Cliff,*" *French Historical Studies* 21, 2 (spring 1998).

12. Carolyn Steedman, "Something She Called a Fever: Michelet, Derrida, and Dust," *American Historical Review* 106, 4 (October 2001): 1159–80.

13. Florencia Mallon, "The Promise and Dilemma of Subaltern Studies: Perspectives from Latin American History," *American Historical Review* 99, 5 (December 1994): 1514.

14. Nicholas B. Dirks, "The Crimes of Colonialism: Anthropology and the

Textualization of India," in Peter Pels and Oscar Salemink, eds., *Colonial Subjects: Essays in the Practical History of Anthropology* (Ann Arbor: University of Michigan Press, 1999), p. 175. For a slightly different view see Saloni Mathur, "History and Anthropology in South Asia: Rethinking the Archive," *Annual Review of Anthropology* 29 (2000): 89-106.

15. For a detailed exposition of the history of history as an archival profession see Bonnie G. Smith, *The Gender of History: Men, Women and Historical Practice* (Cambridge, Mass.: Harvard University Press, 1998), especially chap. 4, and Rosemary Jann, "From Amateur to Professional: The Case of the Oxbridge Historians," *Journal of British Studies* 22 (1983): 122-47.

16. Michel Foucault, *The Birth of the Clinic: An Archaeology of Medical Perception* (New York: Pantheon Books, 1973), and *Discipline and Punish: The Birth of the Prison* (New York: Pantheon Books, 1977). For a useful review of the panopticon and its histories see Roy Boyne, "Post-Panopticism," *Economy and Society* 29, 2 (2000): 285-307.

17. See Jonathan Crary, *Techniques of the Observer: On Vision and Modernity in the Nineteenth Century* (Cambridge, Mass.: MIT Press, 1990).

18. John M. MacKenzie, "Edward Said and the Historians," *Nineteenth-Century Contexts* 18 (1994): 9-26.

19. See Edward Said, *Orientalism* (New York: Vintage Books, 1978); Gayatri Spivak, "The Rani of Sirmur: An Essay in Reading the Archives," *History and Theory* 24, 3 (1985): 247-72; and Dipesh Chakrabarty, "The Death of History? Historical Consciousness and the Culture of Late Capitalism," *Public Culture* 4, 2 (1992): 47-65.

20. See Winks, *The Oxford History of the British Empire*, vol. 5, especially contributions by C. A. Bayly, David Washbrook, and Anthony Hopkins. This was prefigured in the debate between O'Hanlon/Washbrook and Gyan Prakash; see Gyan Prakash, "Writing Postorientalist Histories of the Third World—Perspectives from Indian Historiography," *Comparative Studies in Society and History* (1990) 32 (2): 383-408; Rosalind O'Hanlon and David Washbrook, "After Orientalism—Culture, Criticism, and Politics in the Third World," *Comparative Studies in Society and History* 34, 1 (1992): 141-67; Gyan Prakash, "Can the Subaltern Ride—A Reply," *Comparative Studies in Society and History* 34, 1 (1992): 168-84.

21. For an especially cogent argument about the spatiality of history see Tony Ballantyne, "Aryanism and the Webs of Empire," introduction to *Orientalism and Race: Aryanism in the British Empire* (London: Macmillan, 2002).

22. Alison Light, *Forever England: Femininity, Literature and Conservatism between the Wars* (London: Routledge, 1991). I am grateful to Jed Esty for helping me see their "radically unhinged" subjectivities.

23. Joelle Bahoul, *The Architecture of Memory: A Jewish-Muslim Household in Colonial Algeria 1937-1962* (Cambridge: Cambridge University Press, 1996), p. 13.

24. This is a recurrent complaint among postcolonial critics interested in colonized women's subjectivity and/in fiction; see for example Rey Chow, *Women and Chinese Modernity: The Politics of Reading between East and West* (Minneapolis: University of Minnesota Press, 1991); Deepika Bahri, "Once More with Feeling: What Is Postcolonialism," *Ariel: A Review of International English Literature*

26, 1 (1995): 51–82; and Amal Amireh, "Framing Nawal El Saadawi: Arab Feminism in a Transnational World," *Signs* 26, 1 (2000): 215–49.

25. Kathryn J. Oberdeck, "Class, Place, and Gender: Contested Industrial and Domestic Space in Kohler, Wisconsin, USA, 1920–1960," *Gender and History* 13, 1 (April 2001): 115.

26. The phrase is David Greetham's. See his "'Who's In, Who's Out': The Cultural Poetics of Archival Exclusion," *Studies in the Literary Imagination* (special issue: "The Poetics of the Archive") 32, 1 (spring 1999): 1.

Bibliography

Unpublished Sources

Hosain, Attia. Scripts, payment receipts and correspondence, BBC Written Archives Centre, Caversham Park, Reading.

Majumdar, Janaki Agnes Penelope. 1935. "Family History." Manuscript and type-script copies held privately. To be published as *Janaki Majumdar's "Family History."* Delhi: Oxford University Press, forthcoming.

Sorabji, Cornelia. "Concerning Purdahnashins." September 1917. Typescript. MSS EUR F165, Oriental and India Office Library, London.

Published Sources

Abbas, Ackbar. *Hong Kong: Culture and the Politics of Disappearance.* Minneapolis: University of Minnesota Press, 1997.

Adams, Annmarie. *Architecture in the Family Way: Doctors, Houses, and Women, 1870–1900.* Montreal: McGill-Queen's University Press, 1996.

Adorno, Theodor. *Minima Moralia: Reflections from a Damaged Life.* Surrey: Gresham Press, 1974.

Ahmad, Aijaz. *In Theory: Nations, Classes, Literatures.* London: Verso, 1992.

Alexander, Meena. "Outcaste Power: Ritual Displacement and Virile Maternity in Indian Women Writers." *Journal of Commonwealth Literature* 24 (1989): 12–29.

Alexander, Sally. *Becoming a Woman, and Other Essays in Nineteenth and Twentieth Century Feminist History.* New York: New York University Press, 1995.

Ali, Azra Asghar. *The Emergence of Feminism among Indian Muslim Women, 1920–1947.* London: Oxford University Press, 2000.

Amin, Shahid. *Event, Metaphor, Memory: Chauri Chaura, 1922–1992.* University of California Press, 1995.

Amin, Sonia. "Childhood and Role Models in the Andar Mahal: Muslim Women in the Private Sphere in Colonial Bengal." In Kumari Jayawardena and Malathi de Alwis, eds., *Embodied Violence: Communalising Women's Sexuality in South Asia.* London: Zed Books, 1996, pp. 71–88.

Amireh, Amal. "Framing Nawal El Saadawi: Arab Feminism in a Transnational World." *Signs* 26, 1 (2000): 215–49.

Anagol-McGinn, Padma. "The Age of Consent Act (1891) Reconsidered: Women's Perspectives and Participation in the Child-Marriage Controversy in India." *South Asia Research* 12, 2 (1992): 100–118.

Anand, Mulk Raj. "Attia Hosain: A Profile." In Attia Hosain, *Sunlight on a Broken Column*. Delhi: Gulab Vazirani for Arnold-Heinemann, 1979, pp. iii–xvi.

———. *Conversations in Bloomsbury*. London: Wildwood House, 1981.

———. "E. M. Forster: A Personal Recollection." *Journal of Commonwealth Literature* 18 (1983): 80–83.

———. "In Conversation with H. G. Wells." *Journal of Commonwealth Literature* 18 (1983): 84–90.

Appadurai, Arjun. *Modernity at Large: Cultural Dimensions of Globalization*. Minneapolis: University of Minnesota Press, 1996.

———. "Number in the Colonial Imagination." In Carol Breckenridge and Peter van der Veer, eds., *Orientalism and the Postcolonial Predicament*, pp. 314–40.

———. "The Past as a Scarce Resource." *Man* 16 (1981): 201–19.

———, ed. *The Social Life of Things: Commodities in Cultural Perspective*. Cambridge: Cambridge University Press, 1986.

Appiah, Kwame Anthony. *In My Father's House: Africa in the Philosophy of Culture*. New York: Oxford University Press, 1992.

Appleby, Joyce, Lynn Hunt, and Margaret Jacob. *Telling the Truth about History*. New York: Norton, 1994.

Askeland, Lori. "Remodeling the Model Home in *Uncle Tom's Cabin* and *Beloved*." In Michael Moon and Cathy N. Davidson, eds., *Subjects and Citizens: Nation, Race and Gender from Oroonoko to Anita Hill*. Durham, N.C.: Duke University Press, 1995, pp. 395–416.

Auslander, Leora. "The Gendering of Consumer Practices in Nineteenth-Century France." In Victoria de Grazia, ed., *The Sex of Things: Gender and Consumption in Historical Perspective*. Berkeley: University of California Press, 1996, pp. 79–112.

Azim, Firdous. *The Colonial Rise of the Novel*. London: Routledge, 1992.

Bachelard, Gaston. *The Poetics of Space* (1964). Boston: Beacon Press, 1994.

Bagchi, Jasodhara. "Europe and the Question of Modernity." *Social Scientist* 24, 7–8 (August 1996).

Bahloul, Joelle. *The Architecture of Memory: A Jewish-Muslim Household in Colonial Algeria 1937–1962* (Cambridge: Cambridge University Press, 1996).

Bahri, Deepika. "Once More with Feeling: What Is Postcolonialism?" *Ariel* 26, 1 (1995): 51–82.

Ballantyne, Tony. "Archive, Discipline, State Power and Knowledge in South Asian Historiography." *New Zealand Journal of Asian Studies* 3, 1 (June 2001): 87–105.

———. *Orientalism and Race: Aryanism in the British Empire*. London: Macmillan, 2002.

Banerjee, Sudeshna. "Spirituality and Nationalist Domesticity: Rereading the Relationship." *Calcutta Historical Journal* 19–20 (1997–98): 180–97.

Banerjee, Swapna Mitra. "Middle-Class Women and Domestics in Colonial Calcutta, 1900–1947." Ph.D. diss., Temple University, 1998.

Bannerjee, Nirmala. "Whatever Happened to the Dreams of Modernity? The Nehruvian Era and Women's Position." *Economic and Political Weekly*, April 25, 1998, WS 2–7.

Bannerji, Himani. "Attired in Virtue: The Discourse on Shame (*Lajja*) and Clothing of the *Bhadramahila* in Colonial Bengal." In Bharati Ray, ed., *From the Seams of History*. Delhi: Oxford University Press, 1995, pp. 67–106.

———. "Fashioning a Self: Gender, Class and Moral Education for and by Women in Colonial Bengal." In Kate Rousmanière et al., eds., *Discipline, Moral Regulation and Schooling: A Social History*. New York: Garland, 1997, pp. 183–218.

Bannerji, Himani, Shahrzad Mojab and Judith Whitehead, eds. *Of Property and Propriety: The Role of Gender and Class in Imperialism and Nationalism*. University of Toronto Press, 2001.

Baron, Ava, and Susan E. Klepp. "'If I Didn't Have My Sewing Machine . . .' Women and Sewing Machine Technology." In Joan M. Jensen and Sue Davidson, eds., *A Needle, a Bobbin, a Strike: Women Needleworkers in America*. Philadelphia: Temple University Press, 1984.

Bayly, C. A. *Empire and Information: Intelligence Gathering and Social Communication in India, 1780–1870*. Cambridge: Cambridge University Press, 1999.

Bedford, Ian. "Intizar Husain's 'An Unwritten Epic' and the 'Matter of Pakistan.'" *Journal of Commonwealth Literature* 28 (1993): 16–32.

Bell, Vikki. "Historical Memory, Global Movement and Violence: Paul Gilroy and Arjun Appadurai in Conversation." *Theory, Culture and Society* 16, 2 (1999).

Bhabha, Homi K. "Of Mimicry and Man: The Ambivalence of Colonial Discourse." In *The Location of Culture*. New York: Routledge, 1994, pp. 85–92.

———. "The World in the Home." In Anne McClintock, Aamir Mufti, and Ella Shoat, eds., *Dangerous Liaisons: Gender, Nation and Postcolonial Perspectives*. Minneapolis: University of Minnesota Press, 1997, pp. 445–55.

———, ed. *Nation and Narration*. New York: Routledge, 1990.

Bhandare, Shaila. *Memory in Indian Epistemology, Its Nature and Status*. Delhi: Indian Books Centre, 1993.

Bharucha, Nilufer E. "I Am a Universalist-Humanist" (interview with Attia Hosain). *Biblio* (July–August 1998): 20–21.

Bhatia, Gautam. *Silent Spaces: And Other Stories of Architecture*. New Delhi: Penguin, 1994.

Birdwell-Pheasant, Donna, and Denise Lawrence-Zúñiga, eds. *House Life: Space, Place and Family in Europe*. New York: Berg, 1999.

Bondi, Laura. "An Image of India by an Indian Woman: Attia Hosain's Life and Fiction." M.A. thesis, Facolta di Lingue e Letterature Straniere, Universita Degli Stufio Venezia.

Bonnell, Victoria E., and Lynn Hunt, eds. *Beyond the Cultural Turn*. Berkeley: University of California Press, 1999.

Bonnerjee, Sadhona, and Janaki Majumdar. *W. C. Bonnerjee and Hemangini*. Calcutta: New Sakti Press.

Borthwick, Meredith. *The Changing Role of Women in Bengal, 1849–1905*. Princeton, N.J.: Princeton University Press, 1984.

Bose, Purnima. "Engendering the Armed Struggle: Women, Writing, and the Bengali Terrorist Movement." In Thomas Foster, Carol Siegel, and Ellen E. Berry, eds., *Bodies of Writing, Bodies in Performance*. New York University Press, 1996, pp. 145–83.

Boyne, Roy. "Post-Panopticism." *Economy and Society* 29, 2 (2000): 285–307.

Brown, Judith. "The Mahatma in Old Age: Gandhi's Role in Indian Political Life, 1935–1942." In Richard Sisson and Stanley Wolpert, eds., *Congress and Indian Nationalism: The Pre-Independence Phase*, pp. 271–304.

Burton, Antoinette. *At the Heart of the Empire: Indians and the Colonial Encounter in Late-Victorian Britain.* Berkeley: University of California Press, 1998.

———. *Burdens of History: British Feminists, Indian Women, and Imperial Culture, 1865–1915.* Chapel Hill: University of North Carolina Press, 1994.

———. "From 'Child-Bride' to 'Hindoo Lady': Rukhmabai and the Debate about Sexual Respectability in Imperial Britain." *American Historical Review* 104, 4 (October 1998): 1119–46.

———. "Thinking beyond the Boundaries: Empire, Feminism and the Domains of History." *Social History* 26, 1 (2001): 60–71.

———. "Who Needs the Nation? Interrogating 'British' History." *Journal of Historical Sociology* 10, 3 (1997): 227–48.

Butalia, Urvashi. *The Other Side of Silence: Voices from the Partition of India.* Delhi: Oxford University Press, 1998.

Canclini, Nestor Garcia. *Hybrid Cultures: Strategies for Entering and Leaving Modernity.* Minneapolis: University of Minnesota Press, 1995.

Candy, Catherine. "The Inscrutable Irish-Indian Feminist Management of Anglo-American Hegemony." *Journal of Colonialism and Colonial History* 2, 1 (spring 2001). Available at: http://muse.jhu.edu/jcch.

Carruthers, Mary J. *The Book of Memory: A Study of Memory in Medieval Culture.* Cambridge: Cambridge University Press, 1990.

Chakrabarty, Dipesh. "The Death of History? Historical Consciousness and the Culture of Late Capitalism." *Public Culture* 4, 2 (1992): 47–65.

———. "The Difference-Deferral of (A) Colonial Modernity: Public Debates on Domesticity in British Bengal." *History Workshop Journal* 36 (1993): 1–33.

———. *Provincializing Europe: Postcolonial Thought and Historical Difference.* Princeton, N.J.: Princeton University Press, 2000.

———. *Rethinking Working-Class History.* Princeton, N.J.: Princeton University Press, 1989.

Chakravarti, Uma. *Rewriting History: The Life and Times of Pandita Ramabai.* Delhi: Kali for Women, 1998.

Chartier, Roger. *On the Edge of the Cliff: History, Language, and Practices.* Baltimore: Johns Hopkins University Press, 1997.

———. "The World as Representation" (originally published 1989). In Jacques Revel and Lynn Hunt, eds., *Histories: French Constructions of the Past.* New York: New Press, 1995, pp. 544–58.

Chatterjee, Partha. "The Nationalist Resolution of the Woman Question." In Kumkum Sangari and Sudesh Vaid, eds., *Recasting Women: Essays in Colonial History.* Delhi: Kali for Women, 1989, pp. 233–53.

Chatterjee, Romola. *Courtyards of My Childhood: A Memoir.* New Delhi: Kali for Women, 1996.

Chattopadhyay, Kamal. *Inner Recesses, Outer Spaces: Memoirs.* New Delhi: Navrange, 1988.

Chaudhuri, Amit. "Beyond the Language of the Raj." *Times Literary Supplement,* August 8, 1997, pp. 17–18.

Chaudhuri, Nirad C. *The Autobiography of an Unknown Indian.* Bombay: Jaico, 1971.

Chaudhuri, Nupur. "Nationalism and Feminism in the Writings of Santa Devi and Sita Devi." In Bishnupriya Ghosh and Brinda Bose, eds., *Interventions: Feminist Dialogues on Third World Women's Literature and Film*. New York: Garland, 1997.

Chow, Rey. *Women and Chinese Modernity: The Politics of Reading between East and West*. Minneapolis: University of Minnesota Press, 1991.

Chowdhury, Indira. *The Frail Hero and Virile History: Gender and the Politics of Culture in Colonial Bengal*. Delhi: Oxford University Press, 1998.

Chugtai, Ismat. *The Crooked Line*. New Delhi: Kali for Women, 1995.

———. *Lifting the Veil: Selected Writings*. Selected and translated by M. Asaduddin. New Delhi: Penguin Books, 2001.

———. *The Quilt and Other Stories*. New Delhi: Kali for Women, 1990.

Clifford, James. "On Ethnographic Allegory." In James Clifford and George E. Marcus, eds., *Writing Culture: The Poetics and Politics of Ethnography*. Berkeley: University of California Press, 1986, pp. 98–121.

Coffey, John. "Democracy and Popular Religion: Moody and Sankey's Mission to Britain, 1873–75." In Eugenio Biagini, ed., *Citizenship and Community: Liberals, Radicals and Collective Identities in the British Isles, 1865–1931*. Cambridge: Cambridge University Press.

Cohn, Bernard S. *Colonialism and Its Forms of Knowledge*. Princeton, N.J.: Princeton University Press, 1996.

Cole, Jennifer. *Forget Colonialism? Sacrifice and the Art of Memory in Madagascar*. Berkeley: University of California Press, 2001.

Colomina, Béatriz. "Excerpts from 'The Split Wall': Domestic Voyeurism." In Jane Rendell, Barbara Penner, and Iain Borden, *Gender, Space, Architecture*. London: Routledge, 2000, pp. 314–20.

Coppola, Carlo, ed. "Marxist Influences in South Asian Literatures." Pamphlet. East Lansing, Mich., 1974.

Coundoriotis, Eleni. *Claiming History: Colonialism, Ethnography and the Novel*. New York: Columbia University Press, 1999.

Cousins, Margaret. *The Awakening of Asian Womanhood*. Madras: Ganesh, 1922.

Cowasjee, Saros, and K. S. Duggal, eds. *Orphans of the Storm: Stories on the Partition of India*. New Delhi: UBS, 1995.

Crary, Jonathan. *Techniques of the Observer: On Vision and Modernity in the Nineteenth Century*. Cambridge, Mass.: MIT Press, 1990.

Crosby, Christina. *The Ends of History: Victorians and the "Woman Question."* New York: Routledge, 1991.

Dasgupta, Keya. "A City Away from Home: The Mapping of Calcutta." In Partha Chatterjee, ed., *Texts of Power: Emerging Disciplines in Colonial Bengal*. Minneapolis: University of Minnesota Press, 1995, pp. 145–66.

Datta, Pradip Kumar. *Carving Blocks: Communal Ideology in Early Twentieth-Century Bengal*. Delhi: Oxford University Press, 1999.

Davidoff, Leonore, and Catherine Hall, *Family Fortunes*. Chicago: University of Chicago Press, 1987.

Davis, Natalie Zemon. *Fiction in the Archives: Pardon Tales and Their Tellers in Sixteenth-Century France*. Palo Alto, Calif.: Stanford University Press, 1987.

Derrida, Jacques. *Archive Fever*. Chicago: University of Chicago Press, 1995.

Desai, Anita. Introduction to *Phoenix Fled and Other Stories*, by Attia Hosain. New Delhi: Penguin, 1989, pp. vii–xxi.

————. Introduction to *Sunlight on a Broken Column*, by Attia Hosain. New Delhi: Penguin, 1988, pp. v–xv.

Devereux, Cecily. "A Process of Being Re-Anglicized: 'Colonial' Houses and 'Post-colonial' Fiction." On-line; available at: http://www.arts.uwo.ca/~andrewf/anzsc/anzsc12/devereux12.htm.

Devi, Jyotirmoyee. *The River Churning: A Partition Novel.* New Delhi: Kali for Women, 1995.

Devji, Faisal. "Gender and the Politics of Space: The Movement for Women's Reform, 1857–1900." In Zoya Hasan, ed., *Forging Identities: Gender, Communities and the State.* New Delhi: Kali for Women, 1994.

Devy, G. N. "Indian Literature in English Translation: An Introduction." *Journal of Commonwealth Literature* 28 (1993): 123–38.

Dhareshwar, Vivek. "Caste and the Secular Self." *Journal of Arts and Ideas* 25–26 (December 1993): 115–26.

Dimmitt, Marjorie. *Isabella Thoburn College: A Record from Its Beginnings to Its Diamond Jubilee, 1961.*

Dirks, Nicholas B. "Colonial Histories and Native Informants: Biography of an Archive." In Carol Breckenridge and Peter van der Veer, eds., *Orientalism and the Postcolonial Predicament: Perspectives on South Asia.* Philadelphia: University of Pennsylvania Press, 1993, pp. 279–313.

————. "The Crimes of Colonialism: Anthropology and the Textualization of India." In Peter Pels and Oscar Salemink, eds., *Colonial Subjects: Essays in the Practical History of Anthropology.* Ann Arbor: University of Michigan Press, 1999, pp. 153–79.

————. "History as a Sign of the Modern." *Public Culture* 2, 2 (spring 1990): 25–32.

————. "*The Home and the World*: The Invention of Modernity in Colonial India." In Robert A. Rosenstone, ed., *Revisioning History: Film and the Construction of a New Past.* Princeton, N.J.: Princeton University Press, 1995, pp. 44–63.

Donald, Moira. "Tranquil Havens? Critiquing the Idea of Home as the Middle-Class Sanctuary." In Inga Bryden and Janet Floyd, eds., *Domestic Space: Reading the Nineteenth-Century Interior.* Manchester, England: Manchester University Press, 1999, pp. 103–20.

Dongerkery, Kamala S. *On the Wings of Time (An Autobiography).* Bombay: Bharatiya Vidya Bhavan, 1968.

Duruz, Jean. "Suburban Houses Revisited." In Kate Darian-Smith and Paula Hamilton, eds., *Memory and History in Twentieth-Century Australia.* Melbourne: Oxford University Press, 1994, pp. 173–89.

Dutt (Joshi), Kalpana. *Chittagong Armoury Raiders Reminiscences.* New Delhi: People's Publishing House, 1979.

Dutt, Paramananda, ed. *Memoirs of Motilal Ghose.* Calcutta: Amrita Bazar Patrika Office, 1935.

Dutton, Ralph. *The English Interior, 1500 to 1900.* London: B. T. Batsford, 1954.

Eagleton, Terry. *Criticism and Ideology.* London: Prometheus Books, 1978.

Echevarría, Roberto Gonzalez. *Myth and Archive: A Theory of Latin American Narrative.* Cambridge: Cambridge University Press, 1990.

Edensor, Tim. *Tourists at the Taj: Performance and Meaning as a Symbolic Site.* London: Routledge, 1998.

Engels, Dagmar. *Beyond Purdah? Women in Bengal, 1890–1939.* Delhi: Oxford University Press, 1996.

Felski, Rita. *The Gender.of Modernity*. Cambridge, Mass.: Harvard University Press, 1995.

Forbes, Geraldine. "Goddesses or Rebels? The Women Revolutionaries of Bengal." *Oracle* 11, 2 (April 1980): 1–15.

———. *The New Cambridge History of India: Women in Modern India*. Cambridge: Cambridge University Press, 1996.

———. "The Politics of Respectability: Indian Women and the Indian National Congress." In D. A. Low, ed., *The Indian National Congress: Centenary Hindsights*, Delhi: Oxford University Press, 1988, pp. 54–97.

———, ed. *Memoirs of an Indian Woman* by Shudha Mazumdar. New York: Sharpe, 1989.

Forbes, Geraldine, and Tapan Raychaudhuri, eds. *From Child Widow to Lady Doctor: The Memoirs of Dr. Haimabati Sen*. New Delhi: Roli Books, 2000.

Foucault, Michel. *The Birth of the Clinic; An Archaeology of Medical Perception*. New York Pantheon Books. 1973.

———. *Discipline and Punish: The Birth of the Prison*. New York: Pantheon Books, 1977.

Fox, Richard G. "Gandhi and Feminized Nationalism in India." In Brackette Williams, ed., *Women out of Place: The Gender of Agency and the Race of Nationality*. New York: Routledge, 1996, pp. 37–49.

Fraiman, Susan. *Unbecoming Women: British Women Writers and the Novel of Development*. New York: Columbia University Press, 1993.

Frame, Janet. *An Autobiography*. New York: Braziller, 1991.

Friedman, Susan Stanford. *Mappings*. Princeton, N.J.: Princeton University Press, 1998.

Fritzsche, Peter. "The Case of Modern Memory." *Journal of Modern History* 73 (March 2001): 87–117.

Fukuyama, Francis. *The End of History and the Last Man*. New York: Avon Books, 1993.

Gambrell, Alice. *Women Intellectuals, Modernism, and Difference: Transatlantic Culture, 1919–1945*. Cambridge: Cambridge University Press, 1997.

Geiger, Susan. "Life Histories of Women in Nationalist Struggle in Tanzania: Lessons Learned." Dar Es Salaam: Tanzania Gender Networking Program, 1996.

———. *TANU Women: Gender and Culture in the Making of Tanganyikan Nationalism, 1955–1965*. Portsmouth, N.H.: Heinemann, 1997.

George, Rosemary Marangoly, ed. *Burning Down the House: Recycling Domesticity*. Boulder, Colo.: Westview Press, 1998.

———. *The Politics of Home: Postcolonial Relocations and Twentieth-Century Fiction*. Cambridge: Cambridge University Press, 1996.

Ghosh, Srabashi. "Changes in Bengali Social Life as Recorded in Autobiographies by Women." *Economic and Political Weekly* 21, 43 (October 25, 1986): WS 88–96.

Glushkova, Irina, and Anne Feldhaus, eds. *House and Home in Maharashtra*. Delhi: Oxford University Press, 1998.

Greetham, David. "'Who's In, Who's Out': The Cultural Poetics of Archival Exclusion." *Studies in the Literary Imagination* 32, 1 (spring 1999): 1–28.

Grewal, Inderpal. *Home and Harem: Nation, Gender, Empire and the Cultures of Travel*. Durham, N.C.: Duke University Press, 1996.

Grimshaw, Anna. "The Eye in the Door: Anthropology, Film, and the Exploration of Interior Space." In Marcus Banks and Howard Murphy, eds., *Rethinking Visual Anthropology*. New Haven, Conn.: Yale University Press, 1997, pp. 36–52.

Guha, Ranajit. "The Migrant's Time." *Postcolonial Studies* 1, 2 (1998): 155–60.

Habibullah, Attia. "Seclusion of Women." In Shyam Kumari Nehru, ed., *Our Cause: A Symposium by Indian Women* (Allahabad: Kitabistan, n.d. [1952?]).

Hage, Ghassan. "The Spatial Imaginary of National Practices: Dwelling-Domesticating/Being-Exterminating." *Environment and Planning D: Society and Space* 14 (1996): 463–485.

Hameed, Syeda S., and Sughra Mehdi, eds. *Parwaaz: A Selection of Urdu Short Stories by Women*. New Delhi: Kali for Women, 1996.

Hamilton, Paula. "The Knife Edge: Debates about Memory and History." In Kate Darian-Smith and Paula Hamilton, eds., *Memory and History in Twentieth-Century Australia*. Melbourne: Oxford University Press, 1994, pp. 9–32.

Hancock, Mary. "Gendering the Modern: Women and Home Science in British India." In Antoinette Burton, ed., *Gender, Sexuality and Colonial Modernities*. London: Routledge, 1999, pp. 148–60.

———. *Womanhood in the Making: Domestic Ritual and Public Culture in Urban South India*. Boulder, Colo.: Westview Press, 1999.

Harish, Ranjana. *Indian Women's Autobiographies*. New Delhi: Arnold, 1993.

Hartman, Saidiya V. *Scenes of Subjection: Terror, Slavery, and Self-Making in Nineteenth-Century America*. New York: Oxford University Press, 1997.

Hasan, Mushirul. *Legacy of a Divided Nation: India's Muslims Since Independence*. Boulder, Colo.: Westview Press, 1997.

———, ed. *India Partitioned: The Other Face of Freedom*, 2 vols. New Delhi: Roli Books, 1995.

———, ed. *Inventing Boundaries: Gender, Politics and the Partition of India*. New Delhi: Oxford University Press, 2000.

Hasan, Mushirul, and M. Assaduddin, eds. *Image and Representation: Stories of Muslim Lives in India*. New Delhi: Oxford University Press, 2000.

Hayford, Charles W. "The Storm over the Peasant: Orientalism and Rhetoric in Constructing China." In Jeffrey Cox and Sheldon Stromquist, eds., *Contesting the Master Narrative: Essays in Social History*. Iowa City: University of Iowa Press, 1998, pp. 156–69.

Heehs, Peter. "Shaped Like Themselves." Review of *Creating Histories: Oral Narratives and the Politics of History-Making*, by Wendry Singer. *History and Theory* 39, 3 (2000). 417–40.

Hirsch, Marianne. "The Novel of Formation as Genre: Between Great Expectations and Lost Illusions." *Genre* 12 (fall 1979): 293–311.

Ho Tai, Hue-Tam. "Remembered Realms: Pierre Nora and French National Memory." *American Historical Review* 106, 3 (June 2001): 906–22.

Hogan, Patrick Colm. *Colonialism and Cultural Identity: Crises of Tradition in the Anglophone Literatures of India, Africa and the Caribbean*. Albany: SUNY Press, 2000.

Hosain, Attia. *Phoenix Fled and Other Stories*. New Delhi: Penguin, 1989.

———. "Seclusion of Women." In Shyam Kumari Nehru, ed., *Our Cause: A Symposium by Indian Women*. Allahabad: Kitabistan, n.d. [1952?].

———. *Sunlight on a Broken Column*. New Delhi: Penguin, 1988.

————. *Sunlight on a Broken Column*. Delhi: Gulab Vazirani for Arnold-Heinemann, 1979.

————. *Sunlight on a Broken Column*. London: Chatto and Windus, 1961.

Howell, Martha, and Walter Prevenier. *From Reliable Sources: An Introduction to Historical Methods*. Ithaca, N.Y.: Cornell University Press, 2001.

Hurley, Siobhan. "Out of India: The Journeys of the Begum of Bhopal, 1901–1930." *Women's Studies International Forum* 21, 3 (1998): 263–76.

Hussyen, Andreas. *After the Great Divide: Modernism, Mass Culture, Postmodernism*. Bloomington: Indiana University Press, 1986.

Jain, Jasbir. *Feminizing Political Discourse: Women and the Novel in India, 1857–1905*. Jaipur: Rawat, 1997.

Jalal, Ayesha. "Secularists, Subalterns and the Stigma of 'Communalism': Partition Historiography Revisited." *Indian Economic and Social History Review* 33, 1 (January–March 1996): 93–104.

Jameson, Frederic. "Third-World Literature in the Era of Multinational Capitalism." *Social Text* 15 (fall 1986): 65–88.

JanMohammed, Abdul. "Worldliness-without-World, Homelessness-as-Home: Toward a Definition of the Specular Border Intellectual." In Michael Sprinker, ed., *Edward Said: A Critical Reader*. Cambridge, Mass: Blackwell, 1992, pp. 96–120.

Jann, Rosemary. "From Amateur to Professional: The Case of the Oxbridge Historians." *Journal of British Studies* 22 (1983): 122–47.

Joshi, Sanjay. *Fractured Modernity: Making of a Middle Class in Colonial North India*. New Delhi: Oxford University Press, 2001.

Judt, Tony. "The End of History." *New Republic*, May 14, 2001, pp. 36–41.

Llewellyn-Jones, Rosie. "Lucknow, City of Dreams." In Violette Graff, ed., *Lucknow: Memories of a City*. Delhi: Oxford University Press, 1997, pp. 49–66.

Kale, Madhavi. *Fragments of Empire: Capital, Slavery, and Indian Indentured Labor Migration in the British Caribbean*. Philadelphia: University of Pennsylvania Press, 1999.

Karlekar, Malavika. *Voices from Within: Early Personal Narratives of Bengali Women*. Delhi: Oxford University Press, 1993.

Kapur, Geeta. "Body as Gesture: Indian Women Artists at Work." In Vidya Dehejia, ed., *Representing the Body: Gender Issues in Indian Art*. New Delhi: Kali for Women, 1997, pp. 66–97.

Kaul, Suvir, ed. *The Partitions of Memory: The Afterlife of the Division of India*. Delhi: Permanent Black, 2001.

————. *Poems of Nation, Anthems of Empire: English Verse in the Long Eighteenth Century*. Charlottesville: University Press of Virginia, 2000.

Kingston, Maxine Hong. *The Woman Warrior*. New York: Knopf, 1976.

Kishwar, Madhu. "Gandhi on Women." *Race and Class* 28, 1 (1986): 43–61.

Kosambi, Meera. "Anandibai Joshi: Retrieving a Fragmented Feminist Image." *Economic and Political Weekly* 31, 49 (December 7, 1996): 3189–97.

————. "The Home as Social Universe: Women's Personal Narratives in Nineteenth-Century Maharashtra." In Irina Glushkova and Anne Feldhaus, eds., *House and Home in Maharashtra*. Delhi: Oxford University Press, 1998, pp. 82–101.

————. "The Meeting of the Twain: The Cultural Confrontation of Three

Women in Nineteenth-Century Maharashtra." *Indian Journal of Gender Studies* 1, 1 (1994): 1-22.

———, ed. *Pandita Ramabai through Her Own Words—Selected Works*. Delhi: Oxford University Press, 2000.

Koshy, Susan. "Mother-Country and Fatherland: Re-membering the Nation in Sara Suleri's *Meatless Days*." In Bishnupriya and Brinda Bose, eds., *Interventions: Feminist Dialogues on Third World Women's Literature and Film*. New York: Garland, 1997, pp. 45–61.

Krishnaswamy, N., and Archana S. Burde, eds., *The Politics of Indians' English: Linguistic Colonialism and the Expanding English Empire*. Delhi: Oxford University Press, 1998.

Kristeva, Julia. "Women's Time." In Toril Moi, ed., *The Kristeva Reader*. New York: Columbia University Press, 1986, pp. 187–213.

Kumar, Krishnan. "Home: The Promise and Predicament of Private Life at the End of the Twentieth Century." In Jeff Weintraub and Krishnan Kumar, eds., *Public and Private in Thought and Practice: Perspectives on a Grand Dichotomy*. Chicago: University of Chicago Press, 1997, pp. 204–35.

Kumar, Radha. *Divide and Fall? Bosnia in the Annals of Partition*. London: Verso, 1997.

———. *The History of Doing*. London: Verso, 1994.

Kumar, Sukrita Paul and Sadique, eds. *Ismat: Her Life and Times*. New Delhi: Katha, 2000.

Lal, Vinay. "Genocide, Barbaric Others, and the Violence of Categories: A Response to Omar Bartov." *American Historical Review* 103, 4 (October 1998): 1187–90.

Lateef, Shahida. *Muslim Women in India: Political and Private Realities*. New Delhi: Kali for Women, 1990.

Lee, Leo Ou-fan. *Shanghai Modern: The Flowering of a New Urban Culture in China, 1930–1945*. Cambridge, Mass.: Harvard University Press, 1999.

Lessard, Suzannah. *The Architect of Desire: Beauty and Danger in the Stanford White Family*. New York: Dial Press, 1996.

Levine, Philippa. *The Amateur and the Professional*. Cambridge: Cambridge University Press, 1986.

Light, Alison. *Forever England: Femininity, Literature and Conservatism between the Wars*. London: Routledge, 1991.

Lima, Maria H. "Decolonizing Genre: Caribbean Women Writers and the Bildungsroman." Ph.D. diss., University of Maryland, College Park, 1993.

Lloyd, David. *Ireland after History*. Notre Dame: Field Day, 1999.

Lokugé, Chandani, ed. *India Calling: The Memories of Cornelia Sorabji, India's First Woman Barrister*. Delhi: Oxford University Press, 2001.

Loomba, Ania. *Colonialism/Postcolonialism*. Routledge, 1998.

Looser, Devoney. *British Women Writers and the Writing of History, 1670–1820*. Baltimore: Johns Hopkins University Press, 2000.

Lukács, Georg. *The Historical Novel*. London: Merlin Press, 1962.

Lynd, Alice, and Staughton, eds. *Rank and File: Personal Histories by Working-Class Organizers*. Boston: Beacon Press, 1973.

Lyotard, Jean François. "The Sign of History." In Derek Attridge, Geoff Bennington, and Robert Young, eds., *Post-structuralism and the Question of History*. Cambridge: Cambridge University Press, 1987, pp. 162–80.

MacKenzie, John. "Edward Said and the Historians." *Nineteenth-Century Contexts* 18 (1994): 9–26.

Mahmud, Shabana. "*Angare* and the Founding of the Progressive Writers' Association." *Modern Asian Studies* 30, 2 (1996): 447–67.

Majumdar, Janaki. *Pramila: A Memoir.* Privately printed, 1974.

Makereti [Maggie Papakura]. *The Old-Time Maori.* Auckland: New Women's Press, 1986.

Mallon, Florencia. "The Promise and Dilemma of Subaltern Studies: Perspectives from Latin American History." *American Historical Review* 99, 5 (December 1994): 1491–1515.

Mandal, Tirtha. *Women Revolutionaries of Bengal, 1905–1939.* Calcutta: Minerva, 1991.

Mani, Lata. *Contentious Traditions: The Debate on Sati in Colonial India.* Berkeley: University of California Press, 1998.

Mann, Susan. *Precious Records: Women in China's Long Eighteenth Century.* Palo Alto, Calif.: Stanford University Press, 1997.

Mathur, Saloni. "History and Anthropology in South Asia: Rethinking the Archive." *Annual Review of Anthropology* 29 (2000): 89–106.

Maushart, Susan. *Sort of a Place Like Home: Remembering the Moore River Native Settlement.* N.p.: Freemantle Arts Center Press, 1993.

Mayaram, Shail. *Resisting Regimes: Myths, Memory and the Shaping of a Muslim Identity.* Delhi: Oxford University Press, 1997.

Mazumdar, Shudha. *Memoirs of an Indian Woman.* Edited with an introduction by Geraldine Forbes. New York: Sharpe, 1989.

Mbembe, Achille, and Janet Roitman. "Figures of the Subject in Times of Crisis." In Patricia Yaeger, ed., *The Geography of Identity.* Ann Arbor: University of Michigan Press, 1996, pp. 153–86.

McClintock, Anne. "Family Feuds: Gender, Nationalism and the Family." *Feminist Review* (1993) 44: 61–80.

McLane, John. "The Early Congress, Hindu Populism, and the Wider Society." In Richard Sisson and Stanley Wolpert, eds., *Congress and Indian Nationalism: The Pre-Independence Phase.* Berkeley: University of California Press, 1988, pp. 47–61.

Mehta, Rama. *Inside the Haveli.* New Delhi: Arnold-Heinemann, 1977.

Melosh, Barbara. "Historical Memory in Fiction: The Civil Rights Movement in Three Novels." *Radical History Review* 40 (1988): 64–76.

Menon, Ritu, and Kamla Bhasin. *Borders and Boundaries: Women in India's Partition.* New Brunswick, N.J.: Rutgers University Press, 1998.

Metcalf, Barbara D. "Reading and Writing about Muslim Women in British India." In Zoya Hasan, ed., *Forging Identities: Gender, Communities and the State.* New Delhi: Kali for Women, 1994.

Minault, Gail. "The Extended Family as Metaphor and the Expansion of Women's Realm." In Gail Minault, ed., *The Extended Family: Women and Political Participation in India and Pakistan.* Columbia, Mo.: South Asia Books, 1981, pp. 3–18.

———. "Other Voices, Other Rooms: The View from the Zenana." In Nita Kumar, ed., *Women as Subjects: South Asian Histories.* Charlottesville: University Press of Virginia, 1994, pp. 108–24.

———. *Secluded Scholars: Women's Education and Muslim Social Reform in Colonial India.* Delhi: Oxford University Press, 1998.

————. "Sisterhood or Separatism? The All-India Muslim Ladies' Conference and the Nationalist Movement." In Gail Minault, ed., *The Extended Family: Women and Political Participation in India and Pakistan.* Delhi: Chanaka, 1981, pp. 83–108.

Minault, Gail, and David Lelyveld. "The Campaign for a Muslim University." *Modern Asian Studies* 8, 2 (1974): 145–89.

Mishra, Sudesh. "The Two Chaudhuris: Historical Witness and Pseudo-Historian." *Journal of Commonwealth Literature* 23 (1988): 7–15.

Mitchell, Sally. *Daily Life in Victorian England.* Westport, Conn.: Greenwood Press, 1996.

Mohanti, Prafula. *My Village, My Life: Portrait of an Indian Village.* New York: Praeger, 1973.

Moir, Martin. "Kaghazi Raj: Notes in the Documentary Basis of Company Rule, 1773–1858." *Indo-British Review* 21, 2 (1993): 185–92.

Morrison, Toni. *Beloved.* New York: Knopf, 1987.

————. *Playing in the Dark: Whiteness and the Literary Imagination.* New York: Vintage, 1993.

Mukherjee, Ishanee. "Women and Armed Revolution in Late Colonial Bengal: An Integrated Study of Changing Role Patterns." In Kasturi and Mazumdar, eds., *Women and Indian Nationalism.* New Delhi: Vikas, 1994, pp. 53–71.

Mukherjee, Manickal. *W. C. Bonnerjee: Snapshots from His Life and Letters.* Calcutta: Deshbandhu Book Depot, 1949.

Mukherjee, Meenakshi. *The Perishable Empire: Essays on Indian Writing in English.* New Delhi: Oxford University Press, 2000.

————. *Realism and Reality: The Novel and Indian Society.* New Delhi: Oxford University Press, 1985.

Muthesius, Hermann. *The English House.* New York: Rizzoli, 1979.

Naipaul, V. S. *A House for Mr. Biswas.* London: Harmondsworth Penguin Books, 1969.

Nair, Janaki. "Uncovering the Zenana: Visions of Indian Womanhood in Englishwomen's Writings, 1813–1940." *Journal of Women's History* 2 (spring 1990): 8–34.

Nair, P. Thankappan. "The Growth and Development of Old Calcutta." In Sukanta Chaudhuri, ed., *Calcutta: The Living City.* Vol. 1. *The Past.* Calcutta: Oxford University Press, 1990.

Nanda, Savitri Devi. *The City of Two Gateways: The Autobiography of an Indian Girl.* London: George Allen Unwin, 1950.

Narayan, Uma. *Dislocating Cultures: Identities, Traditions, and Third World Feminism.* New York: Routledge, 1997.

Nawaz, Mumtaz Shah. *The Heart Divided* (1948). Lahore: ASR, 1990.

Needham, Anuradha Dingwaney. "Multiple Forms of (National) Belonging: Attia Hosain's *Sunlight on a Broken Column.*" *Modern Fiction Studies* 39, 1 (1993): 93–112.

Nelson, Cynthia. "Biography and Women's History: On Interpreting Doria Shafik." In Nikki Keddie and Beth Baron, eds., *Women in Middle Eastern History: Shifting Boundaries in Sex and Gender.* New Haven, Conn.: Yale University Press, 1991, pp. 310–33.

Nora, Pierre. "Between Memory and History: Les Lieux de Mémoire." *Representations* 26 (spring 1989).

Oberdeck, Kathryn J. "Class, Place, and Gender: Contested Industrial and Domestic Space in Kohler, Wisconsin, USA, 1920–1960." *Gender and History* 13, 1 (April 2001): 97–137.

O'Hanlon, Rosalind, ed. *A Comparison between Men and Women: Tarabai Shinde and the Critique of Gender Relations in Colonial India.* Madras: Oxford University Press, 1994.

O'Hanlon, Rosalind, and David Washbrook. "After Orientalism: Culture, Criticism, and Politics in the Third World." *Comparative Studies in Society and History* 34, 1 (1992): 141–67.

Paisley, Fiona. *Loving Protection? Australian Feminism and Aboriginal Women's Rights 1919–1939.* Melbourne: Melbourne University Press, 2000.

Pandey, Gyanendra. "Partition and the Politics of History." In Madhusree Dutta, Flavia Agnes, and Neera Adarkar, eds., *The Nation, the State and Indian Identity.* Calcutta: Samya, 1996, pp. 1–26.

———. "The Prose of Otherness." In David Arnold and David Hardiman, eds., *Subaltern Studies 8: Essays in Honor of Ranajit Guha.* New Delhi: Oxford University Press, 1994, pp. 188–221.

———. *Remembering Partition.* Cambridge: Cambridge University Press, 2001.

Passerini, Luisa. *Fascism in Popular Memory.* Cambridge: Cambridge University Press, 1987.

Patel, Sujata. "Construction and Reconstruction of Women in Gandhi." *Economic and Political Weekly* (February 20, 1988): 377–87.

Pearlman, Mickey, ed. *A Place Called Home: Twenty Writing Women Remember.* New York: St. Martin's Press, 1996.

Pederson, Susan. "National Bodies, Unspeakable Acts: The Sexual Politics of Colonial Policy-Making." *Journal of Modern History* 63 (December 1991): 647–80.

Personal Narratives Group, eds. *Interpreting Women's Lives: Feminist Theory and Personal Narratives.* Bloomington: Indiana University Press, 1989.

Pickering, Jean, and Suzanne Kehde, eds. *Narratives of Nostalgia: Gender and Nationalism.* London: Macmillan, 1997.

Pinney, Christopher. *Camera Indica: The Social Life of Indian Photographs.* Chicago: University of Chicago Press, 1998.

Pollock, Griselda. *Vision and Difference: Femininity, Feminism and the Histories of Art.* London: Routledge, 1988.

Pollock, Sheldon. "Cosmopolitan and Vernacular in History." *Public Culture* 12, 3 (2000): 591–625.

———. "Literary History, Indian History, World History." *Social Scientist* 23, 1–2 (October–December): 112–42.

Ponzanesi, Sandra. *Paradoxes of Post-colonial Culture: Feminism and Diaspora in South Asian and Afro-Italian Women's Narratives.* University of Utrecht, 1999.

Poovey, Mary. *A History of the Modern Fact: Problems of Knowledge in the Sciences of Wealth and Society.* Chicago: University of Chicago Press, 1998.

Poulos, Steven Mark. "Feminine Sense and Sensibility: A Comparative Study of Six Modern Women Short Fiction Writers in Hindi and Urdu: Rashid Jahan, Ismat Chughtai, Qurratulain Hyder, Mannu Bhandari, Usha Priyamvada, Vijay Chauhan." Ph.D. diss., University of Chicago, 1975.

Prakash, Gyan. "Can the Subaltern Ride—A Reply." *Comparative Studies in Society and History* 34, 1 (1992): 168–84.

————. "Science between the Lines." In Shahid Amin and Dipesh Chakrabarty, eds., *Subaltern Studies 9: Writings on South Asian History and Society.* Delhi: Oxford University Press, 1996, pp. 59–82.

————. "Writing Postorientalist Histories of the Third World: Perspectives from Indian Historiography." *Comparative Studies in Society and History* 32, 2 (1990): 383–408.

Pratt, Mary Louise. "The Short Story: The Long and the Short of It." In Charles May, ed., *The New Short Story Theories.* Athens, Ohio: Ohio University Press, 1994, pp. 91–113.

Prochaska, David. "History as Literature, Literature as History: Cagayous of Algiers." *American Historical Review* 101, 3 (June 1996): 671–711.

Rajan, Gita. "(Con) Figuring Identity: Cultural Space of the Indo-British Border Intellectual." In Gisela Brinker-Gabler and Sidonie Smith, eds., *Writing New Identities: Gender, Nation, and Immigration in Contemporary Europe.* Minneapolis: University of Minnesota Press, 1997, pp. 78–99.

Rajan, Rajeswari Sunder. "The Feminist Plot and the Nationalist Allegory: Home and World in Two Indian Women's Novels in English." *Modern Fiction Studies* 39, 1 (1993): 71–92.

Ramusack, Barbara. "Catalysts or Helpers? British Feminists, Indian Women's Rights and Indian Independence." In Gail Minault, ed., *The Extended Family: Women and Political Participation in India and Pakistan.* Columbia, Mo.: South Asia Books, 1981.

————. "Embattled Advocates: The Debate over Birth Control in India, 1920–1940." *Journal of Women's History* 1, 2 (fall 1989): 34–64.

Ramusack, Barbara, and Sharon Sievers, eds. *Women in Asia.* Bloomington: Indiana University Press, 1999.

Ranade, Ramabai. *Ranade: His Wife's Reminiscences (Amchya Ayuskahtil Kahi Athvanni).* Delhi: Ministry of Information and Broadcasting, 1963.

Rao, Uma. "Women in the Frontline: The Case of U. P." In Leela Kasturi and Vina Mazumdar, eds., *Women and Indian Nationalism.* New Delhi: Vikas, 1994, pp. 28–52.

Rapoport, Amos. "Housing as Culture." In Lisa Taylor, ed., *Housing: Symbol, Structure, Site.* New York: Cooper-Union Museum with the Smithsonian, 1990), pp. 4–10.

Ray, Bharati. "Calcutta Women in the Swadeshi Movement (1903–1910): The Nature and Implications of Participation." In Pradip Sinha, ed., *The Urban Experience: Calcutta.* Calcutta: Riddhi, 1987, pp. 168–81.

Ray, Sangeeta. *En-Gendering India: Woman and the Nation in Colonial and Postcolonial Narratives.* Durham, N.C.: Duke University Press, 2000.

————. "Memory, Identity, Patriarchy: Projecting a Past in the Memoirs of Sara Suleri and Michael Ondaatje." *Modern Fiction Studies* 38 (winter 1993): 37–58.

Reddy, Muthulakshmi. *Autobiography.* Madras: n.p.,1964.

Reeves, Peter. "Lucknow Politics, 1920–1947." In Violette Graff, ed., *Lucknow: Memories of a City.* Delhi: Oxford University Press, 1997, pp. 213–26.

Reiger, Kerreen. *The Disenchantment of Home: Modernizing the Australian Family Home, 1880–1940.* Melbourne: Oxford University Press, 1985.

Robinson, Francis. "The Re-emergence of Lucknow as a Major Political Centre, 1899–Early 1920s." In Violette Graff, ed., *Lucknow: Memories of a City.* Delhi: Oxford University Press, 1997, pp. 196–212.

Rodriguez, Ileana. *House, Garden, Nation: Space, Gender and Ethnicity in Postcolonial Latin American Literatures by Women.* Durham, N.C.: Duke University Press, 1994.

Rosaldo, Renato. "Imperialist Nostalgia." *Representations* 26 (spring 1989): 107–22.

Roselli, John H. "The Self-Image of Effeteness: Physical Education and Nationalism in Nineteenth-Century Bengal." *Past and Present* 86 (February 1980): 121–48.

Rosenzweig, Roy. "Oral History and the Old Left." *International Labor and Working Class History* 24 (1983): 27–38.

Rosner, Victoria. "Home Fires: Doris Lessing, Colonial Architecture, and the Reproduction of Mothering." *Tulsa Studies in Women's Literature* 18, 1 (spring 1999): 59–90.

Roy, Kumkum. "The King's Household: Structure and Space in the Sastric Tradition." In Kumkum Sangari and Uma Chakravarti, eds., *From Myths to Markets: Essays on Gender.* New Delhi: Manohar, 1999, pp. 18–28.

Roy, Parama. *Indian Traffic: Identities in Question in Colonial and Postcolonial India.* Berkeley: University of California Press, 1998.

Rubin, David, ed. *Widows, Wives and Other Heroines: Twelve Stories by Premchand.* Delhi: Oxford University Press, 1998.

Rushdie, Salman. "Damme, This Is the Oriental Scene for You!" *New Yorker,* June 23 and 30, 1997, pp. 50–61.

———. "Letter from India: A Dream of Glorious Return." *New Yorker,* June 19 and 26, 2000, pp. 95–112.

Russell, Ralph, ed. *Hidden in the Lute: An Anthology of Two Centuries of Urdu Literature.* Delhi: Viking, 1995.

Saha, Suhrita. "Book Review: Tales of a Broken Land." Review of *The Partitions of Memory: The Afterlife of the Division of India,* edited by Suvir Kaul. *London Telegraph,* May 25, 2001.

Said, Edward. *Orientalism.* New York: Vintage Books, 1978.

Samaddar, Ranabir. "The History That Partition Creates." In Ranabir Samaddar, ed., *Reflections on Partition in the East.* New Delhi: Vikas, 1997, pp. 1–34.

Sangari, Kumkum. "The Politics of the Possible." In T. Niranjana, P. Sudhir, and V. Dhareshwar, eds. *Interrogating Modernity: Culture and Colonialism in India.* Calcutta: Seagull, 1991.

———. "Relating Histories: Definitions of Literacy, Literature, Gender in Early Nineteenth-Century Calcutta and England." In Svati Joshi, ed., *Rethinking English: Essays in Literature, Language, History.* New Delhi: Trianka, 1993, pp. 242–72.

Santner, Eric. *Stranded Objects: Mourning, Memory, and Film in Postwar Germany.* Ithaca, N.Y.: Cornell University Press, 1991.

Sarkar, Mahua. "Muslim Women and the Politics of (In)visibility in Late Colonial Bengal." *Journal of Historical Sociology* 14, 2 (June 2001): 226–50.

Sarkar, Tanika. "A Book of Her Own. A Life of Her Own: Autobiography of a Nineteenth-Century Woman." *History Workshop Journal* 36 (1993): 35–65.

———. "The Hindu Wife and the Hindu Nation: Domesticity and Nationalism in Nineteenth-Century Bengal." *Studies in History* 8, 2 (1992): 213–35.

———. "Rhetoric against Age of Consent: Resisting Colonial Reason in the

Death of a Child-Wife." *Economic and Political Weekly* 28, 36 (September 4, 1993): 1869–78.

——. *Wife, Hindu Nation: Community, Religion and Cultural Nationalism.* Delhi: Permanent Black, 2001.

——. *Words to Win: The Making of Amar Jiban: A Modern Autobiography.* New Delhi: Kali for Women, 1999.

Sarker, Sonita. "Unruly Subjects: Cornelia Sorabji and Ravinder Randhawa." In Sonita Sarker and Esha Niyogi De, eds., *Trans-Status Subjects: Gender in the Globalization of South and Southeast Asia.* Durham, N.C.: Duke University Press, forthcoming.

Scott, James. *Seeing Like a State: How Certain Schemes to Improve the Human Condition Have Failed.* New Haven, Conn.: Yale University Press, 1998.

Sekula, Alan. "The Body and the Archive." *October* 39, 3 (1986): 3–64.

Seth, Rumina. "Contesting Identities: Involvement and Resistance of Women in the Indian National Movement." *Journal of Gender Studies* 5, 3 (1996): 305–15.

——. *Myths of the Nation: National Identity and Literary Representation.* Oxford: Clarendon Press, 1999.

Seth, Sanjay. "Rewriting Histories of Nationalism: The Politics of 'Moderate Nationalism' in India, 1870–1905." *American Historical Review* 104, 1 (February 1999): 95–116.

Shah, Nayan. *Contagious Divides: Epidemics and Race in San Francisco's Chinatown.* Berkeley: University of California, 2001.

Shanawaz, Jahan Ara. *Father and Daughter: A Political Autobiography.* Lahore: Nigarishat, 1971.

Sharlet, Jeff. "Should Historians Take the Fiction-Writing Test?" *Chronicle of Higher Education,* May 12, 2000.

Silvestri, Michael. "The Thrill of 'Simply Dressing Up': The Indian Police, Disguise, and Intelligence Work in Colonial India." *Journal of Colonialism and Colonial History* 2, 2 (2001). Available at: http://muse.jhu.edu/jcch.

Singh, Maina Chawla. *Gender, Religion and "Heathen" Lands: American Missionary Women in South Asia (1860s–1940s).* New York: Garland, 2000.

Singh, Radhika. *A Despotism of Law: Crime and Justice in Early Colonial India.* Delhi: Oxford University Press, 1998.

Sinha, Mrinalini. *Colonial Masculinity: The "Manly Englishman" and the "Effeminate Bengali" in the Late Nineteenth Century.* Manchester, England: Manchester University Press, 1995.

——. "Gender in the Critiques of Colonialism and Nationalism: Locating the 'Indian Woman.'" In Joan Scott, ed., *Feminism and History.* New York: Oxford University Press, 1996.

——. "The Lineage of the 'Indian' Modern: Rhetoric, Agency, and the Sarda Act in Late Colonial India." In Antoinette Burton, ed., *Gender, Sexuality and Colonial Modernities.* London: Routledge, 1999, pp. 207–21.

——. "Refashioning Mother India: Feminism and Nationalism in Late-Colonial India." *Feminist Studies* 28, 3 (fall 2000): 623–44.

——. "Suffragism and Internationalism: The Enfranchisement of British and Indian Women under an Imperial State." *Indian Economic and Social History Review* 36 (October–December 1999): 461–84; reprinted in Ian Fletcher, Philippa Levine, and Laura Mayhall, eds., *Women's Suffrage in the British Empire: Citizenship, Race, and Nation.* Routledge: London, 2000, pp. 224–39.

————, ed. *Mother India.* Delhi: Kali for Women, 1998; Ann Arbor: University of Michigan Press, 2000.

Skaria, Ajay. *Hybrid Histories: Forests, Frontiers and Wildness in Western India.* Delhi: Oxford University Press, 1999.

Smith, Bonnie. *The Gender of History: Men, Women and Historical Practice.* Cambridge, Mass.: Harvard University Press, 2000.

Soja, Edward. *Thirdspace: Journeys to Los Angeles and Other Real-and-Imagined Places.* London: Blackwell, 1996.

Sorabji, Cornelia. "A Bengali Woman Revolutionary." *Nineteenth Century and After* 114 (November 1933): 604–11.

————. *Between the Twilights.* 1908.

————. "The Gandhi Apocrypha." *Nineteenth Century and After* 110 (November 1931): 594–601.

————. *India Calling: The Memories of Cornelia Sorabji.* London: Nisbet, 1934.

————. "Indian Women of 'The Outside': The Emancipated Who, with No Book of Rules, Have Attained New Spheres of Freedom." *Asia* (April 1924): 306–32.

————. *India Recalled.* London: Nisbet, 1936.

————. "Mahatma Gandhi." *Nineteenth Century and After* 100 (September 1926): 368–79.

————. "Social Relations—England and India." In *Pan-Anglican Papers: Being Problems for Consideration at the Pan-Anglican Congress.* London: Society for Promoting Christian Knowledge, 1908.

————. *Susie Sorabji: Christian-Parsee Educationalist of Western India: A Memoir by Her Sister.* Oxford: Oxford University Press, 1932.

————. *Therefore: An Impression of Sorabji Kharsedji Langrana and His Wife Franscina.* Oxford: Oxford University Press, 1934.

————. "Zenana Dwellers: The Selfless Women of Hinduism, Keepers of the God-Rules." *Asia* (March 1924).

Spence, Jonathan. *The Memory Palace of Matteo Ricci.* New York: Penguin, 1985.

Spiegel, Gabrielle M. *The Past as Text: The Theory and Practice of Medieval Historiography.* Baltimore: Johns Hopkins University Press, 1997.

Spivak, Gayatri. "The Rani of Sirmur: An Essay in Reading the Archives." *History and Theory* 24, 3 (1985): 247–72.

Srinivasan, Amrit. "The Survivor in the Study of Violence." In Veena Das, ed., *Mirrors of Violence: Communities, Riots and Survivors in South Asia.* Delhi: Oxford University Press, 1990.

Steedly, Mary Margaret. *Hanging without a Rope: Narrative Experience in Colonial and Postcolonial Karoland.* Princeton, N.J.: Princeton University Press, 1993.

Steedman, Carolyn. "Inside, Outside, Other: Accounts of National Identity in the Nineteenth Century." *History of the Human Sciences* 8, 4 (1995): 59–76.

————. *Landscape for a Good Woman: A Story of Two Lives.* New Brunswick, N.J.: Rutgers University Press, 1987.

————. "Something She Called a Fever: Michelet, Derrida, and Dust." *American Historical Review* 106, 4 (October 2001): 1159–80.

Stewart, Susan. *On Longing: Narratives of the Miniature, the Gigantic, the Souvenir, the Collection.* Baltimore: Johns Hopkins University Press, 1984.

Stoler, Ann, and Karen Strassler. "Castings for the Colonial: Memory Work in 'New Order' Java." *Comparative Studies in Society and History* (2000): 4–48.

Stoner, K. Lynn. *From the House to the Streets: The Cuban Woman's Movement for Legal Reform, 1898–1940*. Durham, N.C.: Duke University Press, 1991.

Suarez-Smith, Richard. "Rule-by-Record and Rule-by-Report: Complementary Aspects of the British Imperial Rule of Law." In Veena Das, ed., *The World and the Word: Fantasy, Symbol and Record*. Delhi: Sage, 1986, pp. 153–76.

———. *Rule by Records: Land Registration and Village Custom in Early British Punjab*. Delhi: Oxford University Press, 1996.

Subramanyam, K. G. "Amrita Sher-Gil and the East-West Dilemma." In Vivan Sundaram et al., *Amrita Sher-Gil*. Bombay: Tata Press, 1972, pp. 63–72.

Syal, Meera. *Anita and Me*. London: Flamingo, 1996.

Talbot, Ian. *Freedom's Cry: The Popular Dimension in the Pakistan Movement and Partition Experience in North-west India*. Karachi: Oxford University Press, 1996.

Tate, Claudia. *Domestic Allegories of Political Desire: The Black Heroine's Text at the Turn of the Century*. New York: Oxford University Press, 1992.

Tharu, Susie. "The Impossible Subject: Caste and Desire in the Scene of the Family." In Rajeswari Sunder Rajan, ed., *Signposts: Gender Issues in Post-Independence India*. New Delhi: Kali for Women, 1999, pp. 187–203.

Tharu, Susie, and K. Lalita, eds. *Women Writing in India 600 B.C. to the Present*. Vols. 1 and 2. New York: Feminist Press, 1991.

Tierney-Tello, Mary Beth. *Allegories of Transgression and Transformation: Experimental Fiction by Women Writing under Dictatorship*. Albany: SUNY Press, 1996.

Tilak, Lakshmibai. *I Follow After: An Autobiography*. Delhi: Oxford University Press, 1998.

Tonkin, Elizabeth. *Narrating Our Pasts: The Social Construction of Oral History*. Cambridge: Cambridge University Press, 1992.

Trivedi, Lisa. "Spinning the 'Nation': Swadeshi Politics, Material Culture and the Making of the Indian Nation, 1915–1930." Ph.D. diss., University of California, Davis, 1999.

Urry, John. "The Tourist Gaze 'Revisited.'" *American Behavioral Scientist* 26, 2 (1992): 172–86.

Van Young, Eric. "The New Cultural History Comes to Old Mexico." *Hispanic American Historical Review* 79, 2 (1999): 211–47.

Villa-Vicencio, Charles. "On the Limitations of Academic History: The Quest for Truth Demands Both More and Less." In Wilmot James and Linda Van de Vijver, eds., *After the TRC: Reflections on Truth and Reconciliation in South Africa*. Cape Town: David Philip, 2000; Athens, Ohio: Ohio University Press, 2001, pp. 21–31.

Visram, Rozina. *Ayahs, Lascars and Princess: The Story of Indians in Britain, 1700–1947*. London: Pluto, 1986.

Visweswaran, Kamala. "Small Speeches, Subaltern Gender: Nationalist Ideology and Its Historiography." In Shahid Amin and Dipesh Chakrabarty, eds., *Subaltern Studies 9: Writings on South Asian History and Society*. Delhi: Oxford University Press, 1996, pp. 83–125.

Voss, Paul J., and Marta L. Werner. "Toward a Poetics of the Archive: Introduction." *Studies in the Literary Imagination* 32, 1 (spring 1999): i–viii.

Wadhawan, Jagdish Chander. *Manto Naama: The Life of Saadat Hasan Manto*. New Delhi: Roli Books, 1998.

Walker, Alice. *Revolutionary Petunias and Other Poems*. New York: Harcourt Brace Jovanovich, 1973.

Walsh, Judith. *Growing Up in British India: Indian Autobiographers on Childhood and Education under the Raj.* London: Holmes and Meier, 1983.

——. "What Women Learned When Men Gave Them Advice: Rewriting Patriarchy in Late-Nineteenth-Century Bengal." *Journal of Asian Studies* 56, 3 (1997): 641–77.

Watson, C. W. *Of Self and Nation: Autobiography and the Representation of Modern Indonesia.* Honolulu: University of Hawaii, 2000.

Wiley, Catherine, and Fiona R. Barnes, eds. *Homemaking: Women Writers and the Poetics of Home.* New York: Garland, 1996.

Winks, Robin, ed. *The Oxford History of the British Empire.* Vol. 5. *Historiography.* Oxford: Oxford University Press, 1999.

Woollacott, Angela. "The Fragmented Subject: Feminist History, Official Records and Self-Representation." *Women's Studies International Forum* 21, 4 (1998): 329–39.

——. "Inventing Commonwealth and Pan-Pacific Feminisms: Australian Women's International Activism." *Gender and History* 10, 3 (1998): 425–48.

——. *To Try Her Fortune in London: Australian Women, Colonialism, and Modernity.* New York: Oxford University Press, 2001.

Young, James. *The Texture of Memory: Holocaust Memorials and Meaning.* New Haven, Conn.: Yale University Press, 1993.

Yung, Judy. *Unbound Feet: A Social History of Chinese Women in San Francisco.* Berkeley: University of California Press, 1995.

Index